UNIVERSALISM AND PARTICULARISM
AT SODOM AND GOMORRAH

Society of Biblical Literature

Ancient Israel and Its Literature

Steven L. McKenzie, General Editor

Editorial Board

Suzanne Boorer
Victor H. Matthews
Thomas C. Römer
Benjamin D. Sommer
Nili Wazana

Number 11

UNIVERSALISM AND PARTICULARISM
AT SODOM AND GOMORRAH

Essays in Memory of Ron Pirson

UNIVERSALISM AND PARTICULARISM AT SODOM AND GOMORRAH

ESSAYS IN MEMORY OF RON PIRSON

Edited by
Diana Lipton

Society of Biblical Literature
Atlanta

UNIVERSALISM AND PARTICULARISM
AT SODOM AND GOMORRAH
Essays in Memory of Ron Pirson

Copyright © 2012 by the Society of Biblical Literature

All rights reserved. No part of this work may be reproduced or transmitted in any form or by any means, electronic or mechanical, including photocopying and recording, or by means of any information storage or retrieval system, except as may be expressly permitted by the 1976 Copyright Act or in writing from the publisher. Requests for permission should be addressed in writing to the Rights and Permissions Office, Society of Biblical Literature, 825 Houston Mill Road, Atlanta, GA 30329 USA.

Library of Congress Cataloging-in-Publication Data

Universalism and particularism at Sodom and Gomorrah : essays in memory of Ron Pirson / edited by Diana Lipton.
    p. cm. — (Society of Biblical Literature ancient Israel and its literature ; no. 11)
  Includes bibliographical references and indexes.
  ISBN 978-1-58983-650-1 (paper binding : alk. paper) — ISBN 978-1-58983-651-8 (electronic format)
  1. Bible. O.T. Genesis XVIII–XIX—Criticism, interpretation, etc. 2. Sodom (Extinct city) 3. Gomorrah (Extinct city) 4. Universalism. 5. Particularism (Theology) I. Lipton, Diana. II. Pirson, Ron.
  BS1235.52.U55 2012b
  222'.1106—dc22   2012003015

Printed on acid-free, recycled paper conforming to
ANSI/NISO Z39.48-1992 (R1997) and ISO 9706:1994
standards for paper permanence.

Contents

Acknowledgments vii
Abbreviations viii
Preface ix
Remembering Ron Pirson, by His Life-Partner
   Petra Thijs xi
Ron Pirson: Memories of a Former Colleague
   Pierre Van Hecke xv
Ron Pirson: Publications xvii

Section 1: The Ethics of Preference

The Eternal Liminality of Lot: Paying the Price of Opposing
   the Particular in the Sodom Narrative
   William John Lyons 3

The Limits of Intercession: Abraham Reads Ezekiel at Sodom and
   Gomorrah
   Diana Lipton 25

Changing God's Mind: Abraham versus Jonah
   T. A. Perry 43

Why Did God Choose Abraham? Responses from Medieval
   Jewish Commentators
   Amira Meir 53

Section 2: Justice by the Book

Outcry, Knowledge, and Judgment in Genesis 18–19
   Ellen J. van Wolde 71

Legal and Ethical Reflections on Genesis 18 and 19
   Calum Carmichael 101

Keeping the Way of Yhwh: Righteousness and Justice in
Genesis 18–19
   Megan Warner 113

Section 3: The Ethics of Hospitality

Was Lot a Good Host? Was Lot Saved from Sodom as a Reward
for His Hospitality?
   Yitzhak (Itzik) Peleg 129

Hospitality Compared: Abraham and Lot as Hosts
   Jonathan D. Safren 157

Hospitality and Hostility: Reading Genesis 19 in Light of 2 Samuel 10
(and Vice Versa)
   Nathan MacDonald 179

Beyond Particularity and Universality: Reflections on Shadal's
Commentary to Genesis 18–19
   Harlan J. Wechsler 191

Does Lot Know about *Yada'*?
   Ron Pirson 203

Contributors 215
Index of Primary Texts 219
Index of Modern Authors 231

Acknowledgments

Many thanks to Dr. Sarah Shectman and Dr. Shirly Natan Yulzary for their excellent editorial work on this volume. They made my task infinitely less taxing, and working with each of them proved to be a pleasure. Many thanks also to the SBL team, Kent Richards in particular, who helped me keep my promise to Ron Pirson to try to publish these essays. Warm thanks to all the contributors; their patient support throughout was deeply appreciated. Especially encouraging were Amira Meir and Itzik Peleg, both of whom had been invited by Ron to participate in the first of three ISBL sessions whose proceedings are published here. Finally, warmest thanks to Petra Thijs for her patience, her trust, and her generous spirit.

Diana Lipton, Jerusalem, July 2011

Abbreviations

Please consult the *SBL Handbook of Style* for abbreviations other than those listed here:

ABR	*Australian Biblical Review*
EncJud	*Encyclopaedia Judaica.* Edited by Fred Skolnik. 22 vols. Detroit: Macmillan Reference USA in association with Keter, 2007.
FCB 2	Feminist Companion to the Bible, Second Series
JPSTC	Jewish Publication Society Torah Commentary
KEHAT	Kurzgefasstes exegetisches Handbuch zum Alten Testament
LHB/OTS	Library of Hebrew Bible/Old Testament Studies
SBLAIL	Society of Biblical Literature Ancient Israel and Its Literature
TBN	Themes in Biblical Narrative

Preface

This volume began its life as a proposal made by Ron Pirson for three International Society of Biblical Literature sessions on Gen 18–19. Ron, a young scholar from the University of Tilburg in the Netherlands, had recently published his doctoral dissertation on Joseph's dreams, completed under the supervision of Professor Ellen van Wolde. He had a clear vision of what he wanted to achieve with his proposed ISBL sessions and knew which scholars he hoped would help him in the first instance to bring it to fruition: Itzik Peleg, Amira Meir, and Diana Lipton, all, by coincidence or not, working within different Jewish traditions (Ron was not). His e-mail to share the happy news that his proposal had been accepted came along with another bearing infinitely less-welcome news. At the age of forty, a lifelong nonsmoker and healthy eater, he had just been diagnosed with terminal, untreatable lung cancer. That was January 2006. By the time the first session took place in Edinburgh the following July, Ron had died. His own paper was read by his colleague Professor Pierre Van Hecke, and the session was attended by Petra Thijs, Ron's beloved life-partner of twenty years. We inaugurated a custom that continued in the sessions that followed in Vienna and Rome of singing Ps 23 in Hebrew in Ron's memory and of saying a few words about him. Not all the contributors to this volume knew Ron in person, but without exception, I believe, they formed a strong sense of him at the ISBL meetings at which their papers were originally delivered. Less easy to explain is the extent to which these twelve contributors seem to me to have acquired their own particular distinctiveness as a group, despite their great differences—geographical, professional, religious, and academic. It is a privilege and an honor to publish their essays, along with Ron's own contribution, in the form of a more lasting memorial than the sessions themselves to a wonderfully sensitive scholar and a man of great integrity.

This volume addresses the vexed and relevant question of universalism and particularism in Gen 18 and 19. The traditional paradigm that

Genesis begins as a universalist narrative and narrows into particularism with the call of Abraham has long since been qualified and undermined. Scholars and members of faith communities alike now see that Gen 12–50 is not the story of how one family and people emerged separate and distinguished from all others but is rather a series of complex, enduring interactions—negative and positive, constructive and destructive (and instructive)—between Israel and its significant others. To demonstrate this in relation to Gen 16 and 21 (Sarah and Hagar, Isaac and Ishmael) or 26–32 (Jacob and Esau, Isaac and Laban) is a simple matter. The essays in this volume aim to draw out this complex engagement from the infinitely less-promising material of Sodom and Gomorrah, a story that has generated more exclusionary exegesis than most other biblical narratives put together. To be sure, there is little to be done to repair the reputations of the residents themselves, nor perhaps should we be tempted to try! The narrative itself, however, is the site of multiple borders and boundaries—fluid, porous, and bidirectional—between similar and different and different and different, between men and angels, men and women, fathers and daughters, insiders and outsiders, related and unrelated, proto-Israelites and non-Israelites, hosts and guests, residents and aliens (and resident aliens), "chosen" and nonchosen, and people and God. The contributors who explore these questions reflect immense diversity. Yet it is easy to identify (perhaps indeed to coin) a single methodological approach that unites their work: "significant exegesis." Every observation made in this volume is based on the close reading of a notoriously difficult and undeniably influential biblical text by a scholar who cares what it says and what it means.

This volume is divided into three sections according to themes that emerged organically (and fortuitously!) over the three annual conference sessions that inspired it: the first, "The Ethics of Preference," focuses on the implications of Abraham's chosenness; the second, "Justice by the Book," examines the application to the many of a legal system designed for the few; the third, "The Ethics of Hospitality," looks again at a theme that has preoccupied commentators ancient and modern. What readers of these essays will, I think, experience, is a phenomenon that appears all too rarely in conference sessions and their proceedings: an overwhelming sense of life being lived. This vivacity has, in ways that would require a chapter of its own to articulate, flowed from Ron Pirson, in whose memory these essays are published. May the tributary that Ron divined and tapped become the tribute to him that he so richly deserved.

Remembering Ron Pirson, by His Life-Partner

Petra Thijs

Although I am a psychologist, not a biblical scholar, in the summer of 2006 I traveled to Edinburgh to attend a seminar on Gen 18–19 at the International Society for Biblical Literature's annual conference. I came instead of my husband, Ron Pirson, who initiated the seminar. The idea for this seminar emerged at another ISBL conference, this time in Cambridge, where Ron met Amira Meir and Yitzhak Peleg and discovered common interests. Sometime after that he approached Diana Lipton, whose interests were also similar, and he was soon able to put together a proposal for three conference sessions over three years with Amira, Diana, Yitzhak, and Ron himself as the planned presenters for the first session.

The day Ron received SBL's positive response to his proposal was the day he received the news that what at first had seemed to be a case of pneumonia proved to be lung cancer, untreatable, unbelievable. Ron was a man of forty-two who lived a healthy life, had hardly ever been sick, was no nicotine or stress addict, and who liked to go for long walking holidays; it was like a thunderbolt. Not less so for the people who knew him. Perhaps you are one of them.

In May 2006, half a year after the diagnosis, Ron died, a few months before the first of the three planned yearly seminars. Diana Lipton had been so kind as to take over the responsibility for the things that remained to be arranged, for which Ron was justly grateful, because she did a great job.

The meeting in Edinburgh had been very important to Ron, and it now proved to be very special to me. To meet all those people who knew him as a Bible scholar, to hear Ron's lecture delivered by his colleague and friend Pierre Van Hecke, the moving speech by Diana, and the singing of Ps 23 in Hebrew by all who knew the words and tune was very moving indeed. If you were there, you will remember.

Now, after the three sessions have taken place, it is with pride as well as a combination of sadness and pleasure that I accepted Diana's invitation to write the foreword for this volume. In light of the initial title of this volume (*Know Your Neighbor*), and in light of the title of Ron's own contribution to it, "Does Lot Know about *Yada'*?" I think it is fitting for you to know something more about the man who conceived these seminars.

Ron was a Bible scholar, but his interests were much broader than that. To get to know him a little will take you through a great variety of things. After he finished secondary school, Ron took some time to discover what he would really like to do. He first tried several studies (Dutch, English, religion) at a teacher-training college, although he knew that he didn't want to become a teacher at secondary school. Then he found that many of his interests came together in the study of theology at university, such as language, history, culture, and psychology. That was in 1985, the year Ron and I met, fell in love, and started living together.

So at the age of twenty-two he started his studies at Tilburg University, at first still a bit timid about his capacities but with great determination. This time it didn't take him long to get to know where his heart lay: biblical studies, exegesis of the Old and New Testaments. He specialized in the former. He wrote his thesis about Joseph: *The Lord of the Dreams*. The title is an allusion to one of Ron's other passions: the works of J. R. R. Tolkien, one of many instances in which Ron's interests merged together. Ron wrote quite a few articles about Tolkien and his work, often from a combined literary, theological, and cultural perspective.

Ron liked to delve into ancient texts, but he also wanted to contribute something more immediately meaningful to society. He was a versatile and sensitive person and could just as easily have worked in pastoral care as in the field of exegesis. For some time, he did voluntary work at a home for the elderly, and he hoped later on to do pastoral work in the hospital for people with cancer.

Ron could as easily write for and give lectures to laymen as to experts; he did a lot to interest people in texts of the Bible. He really wanted to share his knowledge, on different terrains and at work as well as outside it. He was an inspiring, enthusiastic teacher. He could bring his subject matter alive and found ways to link these ancient texts to contemporary life, by way of literature, movies, contemporary issues, and so forth. Needless to say, he was a popular teacher who was greatly missed, by students and teachers alike.

Ron had his very own way of reading and interpreting the Bible, always trying to find something original, looking beyond the obvious, crossing borders. He didn't mind stepping on someone's (academic) toes occasionally, but it was always well-argued, well-founded on a close study of the Hebrew text, and written in an engaging style. Read his paper about Lot and see for yourself. His last big project was a Dutch commentary on the book of Genesis, with lots of new insights and written in his fluent and much-praised style.

Ron applied the same inventive thinking-outside-the-box attitude to his daily life; he could appreciate a bit of controversy. Some might have called him obstinate or impertinent, but he never intended to hurt. He was modest, but if he saw injustice being done, he could voice his (sometimes strong) opinions without being deterred by a misplaced awe for status or authority. He always welcomed criticism on his own work and behavior, and although he had little patience with downright incompetence, he had even less with the failure to acknowledge it.

Ron was an open, honest person with great integrity. He liked meeting people and opened himself to their ideas and feelings. Although a serious person, he could enjoy life to the full. He had a great sense of humor, liked to laugh, and was often ironic (which was hard for some people to understand and appreciate). He was always true to himself and greatly valued that quality in others. He simply could not understand people who pretended to be something they were not. It was not only Ron's capacity as a teacher and a scholar that makes people remember him so fondly. Even more important, I think, is that he really cared—about ideas and, more important, about people. He was attentive to their needs, liked to make them happy, and expected nothing back in return for helping others. Of course, he cared very much for his family and friends, just as he empathized with his colleagues in their joys and sorrows. He would help a student on a personal issue or put a coin in a machine at the supermarket so a kid could take a ride on it.

Ron was always conscious about the environment and really liked nature and the spirituality he found there. Every summer Ron and I went walking, preferably in the U.K.: Offa's Dyke Path, Pennine Way, Cambrian Way, Coast to Coast, you name it. Ron loved the green hills, the moors, and woods. He loved to talk to the people we met, and he loved the magic of the landscape. This magic he had experienced for the first time before he had ever even been to Britain: in his room in his parents' house when he was a teenager. It was there that he fell in love with reading and with Tolkien's *The Lord of the Rings*. Around the same time he discovered the music of Mike Oldfield, and it was with Tolkien and Oldfield that he glimpsed for the first time the mystical aspects of the British landscape. He had been intrigued in his youth by Oldfield's album *Hergest Ridge*, and when he found out that it was a real place, he wanted to visit it. And so we did, on the Offa's Dyke Path. At the foot of Hergest Ridge, on the border of England and Wales, Ron and I had our blessing ceremony in 1997 (and even made it into the local paper!). Nine years later it was on top of that hill that another kind of ceremony took place, not one of joining but of parting.

In 1999, after having walked several long-distance paths in the U.K., we took up a new project: we decided to walk across the whole island. We started at Land's End and used several holidays to walk our way up to Scotland. The year before Ron died, there were only twenty kilometers left to our destination, Cape Wrath, when he suddenly got a severe pain in his back. Perhaps it was just that, or perhaps it was the cancer already—he got severe back aches again after the diagnosis. Anyway, with the end of our journey in sight, we had to return home early, and he didn't get the chance to finish it afterwards. For some time he had wanted to write a book about a walk through Britain, a sort of spiritual journey. Unfortunately, the book will never be written, along with other projects Ron already had in mind.

Ron never complained about his fate. With Monty Python, he always looked on the bright side of life. He didn't think (as people around him often did) that forty years had been taken away from him. He saw no injustice, nothing unfair: no one is promised a long life. He had had his share and was grateful for the life that he had lived.

I mentioned earlier that Ron expected nothing in return for what he did for others, but of course he got a lot in return. After we heard the diagnosis, we were overwhelmed by acts of generosity and tokens of sympathy, even from people who hardly knew Ron, which was really heartwarming. You reap as you sow; that was the way it was with Ron. He felt so fortunate and gave so much, and he could only be grateful for what he had been given and achieved. Of course he wanted to live on, for the people he loved and to fulfill his dreams and ambitions, but in different ways he does live on. I am proud and thankful that Ron's Gen 18–19 seminars resulted in this book, one of the many ways in which Ron is with us still.

Ron Pirson: Memories of a Former Colleague

Pierre Van Hecke

Ron Pirson was an excellent colleague. About a year before he passed away, I wrote to tell him that I wished everybody could have a colleague like him. That was no friendly exaggeration. The immediate catalyst for my remark was Ron's discovery of some scholarly opportunity for which he believed I would be eligible. He had even gone to speak with the dean in order to plead my case, without my knowing anything about it. I mention this because it is typical of Ron's approach to his colleagues. He was extremely attentive to our activities, interests, and concerns. Often I would tell him about a project, and months later he would still know all the details and ask how it was going. Laughingly, I told him that if I wanted to know when my next meeting or conference was, I could just ask him! He remembered all these things, just because he was so interested in what his colleagues were doing and because he genuinely sympathized with both their sorrows and their joys. The academic world is often characterized by a spirit of competition—even of envy—between colleagues, but not so with Ron. He would never boast of his own achievements—even though he had enough reasons to do so—nor would he ever begrudge someone else's. He always remained his humble and hard-working self, a kind and engaging person.

This does not mean that Ron had no strong opinions. In many faculty and department meetings, he expressed his sharp views about the future of our teaching and research, and he did not shy away from criticizing plans and decisions when he judged that they were going against the interests of the faculty. On the scholarly level, too, he took strong positions against fixed and established opinions, challenging other scholars to give up the preconceived ideas of which they were sometimes unaware. He was not afraid to defend his own points of view, once he had reached a conclusion after long hours of silent and solitary work (in the tiniest office in the whole faculty, which he liked very much). On the other hand, he had no difficulties in accepting criticism of his own work, as I often witnessed when discussing early drafts of papers he gave me to read.

Ron was an excellent writer, both in Dutch and in English. Here his interest in and his profound acquaintance with both Dutch and English literature became very apparent. The Dutch commentary on Genesis, of which he saw the publication a few months before his death, is one eminent example thereof. It is not only a thorough scholarly work but also a joy to read. I hope it might one day become available in English.

Ron was a good narrator, not only in writing, but also in teaching. His well-prepared courses, his enthusiasm, his ability to interact with his students and to connect with their interests, and his challenging and thought-provoking ideas made him one of the most popular lecturers by far in our faculty. Students liked him very much, not only as a lecturer, but also as a human being, always available and always interested in what students were doing and organizing. He was also active himself in organizing and collaborating in initiatives for the students, the marathon screenings of the *Lord of the Rings* and the *Matrix* cycles, for example.

I miss Ron, and I know I am joined in this by many others, friends, family, colleagues, and students alike.

Ron Pirson: Publications[1]

1. "Een fraaie garderobe." *Schrift* 28, no. 165 (1996): 85–88.
2. "De renovatie van de tempel volgens Haggai." *Schrift* 29, no. 173 (1997): 154–56.
3. "Een andere kant van Jakob." *Schrift* 30, no. 175 (1998): 7–8.
4. "Een bijl op het water." *Schrift* 30, no. 177 (1998): 82–84.
5. "De kaak-slag bij Lechi." *Schrift* 31, no. 185 (1999): 144–46.
6. "De tien geboden binnenstebuiten." *Schrift* 31, no. 186 (1999): 169–72.
7. "The Lord of the Dreams: Genesis 37 and Its Literary Context." Tilburg: Proefschrift Theologische Faculteit, 1999. See also number 16 below.
8. "Getallenspel: De droom-paren in Genesis 37–50." Pages 97–115 in *Over spel: Theologie als drama en illusie*. Edited by H. Beck et al. Leende: Damon, 2000.
9. "Jozef tussen Israël en Egypte, thema-aflevering." *Schrift* 32, no. 188 (2000): 34–61.
10. "Leeftijden in Genesis." *Schrift* 32, no. 189 (2000): 74–77.
11. *De dromer van Hebron: Een herlezing van het verhaal van Jozef en zijn broers.* Kampen: Ten Have, 2001.
12. "De sprekende ezelin." *Schrift* 33, no. 195 (2001): 72–74.
13. "Leviticus en de Tora." *Schrift* 33, no. 196 (2001): 95–99.
14. "The Sun, the Moon and Eleven Stars. An Interpretation of Joseph's Second Dream." Pages 561–68 in *Studies in the Book of Genesis*. Edited by A. Wénin. BETL 155. Leuven: Peeters, 2001.
15. "Het boek Prediker: Salomo en Qohelet." *Schrift* 34, no. 201 (2002): 80–83.
16. *The Lord of the Dreams: A Semantic and Literary Analysis of Genesis 37–50.* JSOTSup 355. London: Sheffield Academic Press, 2002.
17. "Over leven in ballingschap: Overleven na de Ballingschap." Pages 46–67 in *Over leven: Leven en overleven in lagen*. Edited by H. Beck and W. Weren. Budel: Damon, 2002.
18. "Saul in Oxford." *Schrift* 34, no. 199 (2002): 12–17.

---

1. Ron Pirson published extensively on J.R.R. Tolkien as well as on the Bible. This bibliography includes just a few examples of the former.

19. "Dat smaakt naar meer: Over het slot van Genesis." *Schrift* 35, no. 208 (2003): 107–10.
20. "De dood van Saul." *Schrift* 35, no. 209 (2003): 157–60.
21. "Genesis en Exodus 1–18." Pages 61–87 in *De Bijbel literair: Opbouw en gedachtegang van de bijbelse geschriften en hun onderlinge relaties*. Edited by J. Fokkelman and W. Weren. Zoetermeer: Meinema, 2003.
22. "God in Middle-Earth?" Pages 94–111 in *Vreemde verhalen, goed nieuws? Over Harry Potter en andere helden*. Edited by B. Verstappen et al. Nijmegen: Valkhof Pers, 2003.
23. "'Lig met mij': De verleiding van Genesis 39." *Interpretatie* 6 (September 2003): 7–9.
24. "Divine Interventions in Tolkien's Universe." In "Job's God." Edited by Ellen van Wolde. Special issue, *Concilium* 4 (2004): 93–102.
25. "Het demonische in *The Lord of the Rings*." Pages 188–99 in *Idolen en demonen: Gelegenheidsbundel Dag van de Filosofie 2004*. Edited by L. Jansen and N. Oudejans. Tilburg: University of Tilburg, 2004.
26. "Oordeel: Sefanja." Pages 495–502 in *De Bijbel Spiritueel: Bronnen van geestelijk leven in de bijbelse geschriften*. Edited by F. A. Maas, J. Maas, and K. Spronk. Zoetermeer: Meinema; Kapellen: Pelckmans, 2004.
27. Review of W. L. Humphreys, *The Character of God in the Book of Genesis: A Narrative Approach*. *BibInt* 12 (2004): 408–10.
28. "Two Rings to Corrupt Them All?" Pages 110–22 in *Lembas-extra 2004*. Edited by R. Pirson. Leiden: de Tolkienwinkel, 2004.[2]
29. "The Twofold Message of Potiphar's Wife." *SJOT* 18 (2004): 249–60.
30. *Genesis: Belichting van het bijbelboek*. Den Bosch: Katholieke Bijbelstichting, 2005.
31. "Van Middle-earth naar Galilea en weer terug." Pages 62–69 in *Wetenschap en literatuur in discussie*. Edited by Harald van Veghel. Budel: Damon, 2005.

---

[2]. Published in a magazine of the Dutch Tolkien Society.

Section 1
The Ethics of Preference

The Eternal Liminality of Lot: Paying the Price of Opposing the Particular in the Sodom Narrative[*]

William John Lyons

1. Introduction

Attending the first meeting of the Gen 18–19 section at the SBL International meeting in Edinburgh in 2006, and seeing how the topic chosen by Ron Pirson[1]—that of universalism and particularism in the Sodom story—was developed, brought home to me just how flexible that narrative is; small disagreements on minor exegetical points easily lead to significant interpretive variations. With this flexibility in mind, I want to begin this essay by setting the scene for my interpretation, spelling out here just what it is that I am trying to achieve.

First, this interpretation comes from within a very specific framework, the canonical approach of Brevard S. Childs.[2] As most will know, his work

---

[*] Thanks are here offered to Jonathan Campbell, Tim Cole, and James Harding for their comments on versions of this essay. None bear any responsibility for what follows, however.

1. I never met Ron, my first introduction to him being the memorial offered by his colleagues and friends at the seminar in Edinburgh in 2006. Nevertheless, my thanks go to him for his deep and, I suspect, abiding influence on my thinking about this text, a text that has occupied me for a large part of my academic career, but which I can no longer think of as I once did. I like to think he would have found this essay persuasive, but as a fellow academic I would have been equally happy had he simply found it worthy of a critical response!

2. Childs, an American professor of Old Testament, spent virtually all of his academic career at Yale and is perhaps best understood as a biblical theologian standing in the reformed tradition of Calvin and Barth. He wrote a large number of books, including two major commentaries (on *Exodus* [OTL; London: SCM, 1974] and *Isaiah* [OTL; London: SCM, 1999]), introductions to both Old Testament and New Testa-

on the "Old Testament" is set explicitly within a Christian context. For Childs, reading the Scriptures involved an initial descriptive task—a task that he believed was shared with Jewish interpreters—followed by a subsequent reappraisal of the material as it "resonated" in the light of the fullness of the Christian canon.³ Though I do not share Childs's confidence about the task's shared nature, I do want to look at our text as he suggested, taking a first "descriptive" glance, before attempting a second "subsequent" reappraisal.

Second, I want to acknowledge the fact that while some of the exegetical positions taken here will be defended, many of them will not be. Abraham recognizes the deity immediately in 18:1–2.⁴ Lot is not righteous, but he is as good a host as Abraham. His rescue from Sodom is not due to Abraham's intercession, or to his own merit. Anyone seeking justification of such points is directed toward the fuller exposition of chapters 18 and 19 found in my *Canon and Exegesis: Canonical Praxis and the Sodom Narrative* (2002).⁵

Third, as I prepared this essay, I found the setting of its presentation to the second meeting of the Gen 18–19 seminar in 2007, the *Hauptgebäude*, University of Vienna, significant,⁶ a setting that is now hard for me

---

ment (*Introduction to the Old Testament as Scripture* [Philadelphia: Fortress, 1979]; *The New Testament as Canon: An Introduction* [Valley Forge, Pa.: Trinity Press International, 1984]), an Old Testament theology (*Old Testament Theology in a Canonical Context* [London: SCM, 1985]), a biblical theology (*Biblical Theology of the Old and New Testaments* [London: SCM, 1992]), and a volume on the reception history of Isaiah as Christian Scripture (*The Struggle to Understand Isaiah as Christian Scripture* [Grand Rapids: Eerdmans, 2004]). Following his death in 2007, a posthumous volume on the Pauline corpus was also published (*The Church's Guide for Reading Paul: The Canonical Shape of the Pauline Corpus* [Grand Rapids: Eerdmans, 2008]).

3. This approach was outlined in detail in his *Introduction to the Old Testament as Scripture*, the relevant theoretical sections of which have now been reproduced in a recent reader on biblical interpretation (William Yarchin, "Canonical Interpretation: Brevard Childs," in idem, *History of Biblical Interpretation: A Reader* [Peabody, Mass.: Hendrickson, 2004], 307–19, esp. 309–15). On Childs's view of the extent of the canon, see his *Introduction to the Old Testament as Scripture*, 84–106, and his *New Testament as Canon*, 518–30.

4. The name Abraham has been used consistently throughout, with square brackets used to change the alternate usage in quotations.

5. JSOTSup 352; Sheffield: Sheffield Academic Press.

6. In 1997, the rector of the University of Vienna, Alfred Ebenbauer, apologized for "the University's culpable involvement in the horrors of Nazism" and announced

to dissociate from a 1938 image of SA troopers standing, arms linked, on its steps, barring access to Jewish faculty and students.[7] When the city of Vienna appeared on my television screen in early 2007, I called my nine-year-old daughter, Hannah, in to watch. She was accompanying me to Vienna and would, I thought, be interested to see where she was about to go. The BBC program was entitled *Who Do You Think You Are?* and the central figure on screen was the English actor Stephen Fry.[8] What then unfolded as we watched was Fry's search for his Viennese relatives, and his discovery that they had been deported to Auschwitz and died or were murdered there in 1944.[9] Fry is Jewish.

Emil L. Fackenheim once wrote of his appreciation for Childs's canonical project, but expressed concern that he did not engage with the Holocaust.[10] On the one hand, that is understandable. Childs was essentially

---

an investigation into the question of whether or not the bodies of Holocaust victims were used in the creation of a widely regarded anatomical atlas, "Topographical Anatomy of the Human Being," a text first compiled in the late 1930s by Eduard Pernkopf, a Nazi and the university's rector from 1943 to 1945 ("Vienna University Apologizes for Nazi Involvement, Plans Investigation," *Michigan Daily*, 13 February 1997). That such historical issues resulted in this visitor responding to the Viennese setting as follows in this essay should not detract from the hospitable welcome offered to the SBL International Meeting in 2007.

7. See photograph number 45023 in the online catalogue of the United States Holocaust Memorial Museum, Washington, D.C. Online: http://www.ushmm.org/.

8. For further details of the BBC television program, see http://www.bbc.co.uk/whodoyouthinkyouare/past-stories/stephen-fry.shtml.

9. The television show's website's description of the fate of the sister of Fry's maternal grandfather, Martin Neumann, and her family reads as follows: "Martin's sister, Reska, was one of those who chose to stay, marrying a man called Tobias Lamm. The couple had children, but during World War II the whole family was sent to Auschwitz. Some disappeared en route. The others died or were murdered in the camp itself" (online: http://www.bbc.co.uk/whodoyouthinkyouare/past-stories/stephen-fry.shtml).

10. In the context of an endnote for a section about the post-Holocaust role of Esther in his *The Jewish Bible after the Holocaust: A Re-reading* (Manchester: Manchester University Press, 1990), Fackenheim wrote the following: "Somewhat encouraging is also the following in Childs: 'The inclusion of Esther within the Christian canon serves as a check against all attempts to spiritualise the concept of Israel—usually by misinterpreting Paul—and thus removing the ultimate scandal of biblical particularity' ([*Introduction to the Old Testament as Scripture* (Philadelphia: Fortress, 1979)] p. 606). I say 'somewhat encouraging' because—as the parenthesis indicates—for all his monumental attempt to do justice to the Jewish Ta'nach as well as the Christian

a reformed theologian, writing in the tradition of Karl Barth, a theologian whom Fackenheim himself had criticized earlier in the same volume for the smooth "seamless" continuity of his theology, pre- and post-Holocaust.[11] On the other hand, one of the more profound elements of Childs's program, in my opinion, was his claim that "illuminating" these texts is crucial, and that sources for this should be sought wherever they may be found.[12] To my shame, I once claimed a wide search for illumination in my book on this text, but had not read the three essays on Sodom and the Holocaust published in a memorial volume for the Catholic theologian Harry James Cargas in 1998.[13]

How is an initial canonical reading of the role of the universal and the particular in the Sodom story illuminated by the Holocaust? How is the reappraisal of that text in the light of the full Christian canon going to be affected? I do not claim to possess a definitive answer to such questions but offer here instead a few faltering steps on the way toward finding out.[14]

2. Preliminaries

If we ask about the presuppositions needed to interpret our text canonically, I suggest that it is knowledge of the three elements described by David J. A. Clines as the central features of the divine promise made to Abraham in Gen 12:1–3, 7—descendants, relationship with the deity, and land—that is most essential.[15]

Old Testament, Childs *either backs away from the Holocaust or ignores it*" (118–19, emphasis added).

11. *Jewish Bible after the Holocaust*, 22–24.
12. On Childs's concept of illumination, see my *Canon and Exegesis*, 77–78.
13. The volume is *Peace, in Deed: Essays in Honor of Harry James Cargas* (ed. Zev Garber and Richard Libowitz; Atlanta: Scholars Press, 1998); the three essays within it are Zev Garber, "Know Sodom, Know Shoah," 83–98; Rachel Feldhay Brenner, "Rereading the Story of Sodom and Gomorrah in the Aftermath of the Holocaust," 71–82; and James F. Moore, "Going Down to Sodom: Re-thinking the Tradition in Dialogue," 99–117.
14. On reflection, I suspect it should be made explicit here that this essay is not a critical exposition of Gen 18–19, developed from scratch and in full interaction with the current secondary literature. Rather it is something like a meditation upon a preexisting exegesis, formulated in the light of a new question, a new focus, and, in particular, a new context in Vienna.
15. *The Theme of the Pentateuch* (2nd ed.; JSOTSup 10; Sheffield: Sheffield Aca-

It follows then that the reason (or reasons) why that promise was necessary in the first place must also be understood.[16] Clines argues that the promise forms part of the deity's response to two motifs prominent in Gen 1–11, a "spread of sin–spread of grace" theme and a "creation–uncreation–recreation" theme.[17] He writes that "[t]he patriarchal narratives ... function as the 'mitigation' element of the Babel story, and ... [demand] to be read in conjunction with Gen 1—as a reaffirmation of the divine intentions for man."[18] Reconciliation between humankind and the deity will take place through a particular individual, Abraham. From the imperatives that frame the promise, however, it is clear that its fulfillment is contingent upon the behavior of Abraham and his descendants. The promise is not earned, being freely given, but it remains conditional.[19]

Finally, an awareness of the dynamics of the relationship between Abraham and his nephew Lot is required.[20] Lot's absence from Gen 18 and his sudden appearance in Gen 19 presuppose prior knowledge about his relationship to Abraham and to the promise. He first appears alongside his uncle's "barren" wife, Sarah, in Gen 11:27–30. As Naomi Steinberg notes,

> the somewhat awkward manner in which Lot's name suddenly occurs in v. 27 and in which the genealogy mentions [Sarah]'s barrenness in v. 30 suggests that the future of the second generation [from Terah] will probably be secured through Lot; Lot will function as the heir that [Abraham] will never father through his wife.[21]

---

demic Press, 1997), 30; cf. also Lyons, *Canon and Exegesis*, 126–28. On specific formulations for each element, see Clines, *Theme of the Pentateuch*, 32–43 (for descendants, see 32–34; for divine-human relationships, see 34–37; for land, see 37–38; and for allusions to all three, see 38–43).

16. Lyons, *Canon and Exegesis*, 129–31.
17. Clines, *Theme of the Pentateuch*, 66–86.
18. Ibid., 85.
19. Lyons, *Canon and Exegesis*, 127–28.
20. Ibid., 131–35.
21. *Kinship and Marriage in Genesis: A Household Economics Perspective* (Minneapolis: Augsburg Fortress, 1993), 48; cf. the same view expressed in recent works by Mark G. Brett, *Genesis* (London: Routledge, 2000), 56; David W. Cotter, *Genesis* (Collegeville, Minn.: Liturgical Press, 2003), 90; and Nachman Levine, "Sarah/Sodom: Birth, Destruction, and Synchronic Transaction," *JSOT* 31 (2006): 140.

Terence E. Fretheim has suggested that Lot is not Abraham's heir; however, the open-ended nature of the promise and Abraham's failure to complain about his lack of an heir until Gen 15:2 lead him to conclude that the narrative shows Abraham's

This is presumably why the patriarch takes Lot with him despite the divine injunction to leave his "kindred" (מולדת) behind in Haran (12:1), a decision that is, as Laurence A. Turner points out, from a "rigidly literal point of view ... inherently contradictory."[22] When the promise of land uttered by the deity on their arrival in Canaan explicitly states that the land will belong to Abraham's "seed" (12:7), however, the problematic nature of Lot's status as heir is heavily underlined.[23]

Lot is not to be Abraham's presumptive heir for long. Following arguments among their respective workers, Abraham offers his nephew the choice of part of the promised land of Canaan, either to the north, or to the south (13:8–9). Lot, upon seeing the Eden-like, well-watered lands of the Jordan valley, however, chooses instead to go to the east, leaving Canaan and going to live among the cities of the plain (13:12). As Larry R. Helyer puts it, "[Abraham]'s heir-apparent virtually eliminates himself from the promise by leaving the land of promise, Canaan. Now [Abraham] is without an heir."[24] That separating himself from Canaan and leaving Abraham without an heir are bad choices is further emphasized by the narrator's aside about the wickedness of those cities and their later destruction by the deity (13:10, 13).

Even following his rescue from the marauding kings by Abraham (Gen 14:1–16), it turns out that, whatever the patriarch might be hoping for, Lot will not be shaken from his convictions; he apparently returns straight away to his home of choice, Sodom. In Abraham's subsequent complaint to the deity (15:2), a member of his household, Eliezer of Damascus, is now named as his heir and his problematic lack of a familial heir is made explicit.[25] (As time goes by, Lot's absence will also exclude him from the divine covenant concerning land made with Abraham in 15:18 and from

---

"absence of calculation" and his "simple trust" (*Abraham: Trials of Family and Faith* [Columbia: University of South Carolina Press, 2007], 33). But his choice of the trusting Abraham over the calculating Abraham of elsewhere in Gen (e.g. 12:10–13; 16:1–4; 17:18; and 18:24–32) still leaves Lot's illegitimate presence unexplained and ignores the explanation of Gen 15:2 as Abraham's despairing response to Lot's return to Sodom in Gen 14.

22. *Announcements of Plot in Genesis* (Sheffield: JSOT Press, 1990), 62; cf. also Philip R. Davies's "a generous interpretation" of leaving kindred (*Whose Bible Is It Anyway?* [2nd ed.; Sheffield: Sheffield Academic Press, 2004], 97).

23. Brett, *Genesis*, 50–51.

24. "The Separation of Abraham and Lot," *JSOT* 26 (1983): 83.

25. Brett, *Genesis*, 56.

the covenant of circumcision outlined by the deity to the patriarch in 17:2–14.)

By the time we reach the beginning of Gen 18, Lot has been living in Sodom for many years with his (Sodomite?) family[26] and Abraham is seated at the oaks of Mamre in the promised land of Canaan with his present heir, Ishmael, awaiting—though it seems without great enthusiasm—the son promised to Sarah in 17:15–21.

3. Genesis 18

It should already be apparent that these narratives cannot be taken as purely particular. Abraham and Lot's stories are each intertwined with the deity's universal narrative. As we read Gen 18,[27] however, we can begin to see concrete manifestations of that interconnection in the exchanges at Mamre and in Abraham's robust challenge to the deity as they overlook Sodom.

First, the narrative begins with a tale of local hospitality. That the three travellers being welcomed by the patriarch include the deity is made apparent to the reader by the narrator in 18:1, and Abraham's use of אֲדֹנָי in 18:3 signals his own awareness of their true identities. The deity's presence does not in itself indicate universal concerns, however; it could simply be a localized event. But with the mention of a future son for Sarah in 18:10, the story is immediately linked to Abraham's descendants through Isaac (cf. 17:15–21), those through whom the promised blessing will come to the nations (Gen 12:3; cf. 18:17–19).

Second, Sarah's belief that the deity is unable to transcend her barrenness is made plain by her disbelieving laughter. When the potentially limited nature of Abraham's "god" is broached in this way, however, it is rebutted by a divine claim to limitless power (18:14): "Is anything beyond YHWH?"

Third, with the travellers' departure, we arrive at the divine soliloquy of 18:17–21 and the question of whether or not Abraham should be informed about the coming investigation of Sodom. Though it concerns one location, the investigation has universal overtones for three reasons: (1) the sequence of events harks back to Gen 4–11 and the deity's propensity for investigating and judging all of humankind; (2) the decision to include Abraham—the one to whom the promise of blessing to all nations

---

26. Holly J. Toensing, "Women of Sodom and Gomorrah: Collateral Damage in the War against Homosexuality?" *JFSR* 21 (2005): 65–66.

27. Lyons, *Canon and Exegesis*, 150–214.

was given—also serves to make Sodom a symbol of the universal; (3) what happens to Sodom is apparently relevant to Abraham and his descendants as an exemplar of the deity's response to those who choose unrighteousness over righteousness (18:19). Abraham's people are therefore to be seen *with* the nations, and not just *over against* them.

Finally, the deity's repeated universalization of local events in Gen 18 is echoed by Abraham in 18:25, as he explicitly appeals not to "his deity" but rather to the "judge of all the earth." The patriarch has drawn the appropriate conclusion from what has just happened at Mamre and is happening here overlooking Sodom; the deity, Israel, and the other nations, are all inextricably interconnected with each other. In the ideology of Gen 18, events concerning Israel and/or the nations are never to be seen as purely particular or wholly universal, but rather they are always to be understood as being intimately related to both.

4. Genesis 19

Lot has not yet explicitly appeared in our text. Indeed his residency in Sodom apart from Abraham means that he can only appear in Gen 19 *after* the dialogue between Abraham and the deity about the investigation of that city has been concluded.[28]

When the two "angels" arrive at Sodom's gate (with the other traveler presumably having been left behind with Abraham), Lot greets them and—in contrast to Abraham's use of אֲדֹנָי—addresses them simply as human beings (אֲדֹנַי = "my lords"; 19:2). Eventually, they accept his offer of hospitality (19:3). When the men of Sodom come to "meet" his guests (19:4–5), however, Lot's response is less worthy. He immediately offers his daughters to them (19:8), an act that indicates to me at least that the deity must look elsewhere for the righteousness that would save this city. Unplacated even by this appalling offer, the mob try to break in, but are then struck blind and pronounced fit for judgment (19:11–13). Lot and his family are effectively dragged out of Sodom by the two "angels" (19:16). Only then does Lot finally recognize the deity (19:18). At his own request, he is allowed first to go to Zoar (19:18–23), and then with his daughters to the hills (19:30), his wife having been lost en route (19:26). As Abraham gazes out over the scene of destruction, the narrator informs us that his

---

28. Ibid., 215–53.

nephew had been saved by the deity for "the remembrance of Abraham" (19:29), a salvation that Lot's iniquity precludes from being the result of the argument of 18:22–32. Finally, the origins of the ancestors of two of Israel's neighboring nations, Moab and Ammon, are narrated in 19:30–38, with each being conceived incestuously as Lot's two daughters lie in turn with their inebriated father.

5. The Liminality of Lot

To see how Lot fits into the ideology of interrelatedness identified in Gen 18, we must return to Haran and Gen 12. Though apparently excluded by the deity's directive to Abraham to go to Canaan, Lot was brought along—as it were, illegitimately—by the patriarch, presumably as his heir. His liminal status is therefore highlighted at the very beginning; he should not really be with Abraham, but with him he is nevertheless. Despite the patriarch's attempts to keep him close by and within the promise, however, Lot moves away from him as the narrative progresses, both geographically, swapping Canaan for Sodom, and ideologically, discarding the putative role bestowed on him by Abraham as the heir through whom the promise would be fulfilled.

It is not Lot's behavior that differentiates him from Abraham in these narratives. Both acquit themselves well by acting as good hosts in our text, but are also capable of reprehensible behavior, Abraham in giving up his wife, Sarah, to Pharoah in Egypt (12:10–20) and to Abimelech in Gerar (20:1–18), and Lot in giving up his daughters to the mob in Sodom (19:8). "Lot's character flaws … are shared with Abraham," Brett notes, before concluding that "all the main characters are riven with moral ambiguity."[29] What truly differentiates the two men is where they stand in terms of the promise; it is the nature of their relationship with the deity that divides them.[30] Or, put differently, it is where they stand on the relationship

---

29. *Genesis*, 68–69. Cotter's uniformly negative portrayal of Lot—e.g., "confused creature that he is" (93), "feckless and incompetent" (94), and "passive and helpless" (95)—in contrast to a very positive portrayal of Abraham, is in fact based upon a combination of flaws that are largely shared with Abraham *and* the implications of his choice to leave Canaan and abandon the promise (cf., e.g., Cotter's fulsome description of Lot's iniquities on 127).

30. Cf. the discussion in Lyons, *Canon and Exegesis*, 219–25. Helyer provides an English translation of Walter Vogels's excellent summary of Lot's position: "[b]y this

between the particular and the universal that makes one of them "right" and the other one "wrong." As we have seen, Abraham clearly comprehends the interconnectedness of the particular and the universal *and* the need for them also to remain distinct. The deity has chosen to deal with universal humankind through the particularity of the promise to the patriarch. Any attempt to dissolve this distinction goes against the ideology of our text. It is in *not* choosing to leave Canaan in Gen 13 that Abraham plays his role to perfection. But Lot transgresses by his choices and thus takes/is given a very different role in the narrative.

Lot's story is not that of a righteous man living among the unrighteous in Sodom; his offering of his daughters is not the best that he could have done in the circumstances.[31] But since the deity and Abraham both assume that Sodom might contain righteous individuals, neither is his behavior intended to indicate the inevitability of a descent into unrighteousness for those outside the promise. Indeed as many later narratives show, living within the promise is itself no guarantee of good ethics either (cf., e.g., the Levite at Gibeah, Saul, Solomon, and Manasseh, to name but a few). Rather Lot's story is that of a man who has rejected the ideology of the text in which he appears. By leaving Abraham with no heir and thus seemingly with no descendants, Lot denies the necessity for the particular altogether. For him, there is no interconnectedness between particular and universal, nor is there any distinction between them because that which will come to represent the former, "Israel," has been effectively abandoned. Lot's residence in Sodom symbolizes his choice to identify with that nation as a representative of the universal and his personal rejection of the deity's plan to bless the nations through Abraham.

Surely such a clear transgression of our text's ideology demands a fitting narrative punishment. True, Lot is physically transposed into two nations other than Israel; his descendants will not now be the mediators of the divine blessings that were to come through the promise, but only two nations among the many other recipients of them. By rights, however, Lot should have died in the fire that consumed Sodom and all of its other

---

purely human undertaking [i.e., leaving for Sodom] which separates him from Abraham, the man of the promise, Lot separates himself from those promises and consequently is further and further removed from God" ("Abraham et l'Offrande de la Terre [Gn 13]," *Studies in Religion/Sciences Religieuses* 4 [1974–1975]: 55; quoted in Helyer, "The Separation of Abraham and Lot," 78).

31. Cf., e.g., the options listed in Lyons, *Canon and Exegesis*, 222.

inhabitants. He is left alive only because of the deity's remembrance of his uncle (19:29).[32] Moab and Ammon therefore also exist only because of the deity's remembrance of Abraham. And so, instead of Lot being physically annihilated as a fitting punishment, the two "sons"—the two nations—born through the physical interventions of his daughters are each destined to receive future blessings through the very promise that he had once so casually discarded; his descendants will subsequently, for example, be given land by the deity alongside Israel (Deut 2:9, 19), though, of course, not every interaction will be a positive one (cf., e.g., 2 Sam 8:2; 2 Kgs 3:24; Jer 48; Amos 2:1–3). He and his descendants will not just remain on the fringes of the promise as recipient nations, however. Through the Moabitess, Ruth, Lot will once again become deeply embedded within the story of the promise, as an ancestor of King David (Ruth 4:17–22) and, in the Christian canon, as an ancestor of Jesus of Nazareth (Matt 1:5).

Though we might have expected our text's ideology of interrelatedness to have removed Lot from view altogether, he once again remains where he should not be. The story that began with Abraham illegitimately leaving Haran with Lot concludes with the deity's decision to give the wholly undeserving Lot a permanent role in the ongoing internal story of Israel. Despite his rejection of the particular and his repeatedly expressed preference for the universal, Lot's liminal status between the two is finally retained as a feature of the canonical text. Perhaps it is that—Lot's eternal liminality—which is a fitting narrative punishment for a man who has tried so hard to leave the particular behind him.

6. Illumination and the Holocaust

Before turning to the Holocaust itself, it is worth pointing out the obvious. That event was, and is, a vast and complex historical phenomenon, and what follows will barely even begin to scratch its surface. Much more could be said, I am sure.[33] Here, however, a few broad brushstrokes are all that space permits.

---

32. By this point in any suggested interpretation of the Sodom narrative, the meaning of this otherwise ambiguous verse is both obvious and unavoidable (Lyons, *Canon and Exegesis*, 249–50). So Brett, for example, unsurprisingly concludes: "Lot is saved, not as a result of his own worth, but of Abraham's" (*Genesis*, 66).

33. Indeed I now find the three Cargas essays very difficult to interact with, partly because their interpretations are so different from mine and partly because their views

For a few, the illumination of the Scriptures afforded by the Holocaust has effectively destroyed them as a meaningful form of sacred literature. For some, a painful accommodation between text and event has proved possible, perhaps over a long period of extensive readjustment. For others, however, nothing has really changed—the Scriptures remain more or less as they always were, unchallenged and unaltered. The canonical approach falls somewhere between these last two, believing that the final form of these texts has sufficient depth to somehow "deal" with the murderous extermination of approximately six million European Jews, while also implicitly suggesting that such a catastrophe must surely do something to them. But what?

Childs's concept of illumination raises some interesting questions about validity and circularity. If a text is illuminated *and* altered, are there limits beyond which such alterations become illegitimate? And, since exegetes inevitably have present concerns embedded in their heads, can there be a reading that is not conditioned to some degree by those modern concerns and hence already illuminated? My earlier admission about the Cargas essays does at least allow me to begin with something of a disclaimer. The exegesis presented here was not originally constructed in explicit relation to either the question with which the Gen 18–19 seminar was concerned—particular and universal within the Sodom narrative— nor to the Holocaust itself. Since the earlier published version of this exegesis in my *Canon and Exegesis* did not focus on the ideology of interrelatedness and Lot's role within that ideology, however, it could be argued that some circularity inevitably remains. Since Childs himself left no detailed rules for adjudicating levels of illumination, however, a communal discernment as to the legitimacy of the source of illumination involved will have to do, and so I leave such questions to the readers of this essay.

7. The Holocaust and the Sodom Narrative

7.1. The Attempted Destruction of the Particular

One can only wonder at what the result of a "successful" one-thousand-year implementation of a fully fledged National Socialist ideology would

---

on the text's resonances with the Holocaust are very differently framed. Rather than lament this situation, however, I would prefer to see it as evidence of the complexity of both text and event!

have been for the non-Aryan peoples of the world. On 24 June 1941, two days after the launching of the German invasion of Soviet Russia, Adolf Hitler ordered Professor Konrad Meyer, a demographics expert, to produce what would become know as *Generalplan Ost*, a detailed plan for the Germanification of the newly conquered East.[34] *Generalplan Ost* went through a number of revisions due to the speed of developments in the war in the East. At one point, however, it envisaged the deportation of thirty-one million non-Germanic Poles (85 percent of the population) and their dispersal and resettlement in Siberia, the remaining populace being thought suitable "stock" for retention within the new German area.[35] Given the technical and practical issues involved, the development of something like a "Final Solution" for the broader issues of Germanification—that is, the physical destruction of peoples other than the Jews—was largely beyond the capabilities of the Nazis in the 1940s.[36] A millennium of Germanification, however, would surely have given the Nazis sufficient time to fully realize their "racial utopia," subjugating, segregating, and enslaving many of the so-called "lower races," and destroying those other races considered "parasites" and beyond all use (e.g., the *Sinti* and the *Roma*).[37] These last groups would have been systematically "eradicated," their numbers being reduced over time by diverse means—restrictions on child bearing, resource deprivation, murder—and their living space taken up by increased numbers of Aryans.

It is not such additional genocides that resonate with the ideology of our text, however. After all, Sodom, Gomorrah, and the other cities of the plain (Zoar excepted) were completely destroyed by the deity. Rather it is the attempted physical destruction of the one group deemed "particular" by our text—those who both self-identified as *and* were also deemed by Nazi ideologues to be "Israel," the Jews[38]—that brings its ideology into sharpest relief, with the Nazis' murderous development of the *Judenrein*

---

34. Christopher R. Browning, *The Origins of the Final Solution: The Evolution of Nazi Jewish Policy, September 1939–March 1942* (Lincoln: University of Nebraska Press, 2004), 240.

35. Ibid., 240–41.

36. Ibid., 241.

37. Jürgen Zimmerer, "Colonialism and the Holocaust: Towards an Archaeology of Genocide," *Development Dialogue* 50 (2008): 101, 106.

38. Not all of those who traditionally claimed physical descent from Abraham through Isaac and Jacob (Israel) were considered to be Jews by the Nazis, however. The Karaites, for example, were considered by Nazi authorities to be non-Jewish by virtue

principle equating to an almost definitive loss of particularity![39] Though the divine casting of Sodom as an exemplar of judgment relevant to Abraham and his descendants shows that Israel is to be seen *with* the other nations, it is certainly not reducible to being just one of them; the distinction between particular and universal must always be maintained. What Lot did by departing from the land and leaving Abraham with no heir and the promise with no particularity, the Nazis tried to do with all of the murderous technology at their disposal in their "Final Solution" to their "Jewish problem."

7.2 The Destruction of Positive Regard

Other examples of National Socialism's mistreatment of the Jews also resonate with our text, but serve primarily to highlight the implicit inclusion within it of alternative types of transgression of its particularist ideology.

In 1940, with the fall of France and the expected fall of Great Britain in the near future and with access to the French colonies and the world's sea lanes on the horizon, an idea that had been discussed by the British, French, and Polish governments in the late 1930s—the settling of Jews on the island of Madagascar off East Africa—was seized upon by the Nazis. It was rapidly developed into a plan to solve their "Jewish problem" by deporting European Jewry *en masse* to the southern hemisphere, an act aping (and considerably enlarging upon) the expulsions of Jews from parts of medieval Christian Europe.[40] Though such a plan may well retain an ongoing distinction between Israel and the nations, it can scarcely be seen as the positive relationship between the two envisaged by Gen 12–19, however. This is especially the case when one notes the lack of consideration expressed about the likely survival rates for the relocated four million or so Jews within what Franz Rademacher, one of the architects of the scheme, termed a *Grossghetto* ("super-ghetto"), a sealed society under

---

of their "racial psychology," a view which they were "encouraged" to hold by the Jewish historians they consulted on the issue (Schlomo Hoffman, "Karaites," *EncJud* 11:794.

39. Cf. Wolfgang Scheffler, "Judenrein," *EncJud* 11:529.

40. Browning, *Origins of the Final Solution*, 81–89; On expulsions from, e.g., Christian England, Spain, and Portugal in the medieval period, see Haim Hillel Ben-Sasson, "Expulsions," *EncJud* 6:625.

effective police control.[41] (With the failure to conquer Great Britain in 1940, the plan was dropped.)

Neither can such a blessed relationship be seen in the enforced wearing of yellow badges by Jews,[42] the physical destruction of their properties and businesses,[43] and the systematic denial of their civil rights,[44] again acts which repeat aspects of earlier Christian mistreatment of the Jews.[45] Instead what such actions ironically illuminate and emphasize is the mutual blessing between the particular, Israel, and the universal, the nations, that remains integral to our text even while Sodom and the doomed cities of the plain burn before Abraham's very eyes.

7.3 Nazi Supersessionism

National Socialist ideology further clarifies the shape of Gen 12–19 when it implicitly attempts to replace that text's "particularity," Israel, with its own "particularity," the Aryans. That possibility does not even exist within our text, though potential adjustments are seriously entertained by the deity later during the golden calf incident at Sinai (Exod 32:9–14) and in the wilderness (Num 14:11–12), a nation descended solely from Moses being proffered there as an alternative to an errant Israel ("now therefore let me alone, that my wrath may burn hot against them and I may consume them; but of you [Moses] I will make a great nation" [Exod 32:10; RSV]).

---

41. Browning, *Origins of the Final Solution*, 85–86. Rademacher's term for Madagascar is quoted in Browning, *Origins of the Final Solution*, 85, as is his summing up of the aims of the policy as *Alle Juden aus Europa*.

42. Cf. the discussion of the history and implications of this practice by B. Mordechai Ansbacher, "Yellow Badge in the Nazi Period," under "Badge, Jewish," *EncJud* 3:47–48.

43. Examples of these are the many destructive events of *Kristallnacht*, November 9, 1938 (cf. Lionel Kochan and Michael Berenbaum, "Kristallnacht," *EncJud* 12:362–63).

44. In the period post-*Kristallnacht*, for example, insurance payments to Jews for the damages caused were confiscated, Jews were barred from schools, placed under curfew, and had their movements restricted (cf. Kochan and Berenbaum, "Kristallnacht," 362–63).

45. Ansbacher notes that the use of badges originated in the Islamic world before being widely adopted in Christian Europe ("Badge, Jewish," 45). Examples of the denial of other basic civil rights in the early Christian period are outlined by Haim Hillel Ben-Sasson in his "Fourth to Seventh Century" segment in the entry "History," *EncJud* 9:204–8.

As long as Abraham refuses to join Lot in Sodom, however, the ideology of Gen 18–19 demands that it is his descendants who will be the "particular" in relation to the other nations' "universal." Even if Israel eventually does fail to walk in the way of the Lord, there is no suggestion in our text that an alternative "promised people" will necessarily be selected. And when that possibility does arise elsewhere in the Hebrew Bible, the deity does not press the issue against the cogent objections raised by Abraham's descendent, Moses (cf. Exod 32:14; Num 14:13–17). It is Abraham's descendants who remain the "particular" in view (cf. Gen 18:17–19), with no place being left by the canonical text for the usurping Aryans.[46]

7.4. The Potentially Perpetual Role of the Nazi Party

Given its deep hatred of the "particular" identified by our text, National Socialism in 1941–1945 was perhaps as diametrically opposed to the promise of Gen 12:1–3, 7 as it is possible to get. Nevertheless, some Jewish responses to the Holocaust may create a further resonance with our text by ascribing to the Nazis a perpetual role somewhat akin to the eternal liminality of Lot. Take, for example, the implications of Fackenheim's categorization of Auschwitz as an "epoch-making event."[47] This type of event is not, he argues, one of the "root experiences" that create Jewish identity, but rather an event that is, in the words of Steven T. Katz, one of those

> historical occasions that challenge the "root experiences" to answer new and often unprecedented conditions. The destruction of the First and Second Temples are, for example, such events. These occurrences test the foundations of Jewish life, i.e., the saving and commanding God of the Exodus and Sinai, but do not shatter them, as the continued existence of the Jewish people testify.[48]

---

46. In contrast to those texts in which Moses is to become the new father of the nation, remnant ideologies elsewhere in the Hebrew Bible do not tend to see those who remain as displacing Abraham as the father of the nation. The New Testament will be dealt with below.

47. *God's Presence in History: Jewish Affirmations and Philosophical Reflections* (New York: New York University Press, 1970), 8–9.

48. "The Issue of Confirmation and Disconfirmation in Jewish Thought after the Shoah," in *The Impact of the Holocaust on Jewish Theology* (ed. Steven T. Katz; New York: New York University Press, 2005), 22.

The conclusion that Fackenheim draws from this categorization of Auschwitz is that the deity was present during the Holocaust in the form of the "Commanding Voice of Auschwitz," uttering there a "614th commandment," that "Jews are forbidden to hand Hitler posthumous victories."[49] This commandment he sees as operating most fully in its collective form in the modern state of Israel.[50]

Acceptance of and obedience to such a commandment by Jews *in whatever way and for whatever reason*[51] gives Hitler and the Nazis an ongoing role in ensuring the future existence of Abraham's descendants, a role set in perpetuity that these hostile outsiders would certainly not have desired, just as the canonical text finally gives to Lot, the indifferent insider-cum-outsider, an eternally liminal role in the story of Israel that he himself never sought.[52]

8. In the Light of the Christian Canon?

In the Christian canon, we can see subtler forms of the resonances noted above. Rather than systematically demanding the physical destruction of one half of the particular-universal equation, Christian supersessionism—drawing on texts like Luke-Acts and Hebrews—has generally seen the church of the New Testament as the new Israel. The true descendants of Abraham, it is claimed, are the people of Jesus, and Israel as it has tradi-

---

49. *God's Presence in History*, 84. The traditional number of commandments is 613.

50. Cf., e.g., his *The Jewish Return into History: Reflections in the Age of Auschwitz and a New Jerusalem* (New York: Schocken, 1978), 97.

51. Some of the problems with Fackenheim's positing of a Commanding Voice and a 614th commandment are noted by Richard Rubenstein and John K. Roth (*Approaches to Auschwitz: The Holocaust and Its Legacy* [2nd ed.; Louisville: Westminster John Knox, 2003], 349–50; cf. also Katz, *Impact of the Holocaust*, 22–29). They conclude as follows, however: "Fackenheim's 614th commandment is religiously and existentially problematic. That, however, is beside the point. *It is perhaps best to see Fackenheim's 614th commandment as a cri de coeur, a cry of the heart transmuted into the language of the sacred.* That would at least help to explain why it has touched so many Jews so deeply" (350).

52. Haman's place in the Purim festival is a good example of yet another enemy of particularity being given a perpetual role that he would not have sought for himself. On the early linking of Hitler with Haman, see Elliott S. Horowitz, *Reckless Rites: Purim and the Legacy of Jewish Violence* (Princeton: Princeton University Press, 2006), 85–86.

tionally been understood has been permanently replaced. Such a position sits uneasily, however, with the view expressed by the apostle Paul in Rom 11, that the church has not wholly replaced the particular "people of God," that "Israel" still has a purpose in the divine economy. Given that any positivity attached to that purpose has usually been seen as eschatological in focus, however, the fate of Jews sojourning with such forms of Christianity has often been little different to that of those marginalized by the supersessionists. With the rise of the Christian imperial religion and under the influence of Augustine of Hippo especially, the church's treatment of Jews has therefore tended to go hand in hand with their totemic function as evidence of Christian superiority; they should survive, it was thought, but only in stunted forms.[53] (This is not to deny, of course, that Christians have sporadically killed many Jews through the centuries.)

While it is clear that the Nazi ideology of 1941–1945 is incompatible with the physical existence of Abraham's descendants, Israel, the fact that at least some forms of Christianity have been able to acknowledge, however imperfectly, the ongoing theological significance of the Jews means that the potential does exist for rather different resonances to arise between our text and post-Holocaust churches, resonances which may go some way beyond either the defunct and idolatrous Israel of the supersessionists or the stunted totemic Israels of the more "tolerant" Christian traditions. A different response to our text's view of the positive nature of the relationship between "particular" and "universal" could be adopted and enacted by churches in the contemporary world. This could perhaps involve the development of a more nuanced understanding of the church's claimed position as a "spiritual Israel," perhaps as an implicit segment of the explicit physical particularity envisaged by our text. More radically, it could involve instead a full acknowledgement of the liminal status of the church as now being outside that particularity—that is, of its Lot-like

---

53. In attributing this view primarily to Augustine (cf. his *City of God* 18.46), James Carroll draws a stark contrast with what he sees as the lack of any desire to have "Jews survive as Jews" in the writings of John Chrysostom and Ambrose of Milan (*Constantine's Sword: The Church and the Jews* [Boston: Houghton Mifflin, 2002], 215–19, esp. 216). His conclusion, that "it is not too much to say that, at this juncture, Christianity 'permitted' Judaism to endure because of Augustine" (218), is overstated, however; Augustine's absence would not *necessarily* have led to Judaism's destruction by the church.

nature—and the knowing pursuit by it of a positive, though largely undeserved, role in Israel's ongoing future.

Should these more positive alternatives be rejected, however, our text's ideology suggests that by taking such a decision these churches risk the same fate as that suffered by Lot and the Nazis on the basis of their decisions, being incorporated against their own wills into the ongoing story of Israel and provided with a role in ensuring its future.

9. Conclusion

This essay has been an attempt to pursue the ideology of Gen 18–19 in its canonical setting and hence it has tended to explore that text with little or no critical questioning. That said, it could be argued, and with some justification, that other elements of the Holocaust and its aftermath could just as easily have been used to illuminate the shape of the text; Fackenheim's focus on the role of the state of Israel, for example, could have been expanded into an interesting discussion of the role of land/landlessness in our text. The possibilities, if not endless, are nevertheless extensive.

Others, however, might already wish to respond by arguing that the modern world does not need texts containing ideas about "promised peoples," whoever and wherever such peoples might be. Instead they might propose that the ethically responsible choice would be to reject the "ideology of the particular" in every text that encourages its invocation, including this one.

Such a view possesses a certain cogency when it is applied across the board and refrains from descending into its own narrow and racist form of antiparticularism. (Anti-Semitism is the classic example of this, of course, but other "versions" of a selectively focused antiparticularism have been vigorously pursued elsewhere, usually with dire consequences.) Those who would advocate pursuing such a general course of action should perhaps take warning from the experiences of Lot and the Nazis, however. For our text is well aware of such objections to its ideology. You see, it has met these criticisms many, many times before, and it has always managed to triumph over those who espouse them.

And that, it seems to me, is the rub.

How does one defeat any ideology that has seen its opponents come and go for millennia, while always "thinking" to itself—to paraphrase Nietzsche—that any attack that does not destroy it serves only to make it ever more secure? How does one so blot out the very idea of particularity that it can never return and rebuild itself at one's expense? And, since that idea will inevitably have possessed the minds of many actual human beings, what of the potential human price that is involved in indulging one's genocidal impulse to eradicate a chosen people?

Particularism may cost, but attempting to destroy it always costs far, far more.

Bibliography

Ansbacher, B. Mordechai. "Badge, Jewish: Yellow Badge in the Nazi Period." *EncJud* 3:45–48.
Associated Press. "Vienna University Apologizes for Nazi Involvement, Plans Investigation." *Michigan Daily* (13 February 1997): A12.
Ben-Sasson, Haim Hillel. "Expulsions." *EncJud* 6:624–26.
———. "History: Fourth to Seventh Century." *EncJud* 9:204–8.
Brenner, Rachel Feldhay. "Re-reading the Story of Sodom and Gomorrah in the Aftermath of the Holocaust." Pages 71–82 in *Peace, in Deed: Essays in Honor of Harry James Cargas*. Edited by Zev Garber and Richard Libowitz. Atlanta: Scholars Press, 1998.
Brett, Mark G. *Genesis*. London: Routledge, 2000.
Browning, Christopher R. *The Origins of the Final Solution: The Evolution of Nazi Jewish Policy, September 1939–March 1942*. Lincoln: University of Nebraska Press, 2004.
Carroll, James. *Constantine's Sword: The Church and the Jews*. Boston: Houghton Mifflin, 2002.
Childs, Brevard S. *Biblical Theology of the Old and New Testaments*. London: SCM, 1992.
———. *The Church's Guide for Reading Paul: The Canonical Shape of the Pauline Corpus*. Grand Rapids: Eerdmans, 2008.
———. *Exodus*. OTL. London: SCM, 1974.
———. *Introduction to the Old Testament as Scripture*. Philadelphia: Fortress, 1979.
———. *Isaiah*. OTL. London: SCM, 1999.
———. *The New Testament as Canon: An Introduction*. Valley Forge, Pa.: Trinity Press International, 1984.
———. *Old Testament Theology in a Canonical Context*. London: SCM, 1985.
———. *The Struggle to Understand Isaiah as Christian Scripture*. Grand Rapids: Eerdmans, 2004.
Clines, David J. A. *The Theme of the Pentateuch*. 2nd ed. JSOTSup 10. Sheffield: Sheffield Academic Press, 1997.
Cotter, David W. *Genesis*. Collegeville, Minn.: Liturgical Press, 2003.
Davies, Philip R. *Whose Bible Is It Anyway?* 2nd ed. Sheffield: Sheffield Academic Press, 2004.

Fackenheim, Emil L. *God's Presence in History: Jewish Affirmations and Philosophical Reflections*. New York: New York University Press, 1970.
———. *The Jewish Bible after the Holocaust: A Re-reading*. Manchester: Manchester University Press, 1990.
———. *The Jewish Return into History: Reflections in the Age of Auschwitz and a New Jerusalem*. New York: Schocken, 1978.
Fretheim, Terence E. *Abraham: Trials of Family and Faith*. Columbia: University of South Carolina Press, 2007.
Garber, Zev. "Know Sodom, Know Shoah." Pages 83–98 in *Peace, in Deed: Essays in Honor of Harry James Cargas*. Edited by Zev Garber and Richard Libowitz. Atlanta: Scholars Press, 1998.
Helyer, Larry R. "The Separation of Abraham and Lot." *JSOT* 26 (1983): 77–88.
Hoffman, Schlomo. "Karaites." *EncJud* 11:785–802.
Horowitz, Elliott S. *Reckless Rites: Purim and the Legacy of Jewish Violence*. Princeton: Princeton University Press, 2006.
Katz, Steven T. "The Issue of Confirmation and Disconfirmation in Jewish Thought after the Shoah." Pages 13–60 in *The Impact of the Holocaust on Jewish Theology*. Edited by Steven T. Katz. New York: New York University Press, 2005.
Kochan, Lionel, and Michael Berenbaum. "Kristallnacht." *EncJud* 12:362–63.
Levine, Nachman. "Sarah/Sodom: Birth, Destruction, and Synchronic Transaction." *JSOT* 31 (2006): 131–46.
Lyons, William John. *Canon and Exegesis: Canonical Praxis and the Sodom Narrative*. JSOTSup 352. Sheffield: Sheffield Academic Press.
Moore, James F. "Going Down to Sodom: Re-thinking the Tradition in Dialogue." Pages 99–117 in *Peace, in Deed: Essays in Honor of Harry James Cargas*. Edited by Zev Garber and Richard Libowitz. Atlanta: Scholars Press, 1998.
Rubenstein, Richard, and John K. Roth. *Approaches to Auschwitz: The Holocaust and Its Legacy*. 2nd ed. Louisville: Westminster John Knox, 2003.
Scheffler, Wolfgang. "Judenrein." *EncJud* 11:529.
Steinberg, Naomi. *Kinship and Marriage in Genesis: A Household Economics Perspective*. Minneapolis: Augsburg Fortress, 1993.
Toensing, Holly J. "Women of Sodom and Gomorrah: Collateral Damage in the War against Homosexuality?" *JFSR* 21 (2005): 61–74.
Turner, Laurence A. *Announcements of Plot in Genesis*. Sheffield: JSOT Press, 1990.
Vogels, Walter. "Abraham et l'Offrande de la Terre (Gn 13)." *Studies in Religion/Sciences Religieuses* 4 (1974–1975): 51–57.
Yarchin, William. "Canonical Interpretation: Brevard Childs." Pages 307–19 in idem, *History of Biblical Interpretation: A Reader*. Peabody, Mass.: Hendrickson, 2004.
Zimmerer, Jürgen. "Colonialism and the Holocaust: Towards an Archaeology of Genocide." *Development Dialogue* 50 (2008): 95–123.

The Limits of Intercession:
Abraham Reads Ezekiel at Sodom and Gomorrah

Diana Lipton

> *Enter in mourning habits, VIRGILIA, VOLUMNIA, leading young MARCIUS, VALERIA, and Attendants*
>
> My wife comes foremost; then the honour'd mould
> Wherein this trunk was framed, and in her hand
> The grandchild to her blood. But, out, affection!
> All bond and privilege of nature, break!
> Let it be virtuous to be obstinate.
> What is that curt'sy worth? Or those dove's eyes,
> Which can make gods forsworn? I melt, and am not
> Of stronger earth than others. My mother bows;
> As if Olympus to a molehill should
> In supplication nod: and my young boy
> Hath an aspect of intercession, which
> Great nature cries "Deny not." Let the Volsces
> Plough Rome and harrow Italy: I'll never
> Be such a gosling to obey instinct, but stand
> As if a man were author of himself
> And knew no other kin.
>
> Shakespeare, Coriolanus 5.3

Coriolanus's young son is not the only one to have "an aspect of intercession." The entire montage is calculated to affect: mourning habits, assembled generations of a single family, gentle mothers and appealing infants, and a dove-eyed woman to lead them by the hand. Coriolanus resolves to resist, but not before Shakespeare has immortalized the tropes of classical intercession, highlighting in the process the clash, or otherwise, of the personal and political, the emotional and the rational, the familial and the national. In this paper, I want to examine the tropes of intercession in relation to the figure of Abraham. The founding patriarch is frequently associated with intercession on behalf of his descendants, who appeal in their prayers to his merit.[1] Somewhat surprisingly, in view of his activity at Sodom and Gomorrah, Abraham is seldom identified as an intercessor on behalf of the nations. This is the role I shall explore here.

Regardless of its composition history, Gen 12–26 in its final form stages the Abrahamic drama against the backdrop of the nations:

> The LORD said to Abram, "Go forth from your native land and from your father's house to the land that I will show you. I will make of you a great nation, and I will bless you; I will make your name great, and it will be a blessing. I will bless those who bless you and curse him that curses you; and all the families of the earth will be blessed through you." (Gen 12:1–3)

An apparent paradox lies at the heart of God's paradigmatic command that Abraham should leave his home among the nations of the world in order that the nations will be blessed through him. If God wanted Abraham to exist in what amounts to a national vacuum, why insist that he bring blessings to all the families of the earth? And if God wanted Abraham to bring blessing to all the families of the earth, why remove him from their midst? Could Abraham and his descendants not benefit the nations and families of the earth more effectively by living among them? The answer to these questions depends in part on the definition of blessing. Most traditional commentaries equate blessing here with knowledge of God and, in particular, his uniqueness. On this reading, the call to Abraham is hard to understand. It is not clear why Abraham and his descendants required the comparative isolation of their own land, an objection that applies even if the families of the earth are understood as Jews living in the Diaspora. In this paper, I shall complicate the notion of blessing, suggesting that, along with its customary associations of teaching and example, blessing should be equated with intercession. Once intercession has been added to the equation, the need for a land of one's own begins to make sense. Intercession requires a degree of separation between the intercessor and the object of intercession, and this was achieved when Abraham interacted with the nations against the backdrop of his own land, whether land is understood

---

1. This is especially evident in the *selichot* liturgy, the preparation for Rosh Hashanah, Yom Kippur, and the Ten Days of Repentance.

literally or conceptually. Over time, land was used less as a spatial or geographic differentiator, and more as a marker of distinctive identity.

Various explanations can be offered for a biblical interest in intercession on behalf of the nations. On one reading, it could be seen in the light of developing monotheism and peaceful coexistence with foreigners under Persian hegemony. The authors of our texts sought mechanisms for extending to others the benefits they claimed for themselves. Related to this, but less altruistically, they may have been motivated by the need to remove from the land what they saw as the polluting effects of all sin, whether Israelite or non-Israelite. Quite differently, they may have used intercession as part of the process of "transforming the foreigner," according to which "the enemy will be defeated by being transformed so that it is no longer a threat to the Jewish people."[2] This latter explanation seems to fit better with later rabbinic texts than with the biblical ones I shall analyze here, but I mention it at the outset in case the ensuing analysis sheds light on its development.

Abraham at Sodom and Gomorrah

The biblical representation *par excellence* of Abraham as intercessor is found in Gen 18–20.[3] As traditionally read, Abraham functions in the Mosaic model of the classical prophet, arguing with God over Israel's fate. My aim is to present an alternative reading of these texts. Read intertextually with Ezek 14, Gen 18–20 presents Abraham as a new model intercessor for the nations, more priestly than classically prophetic. Genesis 18–20 are rich and redactionally complex; they work on many different levels and address numerous theological questions. Ezekiel 14 is close to pure theology, and has quasi-legal status;[4] Gen 18–20 explores its implications through narrative and, crucially, amends it.[5] The priestly/prophetic

---

2. Daniel L. Smith-Christopher, "Between Ezra and Isaiah: Exclusion, Transformation, and Inclusion of the 'Foreigner' in Post-Exilic Biblical Theology," in *Ethnicity and the Bible* (ed. Mark G. Brett; Leiden: Brill, 1996), 130.

3. For reasons I discuss in detail in *Revisions of the Night: Politics and Promises in the Patriarchal Dreams of Genesis* (JSOTSup 288; Sheffield: Sheffield Academic Press, 1999), 35–62, and outline below, Gen 20 belongs in the unit with Gen 18 and 19.

4. Paul M. Joyce, *Divine Initiative and Human Response in Ezekiel* (JSOTSup 51; Sheffield: Sheffield Academic Press, 1989), 72, aptly describes this passage as "priestly case law."

5. Gen 18 is often seen as a "midrash" on Gen 19. See, e.g., Joseph Blenkinsopp,

dimension of Abraham's character may have been developed in response to a theological conundrum that arose in a particular historical setting. Once God was understood as the God of all the earth and its inhabitants, and once Israelites were envisaged as coexisting peacefully alongside non-Israelites, whether in the Diaspora or in the land, the following question demanded an answer: How can non-Israelites (in contrast to Israelites) atone for their sins, and how can the land in which they live, whether Diaspora or Israel, be cleansed from the polluting effects of sin? In this paper I shall formulate responses to these questions by reading Gen 18–20, involving non-Israelite regions whose inhabitants have sinned and are punished via natural disaster, in the light of Ezek 14, involving a foreign land whose inhabitants have sinned and are punished by four disasters (sword, famine, beasts, and disease),[6] and Gen 18 (Isaac's birth announcement) and 20, involving a foreign king in the land of Canaan whose line is threatened. Needless to say, other biblical texts answer these questions differently, especially those that presuppose the cult.[7] There are, in addition, texts that address issues that are similar yet different in important ways. Jonah, for example, is a prophet who intercedes for a non-Israelite people, but the land is distant and remote, and prophetic intervention leads to repentance, which is not an option in Gen 18–20. The location of the land in Ezekiel is not specified, and although the particular inhabitants mentioned are non-Israelite, and although Israelites are mentioned only in relation to what I read as a contrasting case, namely, Jerusalem,[8] the national status of the land is not explicitly stated. This ambiguity is in keeping with Gen 18–20, where the locations and people in question are clearly non-Israelite—Sodom and Gomorrah are in the region chosen by Lot, not Abraham (Gen 13:10–13), and Abimelech self-identifies as a nation (20:4). Yet perhaps not surprisingly in view of their context in the

---

"Abraham and the Righteous of Sodom," *JJS* 33 (1982): 121–22. I see textual and theological indications that both Gen 18 and 19 in their final form respond to Ezek 14.

6. Few commentators note the land's foreignness and its implications, but see Moshe Greenberg, *Ezekiel 1–20: A New Translation with Introduction and Commentary* (AB 22; New York: Doubleday, 1983), 256: "the only passage in scripture in which trespass ... is predicated of a *non-Israelite subject*" (emphasis added).

7. Jacob Milgrom, *Numbers* (JPSTC; Philadelphia: Jewish Publication Society, 1990), 124–25, on Num 15:29: "The *ger* ... is equally liable as the citizen to bring the sacrifice. The implicit reason is the Holy Land will become polluted by sins committed upon it, be they ritual or ethical, whether by the citizen or the stranger."

8. I defend this reading below.

patriarchal narratives, where a national identification would be anachronistic, neither Gerar nor Sodom and Gomorrah is explicitly identified as non-Israelite.

There remains one important preliminary question: Is the sin of non-Israelites an issue that these texts would plausibly address? The case for the prophetic text is strong; on almost any plausible dating, Ezekiel either anticipates or describes a return to the land under Persian hegemony. The case for reading Genesis with these concerns in mind is inevitably weaker—the dating of Genesis is so much less certain. I see Genesis in its final form as a late exilic or early postexilic production that explores the possibility of peaceful coexistence with foreigners under projected Persian rule. Yet even if Genesis is predominantly anti-Persian, and thus more narrowly nationalist than I allow,[9] a mechanism for dealing with non-Israelite sin within and outside the land was almost certainly required. Indeed we see this concern emerging in texts identified with this period. Given the speculative nature of the enterprise of dating of biblical texts, and since my view is hardly a minority position, I shall proceed on the assumption that Gen 18–20 were at the very least redacted after Ezek 14 and develop its theology.

It is not difficult to justify reading passages of Ezekiel in relation to Gen 18 and 19. Ezekiel is one of the few prophets to mention Abraham (33:23), and scholars often comment on links between Gen 18 and Ezek 18, in which transgenerational punishment is precluded. Connections between Ezek 14:12–23 and Gen 18 and 19 have also been made, albeit less often and in fairly general terms.[10] Nevertheless, I want to make my case clear, and thus set out below in table form the explicit verbal and thematic links I see between these texts. The precise nature of their relationship cannot be established with certainty. On one reading, Ezekiel may elaborate and explain Genesis from a shared theological perspective. This, however, seems unlikely. As I shall show, Ezekiel represents a restriction of the theology implicit in Gen 18–20. Had Ezekiel been written with Genesis in mind, it would more accurately be characterized as an opposing point of view. On another reading, then, Ezekiel may polemicize against Genesis; it is hard to rule this out. Alternatively, Genesis may elaborate and

---

9. See, e.g., Mark G. Brett, *Genesis: Procreation and the Politics of Identity* (London: Routledge, 2000).

10. Several commentators discuss Ezek 14 in relation to Gen 18–19; see, e.g., Greenberg, *Ezekiel 1–20*, 258; and Joyce, *Divine Initiative*, 72–73.

explain Ezekiel from a shared perspective, and this is my preferred understanding of the relationship between these texts. In other words, Genesis corrects Ezekiel sympathetically. I assume, then, that Gen 18–19 in its final form is later than Ezekiel, and that Genesis is working through theological issues raised by Ezekiel. Some redactional difficulties in Genesis may thus be explained by the desire to forge a connection with Ezekiel, and even the particular placement of Gen 18–19—in some respects a bizarre interruption of the narrative flow—is affected by Ezekiel.

My first table deals with vocabulary and concepts that are shared by the two texts:

Ezekiel 14	Genesis 18–19
Non-Israelite land (v. 13), though Israelite equivalent is a city (v. 21).	Non-Israelite cities (18:20) and God called judge of all the earth.
Inhabitants sin, ארץ כי תחטא־לי (v. 13).	Inhabitants sin, וחטאתם כי כבדה מאד (18:20).
Punishment speculated, e.g., לו (v. 15).	Speculation over punishment (18:21).
Three men, שלשת האנשים (v. 14).	Three men/angels, שלשה אנשים (18:22; cf. v. 2). In 19:1 two messengers/angels, שני המלאכים.
In it (the city), בתוכה (v. 14).	In the city, בתוך העיר (18:26).
Righteousness, צדקה (vv. 14, 20).	Righteous, צדיק (18:23, 24, 25, 26, 28).
Sons and daughters (vv. 16, 18, 20, 22).	Sons-in-law, sons and daughters (19:12, 14 [x 2], 15—the two married daughters stay with their men, 19:14).
Survivors, נותרה־בה פלטה (v. 22)	המלט flee (19:19, 20, 22) but do not in the end survive

Almost all exegetes see individual versus collective responsibility (cf. Ezek 18)[11] and vicarious punishment[12] as the key theological themes of these texts. I prefer to highlight the interplay of divine justice and human intercession in relation to Israelites versus non-Israelites. One possible explanation for why this contrast is so often overlooked is grammatical. The subject shift from the generic land to Jerusalem in verse 21 is awkward, though I see אף כי as marking an emphatic turning point.[13] Another explanation is theological. For different reasons, differentiating responses in the Hebrew Bible to Israelite and non-Israelite sin have been of little interest to exegetes of any faith background, though they are a preoccupation of Jewish texts such as b. Avodah Zarah 4a, b (which, fascinatingly, draws prooftexts from precisely the range of texts that interest me here: Ezek and Gen 18–19) and Christian texts such as Rom 4.[14]

A second table reveals the extent to which intercession for non-Israelites is a shared thematic concern of these two texts. I follow Greenberg in emphasizing the "extra-Israelite" identity of all three men mentioned by Ezekiel. Job is not obviously Israelite, Noah is pre-Israelite, and Daniel (of Ugaritic myth, not the biblical book) is almost certainly non-Israelite.[15] If Lot's national/ethnic status is at first unclear, he emerges from Gen 19 as the father of the Moabites and Ammonites, two significant enemies of Israel. For the Genesis authors, Lot too was surely a non-

---

11. Joyce, *Divine Initiative*, 72.

12. See Nathan MacDonald, "Listening to Abraham—Listening to YHWH: Justice and Mercy in Genesis 18:16–33," *CBQ* 66 (2004): 27, discussing Brueggemann et al. and the "eastern bazaar."

13. I thus combine Joyce, *Divine Initiative*, 73, who reads "how much more so," and Walther Zimmerli, *Ezekiel 1* (Hermeneia; Minneapolis: Augsburg Fortress, 1979), 311, who reads it as emphatic.

14. Following the presentation of a short version of this paper (ISBL, Edinburgh, July 2006), Bruce Rosenstock suggested to me that Rom 3 carries over a hermeneutic framework from Gen 18, examining the nature of God as judge of the world (judge of the cosmos in Paul), and asking if Jews have any advantage over gentiles. Rom 4 evokes Gen 15–18 in order to argue that Abraham provides a model for both Jews and Gentiles to find justification before God. Of course, he is not an intercessor – that function was taken over by Christ, as the last verse of the chapter states. Paul in ch. 11 will take up the further question of whether a remnant of the Jews will remain despite their failure to find justification through faith.

15. Greenberg, *Ezekiel 1–20*, 257.

Israelite, albeit one with a complex identity (not unlike the matriarchs, in some respects).

Ezekiel 14	Genesis 18–19
Three save only themselves (vv. 14, 19, 20).	Two save the members of Lot's family (19:12, 13) who do not exclude themselves (sons-in-law/wives, v. 14, and wife, v. 26).
Righteousness saves (vv. 14, 20).	Righteousness could save (v. 23, etc.).
Family members not saved (vv. 16, 18, 20).	Family members saved initially, apparently for Abraham's sake (19:29), but those who do not exclude themselves are excluded via their offspring (Deut 23:4), including Lot.

Ezekiel makes it crystal clear that non-Israelites can save only themselves, and that this is achieved through their own righteousness. Genesis is much more complex; it is not easy to know in the end what its authors had in mind. Were Lot's family saved from destruction by the angels, or perhaps by Abraham? Were some saved and others not? Or, as seems to me most likely, did the entire family exclude themselves one by one through their failure to match intercession with righteousness? On this reading, Lot and his daughters were the last to rule themselves out, excluded on account of their incestuous relations. As far as Israelites are concerned, Ezekiel is less clear. Ezekiel 14:21 indicates that some descendants will be saved from destruction in the city, though not for their righteousness: "Assuredly, thus said the LORD God: How much less should [should any escape] now that I have let loose against Jerusalem all four of my terrible punishments—the sword, famine, wild beasts and pestilence—to cut off man and beast from it."

A third table reveals another shared concern: survival and continuity after divine punishment. Once again, Ezekiel is unambiguous. The three righteous individuals will survive, but no one else will survive on their merit, not even their children. Once again, Genesis is ambiguous. Lot's children survive, at least in the first instance, and he even has children/grandchildren (at one fell swoop). Yet, as noted above, the children are gradually eliminated from the picture, and although Lot's descendants do survive as nations in their own right, they are permanently excluded from joining the congregation of Israel, an indication that, in the context of the Bible at least, their survival was only skin-deep.

Ezekiel 14	Genesis 18–19
Three men will survive.	The angels survive, and Lot survives in a designated city, Zoar (19:22).
Next generation excluded (vv. 16, 18, 20).	Offspring of Lot's saved daughters are permanently excluded from Israel (Deut 23:4).
Survivors in Jerusalem (v. 22), including sons and daughters.	Gen 18–19 is embedded in a narrative in which the next generation looks precarious (Sarah is childless in 18 then taken by Abimelech in 20), but survives.

In a nutshell, the Ezekiel gap that Genesis fills is the lack of an intercessor for non-Israelites. The problem that this addresses concerns how sin may be removed from the nations, a crucial matter when Israelites and non-Israelites are envisaged as living alongside each other, whether in the land or in the Diaspora. The following tables summarize the differences between Ezekiel and Gen 18–19 as outlined above.

Removing sin from the nations: Ezekiel 14 versus Genesis 18–19:

	Ezekiel 14	Genesis 18–19
Punishment via natural disasters	Yes	Yes
Righteous preserved	Yes	Yes
People saved on merit of others	No	Yes
Future generations included	No	Yes
Vicarious punishment	No	No
Prophetic intercessor	No	Yes

Removing sin: Israel versus the nations in Ezekiel 14 and Genesis 18–19 read intertextually:

	Israel (implied)	Nations
Punishment via natural disaster	Yes	Yes
Survivors (not merit-based)	Yes	No
Righteous individuals preserved	No	Yes
Future generations preserved	Yes	Yes
Prophetic intercessor	Yes	Yes
Vicarious punishment	No	No

What emerges clearly from these tables is that the situation for non-Israelites is better in Ezekiel and Genesis read intertextually than in Ezekiel alone. In Ezekiel read alone, nonrighteous non-Israelites cannot be saved on the merits of others, and, in particular, righteous non-Israelites cannot preserve their descendants. The explanation for this improvement lies in the presence of the intercessor for non-Israelites, for which no provision is made in Ezek 14, but which Gen 18 and 19 supplies in the figure of Abraham. The dynamic is transformed by Abraham's role, and he is established here as a prototype for prophetic intercession on behalf of the nations.

In his transformative discussion of prophetic intercession, Yochanan Muffs offers four basic mechanisms for averting or limiting divine punishment: punishment is exacted little by little (Num 14:19); punishment is transferred (2 Sam 12:14); God limits his own anger (Ps 78:38; Hos 11:9); and divine love trumps divine anger (only postbiblical examples given).[16] In narrative terms, Exod 32–33 (golden calf) serves as a manual for prophetic intercession. Moses tells God: calm down (32:11); they are *Your* people (32:11); *You* brought them out of Egypt (32:11); think what the Egyptians will say (32:12); remember the patriarchs (32:13); keep *Your* promises (32:13); let the Levites kill three thousand people (32:27); kill

---

16. Yochanan Muffs, *Love and Joy: Law, Language and Religion in Ancient Israel* (New York: Jewish Theological Seminary of America; Cambridge: Harvard University Press, 1992), 9–48.

me instead (32:32). A crucial parallel between Moses and Abraham is that both address themselves exclusively to God. Whether because it was too late in the game or because they considered it to be a waste of breath, neither attempts to change human behavior, nor do they even hint to God that people might behave better in future. But this parallel is outweighed by a crucial difference. Moses utters not a word about divine justice, but Abraham makes divine justice the very basis of his intercession: How can a just God punish righteous people (Gen 18:25; 20:4)? The difference may proceed from the universalist perspective of our texts versus the highly particularist calf narrative.[17] The comparison with Moses highlights another important feature of Abraham's intercession, namely, that it owes as much to the "priestly" model as to the prophetic. This may explain the use in Gen 18:26 of ונשאתי לכל־המקום בעבורם, "I will forgive (literally, raise [the sin of]) the whole place for their sake." The verb נשא is typical of priestly texts, especially Ezekiel, with the difference already noted that the nations, unlike Israel, must be righteous. The requirement for righteousness is underlined when God saves Lot and his daughters because of Abraham (Gen 19:29), but they effectively exclude themselves through unrighteous acts (drunkenness and incest, 19:30–38).[18]

Abraham's intercession on behalf of the nations is consistent with God's promise in 12:1 that Abraham will bless (or cause to bless themselves) those who bless him and curse (or cause to curse themselves) those who curse him, which is alluded to in Gen 18:18: ואברהם היו יהיה לגוי גדול ועצום ונברכו בו כל גויי הארץ, "And Abraham will become a great and populous nation and all the nations of the earth will bless themselves through him." Intercession, especially of a priestly nature, is suggested by 18:22, ואברהם עודנו עמד לפני יהוה, "And Abraham continued to stand before the LORD,"[19] and is further emphasized by the placement of Gen 18–19 between one narrative featuring a tent (Gen 18:1, 2, 6, 9, 10, cf. perhaps the tent of meeting)[20] and another about intercession. Genesis 20:7 explicitly

---

17. Zimmerli, *Ezekiel 1*, 315, makes the same contrast, but from a perspective I clearly do not share: "By this [universal] emphasis, Ezekiel stands in clear opposition to the selfish assurances of Israel which sought to rely on the efficacy of its great men of piety."

18. Space does not permit discussion of Noah, the righteous survivor we last see drunk and sexually compromised, but that is required.

19. MacDonald, "Listening to Abraham," 27.

20. Brian Doyle, "'Knock, Knock, Knockin' on Sodom's Door': The Function of

identifies Abraham as a prophet, and the text proceeds to define a prophet as one who intercedes: Abraham intercedes for Abimelech, a foreign king, following his failed intercession on behalf of Sodom and Gomorrah, foreign cities. All three narratives deal with the continuation of families and lines:[21] this is highlighted by God's reference to descendants in his initial justification for telling Abraham his plans for Sodom and Gomorrah: כי ידעתיו למען אשר יצוה את בניו ואת ביתו אחריו, "For I have known him so that he can command his sons and his [dynastic] house after him..." (18:19). By contrast, Sodom and Gomorrah are wiped out. Even Lot is excluded on several counts from being a long-term survivor and, as noted above, his Moabite and Ammonite descendants are excluded permanently from the congregation of Israel (Deut 23:4).

Descendants are central in Gen 20, which bridges the announcement that Sarah's barrenness will end and the confirmation of her pregnancy. Her short stay with Abimelech could have resulted in pregnancy, jeopardizing Abraham's line, but the first few verses of Gen 21 confirm in seven different ways that Abraham is Isaac's father. Abimelech's line is correspondingly threatened. God punishes Abimelech by closing up all the wombs in his house (palace *and* dynastic house), and they are opened through intercession: ויתפלל אברהם אל האלהים וירפא אלהים את אבימלך ואת אשתו ואמהתיו וילדו, "Abraham then prayed to God, and God healed Abimelech and his wife and his slave girls, so that they gave birth" (20:17). This time, the intercession is matched by Abimelech's own righteousness, demonstrated through his own claim (ignorance is a defense), and validated by God: ואבימלך לא קרב אליה ויאמר אדני הגוי גם צדיק תהרג (20:4). The NJPS translation—"Now Abimelech had not approached her. He said, 'Will you slay people even though innocent?'"—obscures both the link to Sodom and Gomorrah and the national component. But both are strongly present: "He said, 'O LORD, will you slay a righteous nation?'" Abimelech thus *corrects* Sodom and Gomorrah; Israelite intercession combined with non-Israelite righteousness secures non-Israelite continuity. Genesis 20 reinforces the contrast I have outlined above regarding expected standards of righteousness for non-Israelites versus Israelites. Non-Israelites

---

פתח/דלת in Genesis 18–19," *JSOT* 28 (2004): 431–48, for whom Gen 18 "serves as a loud echo of the Tent of Meeting" (442).

21. Greenberg, *Ezekiel 1–20*, 258, cites Shalom Spiegel on the links between the choice of Noah, Job, and Daniel in Ezek 14 and their respective roles in saving their own offspring.

must be righteous, even in the presence of an intercessor, which is why there are no survivors at Sodom and Gomorrah while Abimelech and his household (and future descendants) survive divine anger. Israelites need not be righteous, which is why Abraham survives at Gerar, despite lying about the identity of his wife, and despite his admission that their marriage is incestuous (20:12).[22] In this respect, Abraham contrasts with Lot as well as with Abimelech. The descendants of Lot's incestuous relationship with his daughters are barred permanently from the congregation of Israel, while the descendants of Abraham's incestuous relationship with Sarah (they had the same father though different mothers, a form of incest worse than Lot's for being explicitly prohibited, Lev 18:9) are the vehicles through which God's blessing is transmitted. And what explains the opposing narrative judgments on these two men and their descendants? Lot, a non-Israelite, must be righteous in order to secure (with the help of an intercessor) continuity through survivors. Since he was not righteous (incest), his descendants are excluded. Abraham, an Israelite, does not depend on righteousness when it comes to survival, which means that his descendants can survive and even thrive despite his incestuous liaison with Sarah. The authors' interests in developing a system of theodicy that incorporates Israelites and non-Israelites may thus explain apparent anomalies such as Abraham's claim that Sarah is in reality his sister.

Prophetic intercession for Israelites secures a numerically significant group of survivors who guarantee continuity: ועוד בה עשריה ושבה והיתה לבער כאלה וכאלון אשר בשלכת מצבת בם זרע קדש מצבתה, "But while a *tenth* part yet remains in it, it shall turn back. It shall be ravaged like the terebinth and the oak, of which stumps are left even when they are felled. Its stump shall be a holy seed" (Isa 6:13).[23] Israelite survivors are not typically selected for their righteousness. There are no numerically significant, long-term survivors in Sodom and Gomorrah, as is emphasized when Abraham stops at *ten* (Gen 18:32). Lot and his daughters do not count;

---

22. For the case that Abraham is not lying and that Sarah is, in fact, his half-sister, see Gershon W. Hepner, "Abraham's Incestuous Marriage with Sarah: A Violation of the Holiness Code," *VT* 53 (2003): 143–55.

23. In an earlier draft of this chapter, I had used the term "remnant" in place of "numerically significant survivors." I am grateful to Sara Japhet for pointing out to me (personal communication, August 2006) that remnant is not the appropriate term here. Even though I can see that she is correct, I cannot find another that conveys precisely the meaning I seek.

their descendants are excluded from the congregation of Israel, even to the *tenth* generation, for failing to be hospitable in the wilderness and because they cursed Israel:

לא יבא עמוני ומואבי בקהל יהוה גם דור עשירי לא יבא להם בקהל
יהוה עד עולם: על דבר אשר לא קדמו אתכם בלחם ובמים בדרך
בצאתכם ממצרים ואשר שכר עליך את בלעם בן בעור מפתור ארם
נהרים לקללך
(Deut 23:4–5)

And besides, Lot is not righteous;[24] the Deuteronomic ruling casts a shadow over Lot's hospitality, as does the measure-for-measure dimension of his daughters' sexual exploitation (Gen 19:8; cf. 19:31, 32). Finally, Gen 18 logically excludes significant survivors; had ten survived, they would have saved the whole city, and thus would not have constituted numerically significant survivors, but a mechanism for saving the whole.

The preceding discussion raises an important question: how can the righteousness of non-Israelites be quantified and measured? This is a huge and complex subject that demands a great deal more space than I can devote here. It seems clear that, according to Ezekiel at least, non-Israelites are not expected to keep Israelite law, and where we find narrative evidence of their so doing, it serves mainly to discredit Israelites for their failure to keep the same laws. Evidence for this reading may be found in Ezek 33, where an explicitly Israelite audience (vv. 2, 7, 10, 11, 12) is told that righteousness cannot save them, neither their own, nor the righteousness of others (33:12–13). For Israelites, sin is the cause of death and repentance the only remedy (vv. 14–15), and not even the merit of Abraham can save them (v. 24). And how are righteousness and sin defined according to Ezekiel? Apparently with reference to a guide that sounds suspiciously like the Holiness Code (Lev 17–26): "If the wicked man restores a pledge, makes good what he has taken by robbery, follows the laws of life, and does not commit iniquity, he shall live, he shall not die" (v. 15). And again in v. 25: "You eat with the blood and raise your eyes to your fetishes, and you shed blood—yet you expect to possess the land! You have relied on your sword, you have committed abominations, you have all defiled other

---

24. Thomas M. Bolin, by contrast, equates Lot with Abraham in terms of hospitality, in "The Role of Exchange in Ancient Mediterranean Religion and Its Implications for Reading Genesis 18–19," *JSOT* 29 (2004): 37–56 (48).

men's wives—yet you expect to possess the land." The emphasis in Ezek 33 on the keeping and breaking of laws with reference to Israelites contrasts sharply with the absence in Ezek 14 of allusion to law with reference to non-Israelites. By implication, then, Israelites are judged according to their capacity to live by the law, and non-Israelites are not. Ezekiel, so far as I can see, goes no further than this in quantifying the righteousness of non-Israelites, but Genesis, of course, does. To oversimplify in the interests of economy, the righteousness of non-Israelites is measured in terms of their hospitality to strangers, which may be learned from, and reinforced by, Israelite example (Abraham's hospitality to the angels, cf. Gen 18:2–8 and Gen 18:19) but does not depend on it.[25] Oppression of strangers is hospitality's polar opposite (exemplified here by the Sodomites' demands in Gen 19:4–11, but cf. also Amalek, Deut 25:17–19),[26] and non-Israelites can be punished for oppressing others, just as they can be rewarded for being hospitable toward them. This, then, is another important respect in which Gen 18–20 refines and develops the attitude outlined in Ezekiel toward non-Israelite sin.

The different place of law in determining Israelite versus non-Israelite righteousness almost certainly explains another substantive difference between what Abraham can do for non-Israelites and what prophets such as Ezekiel can do for Israel. Once Abimelech's righteousness is established, God instructs Abraham to intercede, but Abraham does not engage substantively (cf. prophets with Israel). In particular, he is not required to judge the people; God is the judge, and Abraham's task is merely (!) to influence God (18:27). Indeed, the Sodom and Gomorrah narrative may implicitly disqualify people from judging members of other nations: ויאמרו האחד בא לגור וישפט שפוט עתה נרע לך מהם, "They said, 'This one came to live temporarily and now he acts as a judge; we will do worse with you than with them'" (19:9). Prophetic intercession for Israel usually involves a warning (Isa 6:8–10; Jer 4:5–9; Ezek 3:6–21), but this is conspicuously absent at Sodom and Gomorrah. God tells Abraham (memorably) what he is about to do, but Abraham does not warn God's potential victims. On

---

25. See Bolin, "The Role of Exchange," esp. 48–49, on hospitality and justice.

26. It would be illuminating to explore this elsewhere via b. B. Bat. 10b on Prov 14:34, "Righteousness exalts a nation; sin is a reproach to a people," expounded in relation to Israelite/non-Israelite eschatology: "R. Johanan b. Zakkai said to them: Just as the sin-offering makes atonement for Israel, so charity [righteousness] makes atonement for the nations."

Ezekiel's terms, he thus fails: בחטאתו ימות... ועשה עול ובשוב צדיק מצדקו ולא תזכרן צדקתו אשר עשה ודמו מידך אבקש, "If a righteous man turns away from his righteousness and does wrong ... he shall die for his sins; the righteous deeds he did will not be remembered; and because you did not warn him, I will require a reckoning for his blood from you" (Ezek 3:20).

Yet no reckoning is required of Abraham, it seems. The absence of judgments and warnings may be taken as reinforcement for Walzer's claim that prophecy of the usual Israelite kind is incompatible with universalism.[27] Whereas Israel has a clearly defined set of rules to which it may be held accountable, the nations have no comparable standards and are thus exempt from the cajoling attempts of outsiders to make them conform, which would in any case be ineffectual.

Many commentators see justice as the central theme of Gen 18–19. I have tried to show that it is rather the relationship between justice and intercession in relation to non-Israelites. Will not the judge of all the earth do justice? For Brett, "The answer of these narratives seems to be a resounding 'yes': judgment will fall only on the guilty not the innocent, and it will fall only after due process."[28] But apart from the escape of Lot's daughters and their descendants, issues Brett goes on to discuss, are questions about what would have happened had ten righteous people lived in Sodom and Gomorrah—the guilty would have evaded punishment for their sake—and about the inhabitants numbering between one and nine who *may* have been righteous (Abraham stops negotiating at ten, 18:32–33). Justice is a two-way process: the righteous are protected and the guilty punished. This is the message of Ezek 14, but Gen 18–19 complicates that simple message; Abraham's intercession could potentially have saved the guilty from justice. Yet as the story unfolds, we see how those who are not righteous bring justice upon themselves through a process combining natural law and measure for measure. Lot's surviving daughters repay their father for (indirect) sexual exploitation, and their offspring are excluded both from joining Israel and from being blessed via Israel: לא תדרש שלמם וטבתם כל ימיך לעולם, "You shall never concern yourself with their welfare

---

27. Cf. Michael Walzer, "The Prophet as Social Critic," in *Interpretation and Social Criticism* (Cambridge: Harvard University Press, 1987), 69–94, on the essential particularism of prophecy; criticism must come from within a system and be directed toward a group with shared values.

28. Brett, *Genesis*, 65–66.

or benefit as long as you live" (Deut 23:7). Genesis 18–19, read intertextually with Ezek 14 and in light of Gen 18:1–16 and Gen 20, is one of many Genesis texts that explore the implications for non-Israelites of interaction with Israel. Shall not the judge of all the world do justice? Yes, but doing justice for *all the world* is not as straightforward as it sounds and God needs the help of Abraham, not as a light to the nations, nor even as their teacher of righteousness, but to act as an intercessor on their behalf.

Bibliography

Blenkinsopp, Joseph. "Abraham and the Righteous of Sodom." *JJS* 33 (1982): 119–32.
Bolin, Thomas M. "The Role of Exchange in Ancient Mediterranean Religion and Its Implications for Reading Genesis 18–19." *JSOT* 29 (2004): 37–56.
Brett, Mark G. *Genesis: Procreation and the Politics of Identity*. London: Routledge, 2000.
Doyle, Brian. "'Knock, Knock, Knockin' on Sodom's Door': The Function of פתח/דלת in Genesis 18–19." *JSOT* 28 (2004): 431–48.
Greenberg, Moshe. *Ezekiel 1–20: A New Translation with Introduction and Commentary*. AB 22. New York: Doubleday, 1983.
Hepner, Gershon W. "Abraham's Incestuous Marriage with Sarah: A Violation of the Holiness Code." *VT* 53 (2003): 143–55.
Joyce, Paul M. *Divine Initiative and Human Response in Ezekiel*. JSOTSup 51. Sheffield: Sheffield Academic Press, 1989.
Lipton, Diana. *Revisions of the Night: Politics and Promises in the Patriarchal Dreams of Genesis*. JSOTSup 288. Sheffield: Sheffield Academic Press, 1999.
MacDonald, Nathan. "Listening to Abraham—Listening to YHWH: Justice and Mercy in Genesis 18:16–33." *CBQ* 66 (2004): 25–43.
Milgrom, Jacob. *Numbers*. JPSTC. Philadelphia: Jewish Publication Society, 1990.
Muffs, Yochanan. *Love and Joy: Law, Language and Religion in Ancient Israel*. New York: Jewish Theological Seminary of America; Cambridge: Harvard University Press, 1992.
Smith-Christopher, Daniel L. "Between Ezra and Isaiah: Exclusion, Transformation, and Inclusion of the 'Foreigner' in Post-Exilic Biblical Theology." Pages 117–42 in *Ethnicity and the Bible*. Edited by Mark G. Brett. Leiden: Brill, 1996.
Walzer, Michael "The Prophet as Social Critic." Pages 69–94 in idem, *Interpretation and Social Criticism*. Cambridge: Harvard University Press, 1987.
Zimmerli, Walther. *Ezekiel 1*. Hermeneia. Minneapolis: Augsburg Fortress, 1979.

Changing God's Mind: Abraham versus Jonah*

T. A. Perry

Like Gen 18–19, the book of Jonah focuses on the prophet's ability to reveal, or perhaps negotiate, the terms of pardon. Yet repentance occurs only in Nineveh, not in Sodom, and only the book of Jonah can move on to consider the status of a postrepentant city. The discussion takes the form of a debate between two valid but not entirely compatible points of view: that of God, who is content to let the Ninevites live as innocent animals and children; and that of Jonah, who has more "spiritual" goals in mind for humanity. It is, I think, illuminating for both texts to read about Jonah and Nineveh in the book of Jonah while thinking about Abraham and Sodom in Gen 18–19.

1. Narrative Provocation

If God commands a prophet to get up and go, either the prophet gets up and goes (e.g., Elijah in 1 Kgs 17:9–10) or at least has a discussion about it:

> Now God said to Jonah: "Get up and go to Nineveh. ..."
> And Jonah got up and went to Tarshish! (Jonah 1:2–3)

And without saying a word: no explanation and no discussion.

My first point is that the reader's astonishment is narratively contrived. At the very start of the book the main issue of Jonah's motivations is presented in a deliberately detective story–like way, so that by the time we reach the final chapter we are athirst for an answer. We of course rush to

---

* This work is a revised version of my paper "Jonah's Theology," delivered at the Society for Biblical Literature International Meeting in Rome, July 2009. Many of the issues relating to Jonah are discussed at greater length in T. A. Perry, *The Honeymoon Is Over: Jonah's Arguments with God* (Peabody, Mass.: Hendrickson, 2006).

judgment—Jonah is disobedient, rebellious, sinful—although to my mind the appropriate move would be reflection and speculation and suspension of judgment, noticing both the text's sophistication and the complexity of the prophetic situation. Indeed, from the very start, it is good to postulate that the best solution to grasping Jonah's motivations is the absence of one, for, as Ehud Ben Zvi puts it, "the reason for his flight is not textually inscribed in the book."[1]

2. Jonah's Admission of Guilt (4:2)

Until chapter 4, that is to say, for here Jonah explicitly gives his reason. Here is the opening of chapter 4:

> When God saw what they did, how they turned from their evil ways, God changed his mind about the calamity that he had said he would bring upon them; and he did not do it. But this was very displeasing to Jonah, and he became angry. He prayed to the Lord and said: "O Lord! Is this not what I said [i.e., thought] while I was still in my own country? *That is why I fled to Tarshish at the beginning*; for I know that you are a gracious God and merciful, slow to anger, and abounding in steadfast love, and ready to relent from punishment. And now, O Lord, please take my life from me, for it is better for me to die than to live." (Jonah 3:10–4:3, NRSV, emphasis added)

Here we finally seem to have solved the problem of motivation, and in Jonah's own words. Where is Jonah at this point? Still in Nineveh (as per 4:5), presumably on or right after the fortieth day when the destruction was scheduled to occur and did not. If we are to believe the exegetes and translators, his motive is one of disappointment and upset over God's mercy (Oh, Abraham, where art thou?). If this is believable, however, then God certainly made the wrong choice of prophet!

Of course, I quoted the text after the manner of those exegetes who wish to bolster a particular theological agenda. I quoted the last verse of chapter 3 and made the transition to chapter 4 seamless by adding words that are neither in the text nor intended. The good folks who divided the

---

1. Ehud Ben Zvi, *The Signs of Jonah: Reading and Rereading in Ancient Yehud* (JSOTSup 367; Sheffield: JSOT Press, 2003), 59.

chapters thought differently; they made the ending of the plot coincide with the ending of chapter 3:

> When God saw what they did, how they turned from their evil ways, God changed his mind about the calamity that he had said he would bring upon them; and he did not do it. (Jonah 3:10)

That is the end of chapter 3 and the end of the plot. Period. To start chapter 4 with additional words such as "But *this* was very displeasing to Jonah" are interpretations disguised as the *peshat* or literal reading.

What then *does* the text say? Let us revisit the start of chapter 4, with Nineveh behind us, and reread the start of a new episode, or rather the return to Jonah's overriding issues—both psychological and theological—with God:

> Now Jonah [became aware that he had] committed a very great sin,[2] and he was distressed [i.e., with himself]. And he pleaded with the Lord, saying: "Please, Lord, was this not my issue [with you] while still in my land! And the reason why I arose and fled to Tarshish is because *I knew* that you are a 'gracious and compassionate God, very patient and full of mercy, and who repents of retribution.' And now, Lord, please take my life from me, for my death is better than my life." (Jonah 4:1–3)

Indeed, Jonah *knew* that God is merciful and accepts repentance: "I knew it [ידעתי]." How did he know it? Perhaps intuitively, most likely he learned it from tradition or in Sunday school. Did Jonah then, well, momentarily forget—or, more likely, repress—his lessons?

Probably, but for reasons that have to be pondered. A cardinal rule for prophets is authentication: be sure you *know* who is speaking, where the voice or vision is coming from.[3] Like all prophets and as per God's programmatic announcement in Gen 18, Jonah has both a friendly relationship with the Holy One and a sophisticated religious upbringing. Now a voice comes to him and orders him, categorically and with no wiggle room, to go to a foreign nation and preach fire and brimstone and destruction:

---

2. וירע (4:1) is to be referred to the opening sins of the Ninevites (1:2); see Perry, *The Honeymoon Is Over*, 138–39.

3. A moving example is the lad Samuel's perplexity in 1 Sam 3.

"Go to Nineveh and preach *against* it [עליה]."[4] (Jonah 1:2)

The content of the message—

"In forty days Nineveh will be annihilated [נהפכת]" (Jonah 3:4)—

is an unmistakable linguistic reference to Sodom (Gen 19:21; also Deut 29:22), whose destruction could not be averted even by Abraham. The bottom line: Jonah did not recognize the voice as that of a loving and merciful God. One distinguished critic (Meir Sternberg) even considers the motive of Jonah's flight to be self-evident: "Jonah is too tender-hearted to carry a message of doom to a great city. He obviously protests against a wrathful God not with words, like Abraham or Moses or Samuel, but with his feet."[5] The interesting question then becomes:

3. Why Did Jonah Change His Mind and Go to Nineveh?

Now God said to Jonah: "get up and go to Nineveh. ..."
And Jonah got up and went to Nineveh. (Jonah 3:2–3)

Let me explain.[6] The book of Jonah is composed of two distinct and parallel narratives, each of which occupies half of the book. In the first, commanded to go to Nineveh and announce its destruction, Jonah flees to the sea and is brought back to dry land. The second part begins exactly as the first and in virtually the same language, except that this second time around Jonah accepts the mission, Nineveh repents and is spared. So much for the plot. This hardly explains the main question: what has he learned that makes him change his mind? For his career, at the end of part 1, has returned to point zero. What has changed, that he should try again?

One theory is that of a divine omnipotence that requires obedience. Through his agent the great fish, God terrorized Jonah to such an extent—perhaps the first example of waterboarding in world literature—that poor Jonah had no choice: he thus knuckled under, learned his lesson, and was spared. The weakness of this reading is twofold: on the one hand, Jonah

---

4. See Perry, *The Honeymoon Is Over*, 44, 140 n. 21, 172.

5. Meir Sternberg, *The Poetics of Biblical Narrative* (Bloomington: Indiana University Press, 1985), 318.

6. See Perry, *The Honeymoon Is Over*, xxxii–xxxv.

was suicidal from (almost) the very start and cared little for his life (in his later formulation: "my death is better than my life," 4:3, 8). On the other, it casts God in the position of speaking power to truth (if you will permit the reversal of the usual expression), of being the very embodiment of "might makes right."[7] What does intervene between Jonah's being returned to dry land and his second chance at a Nineveh mission is chapter 2, a series of astonishing prayers that some would like to excise. What Jonah learned, as Emerson said, is that God always answers prayers.[8] Here Jonah first sought to die and God obliged; then he asked to be saved and God again obliged. This means that God has reestablished dialogue with him and, seeing that Jonah is dead serious, as it were, may now be willing to negotiate, exactly as Abraham did.

Indeed, there is a slight but momentous change in God's second directive, a sign that different terms have been negotiated. Whereas the original divine command left no room for repentance, "preach *against it* [עליה]," the second time around Jonah is to preach *to it* (i.e., to Nineveh; אליה). Secondly, instead of an unspecified but Sodom-like punishment to be visited upon Nineveh, a precise text now appears. The rabbis, followed most notably by Sasson, put great stress on a kind of oracular ambiguity embedded in the command: in forty days they will be "overthrown" one way or another, either by annihilation or "overthrown" by repentance.[9] Thus, when Jonah finally admits wrongdoing, it is not because he disregarded God's command to go to Nineveh but rather because, puzzled and even horrified by the uncompromising stringency of the demand, he momentarily lost faith in God's essentially merciful nature. Or because, like Abraham, he needed to negotiate more lenient terms.

This latter possibility offers some legroom to those readers who are ritually pleased whenever the "God of the Old Testament" is angry about something. Although this aspect makes no literal appearance in Gen 18–19 or in Jonah either—in our text it is always the prophet who is upset

---

7. Our prophet's name is Jonah ben Amittai (1:1; also 2 Kgs 18:1), literally "son of truth."

8. Quoted in Perry, *The Honeymoon Is Over*, 13.

9. Jack M. Sasson, *Jonah: A New Translation with Introduction, Commentary, and Interpretation* (AB 42B; New York: Doubleday, 1990), 234–35. For this second emendation in the original command (the word occurs only in ch. 3, and there is no proof that it was used earlier) to have maximal effect, both Jonah and the Ninevites must be aware of the ambiguity. See Perry, *The Honeymoon Is Over*, 168.

about something—some form of divine anger, or at least disapproval and disappointment, may be projected. For, surely, the wicked cannot always be let off the hook for nothing—God does have standards, after all! Let us then imagine that, because of the peremptory manner of God's opening presentation as well as the harshness of his language, Jonah decides that God is again blowing his stack, thinking: "I knew all along that you are a merciful God and would forgive them, but you had to calm down a bit first, so I ran away to give you a chance to cool off."[10] This reading gives a heightened twist to the concluding dialogue in chapter 4, where Jonah is invited to consider, by a God who is a pedagogue who controls his anger and now seeks to justify it in terms of Jonah's own feelings and reactions:

"Jonah, try to understand why I was angry." (Jonah 4:4)

4. The Ending

At the end of part 1 (chs. 1–2) God has the last word, so to speak: Jonah is brought back to the start and God is to be obeyed. So too at the end of the book, God again has the last word—literally this time—and here the situation is most complex and unusual, for God asserts nothing and projects no finality: a last word which is not a final one. Rather, he asks a question!

Emmanuel Levinas, commenting on Descartes' view of the idea of the infinite as implanted in humans, summarizes its importance as follows:

> Descartes has thus rendered thinkable a relation with the more, with the non-containable. ... A patience with the *question* is thus rehabilitated. With the question which is too large for an answer. Philosophy tends to see in this the absence of an answer. ... whereas it really signifies the infinite.[11]

Where does all this leave our Prophet? Not back in rapt contemplation and divine service at the temple (or in heaven), and not in Sheol at the bottom of the sea.[12] Rather, he is still where we leave him at the book's last words, sit-

---

10. I owe this reading to Avi Perry, a student at Yale Law School.

11. Emmanuel Levinas, *Dieu, la mort et le temps* (Paris: Grasset, 1993), 165. It should be noted that the idea also occurs in Qoh 3:11, where the infinite is rendered by הָעֹלָם.

12. For the possibility that Jonah's final conversation with God takes place in heaven, see Perry, *The Honeymoon Is Over*, 199.

ting east of Nineveh and waiting to see what will be concerning Nineveh:[13] the infinite unfolding of history under the opaque but delighted sponsorship of the Creator God-of-not-yet. Jonah the visible prophet: standing before us to engage our encounter with a world of adventure.

Fine, God lets the Ninevites live (but not the Sodomites …), while Jonah peers out of his hut and says: "Let's wait and see." Is there then no concluding agreement? Does God's question then imply an acceptance as infinite as it is spontaneous? This seems to be the meaning of the concluding *kikayon* (small plant) episode, where Jonah is tricked into loving a transient thing. For in accepting and indeed enjoying the *kikayon* gift, Jonah has moved beyond reward and punishment (based strictly on one's effort and merit) and has entered a neutral zone, in which case he cannot object to the *kikayon*'s demise. And yet he does, spontaneously and in proportion to his great joy at the *kikayon*'s appearance. Why? Because he can now accept and admire the beauty of something that he did not work at or grow. However, this means that Jonah is now completely at God's mercy, not of God the Judge but rather of God the Creator, who can give and take as it pleases and without any consideration of right and wrong. This argument has such resonance because the Ninevites live through the grace of God the Creator. It is true that the Judge may have intervened, but only to certify their wickedness and allow its consequent destruction to occur. Once they have recovered their original innocence, however, then the original (gratuitous) goodness of the Creator is restored. In other words, their merit is purely negative, involving a removal of evil. To follow this logic, should we then agree with God and be content to live as innocent animals and children? Or should we, as Jonah has held until this point, strive to the ideal ends of grace and effort? Or, in a modern context, is it enough to be harmless consumers or should we put our sights on saving the world? Again, this time theologically formulated: should we fear God only because we love life, or should we love God without motive, because we fear nothing? As a loving parent, God's concluding point is that he

---

13. Jonah sits in his booth in order to see "what will be *concerning* the city [of Nineveh]" (4:5). Although the preposition *b-* is typically understood as "*in* the city" (בעיר), that cannot be the case here, since Jonah both was in the city at the time of the averted destruction and is now outside it. The issue is thus not his curiosity about its repentance, since that has already occured and the city has been saved. Rather, the question is the status of post-repentance Nineveh, whether they will backslide or not in the future. See Perry, *The Honeymoon Is Over*, 130, 148–50, 169–71.

would be content with the first. But as the Creator of free humans, he leaves the choice up to Jonah.

In the real world of Nineveh, however, the Judge must always hover just behind or over the Creator. If life is given as a gift, it still must be accepted and deserved. This complex situation can perhaps be clarified by taking another look at the concluding *a fortiori* argument that sustains God's point of view.[14] God observes to Jonah:

(a) You admired[15] the small plant
(b) which you did not work for or grow,
(c) which both appeared and perished overnight. (Jonah 4:10)

God then asks:

(a) should I also not admire (by not destroying) that large city
(b) ─────────
(c) and which was not destroyed over many generations? (Jonah 4:11)

This purported *a fortiori* is based on two observations, which are seen as reasons: size and transience. We are asked to believe that God, who created everything in its own way, still prefers

(a) size (large over small)
(c) permanence (e.g., stones) over transience as exemplified by plants.

Critics, however, admitting that this antiparallelism is less than perfect, invent a telling opposition to perpetrate the structural balance that is felt to be needed:[16]

(b) which required no effort on your part, Jonah
(b) *but which I, God, did nurture and grow.*

---

14. For a discussion of the theory of the concluding *a fortiori* argument, see Perry, *The Honeymoon Is Over*, 166–69.

15. This crucial verb חום is often understood as a compassionate refusal to harm. Uriel Simon, however, gets it just right, referring to the "primary sense of averting destruction and waste *because of appreciation and esteem*" (*Jonah: The Traditional Hebrew Text* [trans. Lenn J. Schramm; JPSTC; Philadelphia: Jewish Publication Society, 1999], 44, emphasis added).

16. Simon, *Jonah*, 45–46.

The question to be asked—even at the risk of putting the desired *a fortiori* at risk—is: Is God tooting his own horn here, or is the driving focus elsewhere? Note that in both (a) and (b) God is not praising himself but the Ninevites.

I think that the *a fortiori* argument stands as it is and without any need of emendation or added suppositions. Points (a) and (c) are comprehensible and reasonable: if Jonah can admire and enjoy a small and fleeting plant, all the more reason that he should appreciate the qualities of Nineveh, that great and enduring city. What, however, is God's point in (b) about Jonah's enjoyment in spite of his lack of effort in its creation? For the sequence to be consistent, note again that (a) and (b) offer contrasts not between God and Jonah but between Jonah and Nineveh. So too for the (b) segment:

(b) which required no effort on your part, Jonah
but which the Ninevites themselves did nurture and grow.

It is here argued not that Nineveh is God's creation but rather that it grew of its own accord, and that in fact is God's point here. We thus understand more keenly God's great disappointed anger over the Ninevites' wickedness because he first admired what they achieved on their own: a large metropolis, a smoothly functioning society, respect for the king, everyone doing assiduously what comes naturally (i.e., Gen 1:22; 9:1; Exod 1:7). Wow! From this perspective, size and permanence do matter to the Creator.

In short, the book's ending focus, coming from God but which the prophet is invited to share, is that the Jonah story is not all about Jonah (read: Israelites?) and not all about God and his mercy either. It is about תיקון עולם, the maintenance of this world as instanced by ... repentant Nineveh! This lesson from Jonah should surely be borne in mind when weighing the delicate balance of particularism and universalism in Gen 18–19.

5. The Disobedience Theory

I would like to append a brief concluding word on the almost universal theory of Jonah's rebellious disobedience and of God's purported need to teach him a lesson. There is a traditional and central principle in religious culture and education, that of *imitatio Dei*, of walking in God's ways. Who then is Jonah's God, that he should be imitated? From the critical literature I take note of the following favorites:

- a deity who waterboards his emissary into compliance
- a dictator who holds to the doctrine of "Might makes right" and must be obeyed at all costs
- a pedagogue who would rather be feared than loved

Of course, such divine features are not typically directed against God but arise as a corollary to the wish to demean and even caricature Jonah: that servant of God who did go to distant Nineveh, who persuaded the entire population to change their ways, and who was thought to have gone to heaven without suffering death.[17] But when the chosen servant is diminished, so too is the master. I find these unsavory characterizations of God in much of the critical literature; I find none of them in the book of Jonah. Quite the contrary, the Jonah-God dialogue models an adult relationship based on openness and mutual respect for strongly held principles that may be both valid while not entirely compatible. This paradox is compounded by another, this one more within our power to rethink. Jonah succeeds in saving his sinful city, but Abraham fails to save his. And yet Abraham is revered as a model of obedience, while Jonah, at least in much of our critical literature, stands condemned.

Bibliography

Ben Zvi, Ehud. *The Signs of Jonah: Reading and Rereading in Ancient Yehud*. JSOTSup 367. Sheffield: JSOT Press, 2003.
Levinas, Emmanuel. *Dieu, la mort et le temps*. Paris: Grasset, 1993.
Perry, T. A. *The Honeymoon Is Over: Jonah's Arguments with God*. Peabody, Mass.: Hendrickson, 2006.
Sasson, Jack M. *Jonah: A New Translation with Introduction, Commentary, and Interpretation*. AB 42B. New York: Doubleday, 1990.
Simon, Uriel. *Jonah: The Traditional Hebrew Text*. Translated by Lenn J. Schramm. JPSTC. Philadelphia: Jewish Publication Society, 1999.
Sternberg, Meir. *The Poetics of Biblical Narrative*. Bloomington: Indiana University Press, 1985.

---

17. Along with Enoch and Elijah; see Perry, *The Honeymoon Is Over*, 101–2.

Why Did God Choose Abraham?
Responses from Medieval Jewish Commentators

Amira Meir

כי ידעתיו למען אשר יצוה את בניו ואת ביתו אחריו ושמרו דרך יהוה לעשות
צדקה ומשפט למען הביא יהוה על אברהם את אשר דבר עליו (Gen 18:19)

My question in this paper is, Why did God choose Abraham? More specifically, why, according to medieval Jewish commentators, did God choose Abraham, distinguishing him and singling him out from among all people of the world? Did these Jewish commentators think that God chose Abraham because of a natural characteristic, or rather because of a decision that Abraham made that reflected the way of life he chose to lead?

The Hebrew Bible itself gives no clear answer to this basic question. The only biblical verse that mentions the verb בחר "to choose" in relation to Abraham is in Neh 9:7–8:

אתה הוא יהוה האלהים אשר בחרת באברם והוצאתו מאור כשדים ושמת
שמו אברהם: ומצאת את לבבו נאמן לפניך וכרות עמו הברית

> You are the Lord God, who chose Abram, who brought him out of Ur of the Chaldeans and changed his name to Abraham. Finding his heart true to you, you made a covenant with him.

According to Nehemiah, then, God chose Abraham because he found Abraham's heart to be true to Him. Yet even if this is God's reason, what precisely does this phrase mean: ומצאת את לבבו נאמן לפניך "and you found his heart true to you"?

A more detailed discussion of what attracted God to Abraham can be found in postbiblical literature, such as the Apocalypse of Abraham, the *Fragments* of Pseudo-Philo, and the book of *Antiquities* of Flavius Josephus. In the Bible itself, however, there appears to be no clear explanation for choosing Abraham.

Chapters 18–19 constitute a distinct unit in the book of Genesis. Chapter 18 includes three verses of special importance, verses 17–19. These are the only verses in chapters 18–19, indeed in all the chapters that recount the stories of the patriarchs, which articulate clearly Israel's oral-religious destiny. I believe that they may relate to our question concerning why God chose Abraham.

Verse 17 opens with the words ויהוה אמר "and God said." As Robert Alter points out,[1] the verb אמר "said" is sometimes used elliptically for אמר בליבו "said in his heart," and that seems clearly to be the case here, since verses 17–19 represent a divine soliloquy.

Many scholars see these verses as an interruption of the narrative flow of verse 16 and verses 20–21 and identify them as a later addition to the text.[2] John Skinner and others claim that the language and the thought show signs of Deuteronomistic influence, but this is not my present interest.[3] My focus here is that these verses, whatever their origin, describe God's thoughts about Abraham and so, as Gordon Wenham points out, make the reader wiser than Abraham at this point.[4]

Verses 17–18 discuss God's determination not to conceal (לכסות) anything from Abraham, since Abraham will become a great and mighty nation, and all the nations of the earth will be blessed through him.

The central verse here, I think, is verse 19. This verse gets to the very heart of the covenant and informs the reader why Abraham was chosen by God to begin a special nation. The verse has some semantic difficulties, generated in part by its unusual grammatical structure; it seems to be packed with meaning and to cry out for interpretation. To use Rashi's language in his commentary to Gen 25:22: על כרחך המקרא הזה אומר דורשני, "even against your will, this verse pleads: interpret me!"

---

1. *Genesis* (New York: Norton, 1996), 80.

2. For instance, J. Estlin Carpenter, *The Composition of the Hexateuch* (New York: Longmans, Green & Co., 1902), 197–98, and others.

3. John Skinner, *Genesis* (ICC; Edinburgh: T&T Clark, 1980), 303. See also Hermann Gunkel, *Genesis* (trans. Mark E. Biddle; Macon, Ga.: Mercer University Press, 1997), 201.

4. *Genesis 16–50* (WBC 2; Dallas: Word, 1994), 50.

In order to get as close as possible to the meaning of the verse as a whole, it is crucial to understand the meaning of each individual word, as well as the grammatical structure of the unit that the words compose.

The vocabulary of this sentence presents several difficulties: (1) What is the meaning of the verb ידעתיו? (2) What is ביתו "his house" or "his household"? (3) What is דרך יהוה "the way of the Lord"? (4) What precisely is צדקה ומשפט "righteousness and justice"?

The grammatical structure of this verse is unusual; it contains a main clause, כי ידעתיו, and this main clause has two subordinate clauses: (1) למען אשר יצוה את־בניו ואת־ביתו אחריו ושמרו דרך יהוה לעשות צדקה ומשפט "*that* he may instruct his children and his posterity to keep the way of the Lord by doing what is just and right"; and (2) למען הביא יהוה על־אברהם את אשר־דבר עליו "*in order* that the Lord may bring about for Abraham what he has promised him."

Steven Fassberg deals with this pattern of למען.[5] He notes that there are only two other verses in the Bible where this pattern (למען "in order that" + verb = למען קטל) appears twice in one verse: Deut 8:16 and Ezek 21:15. In these verses, however, the second occurrence of למען is either a repetition or a parallel to the first. Genesis 18:19 is then the only verse in the Bible in which the main clause has two subordinate sentences starting with למען "for the purpose of/in order that" in a single sentence and with two different meanings. So the question is: What is the "reason for which" or perhaps "because of which" (למענה) God chose Abraham?

I turn now to answers to this precise question offered by a range of medieval Jewish commentators who lived between the tenth and sixteenth centuries in Egypt, France, Spain, and Italy: Rabbi Sa'adia Ga'on,[6] Rabbi Shelomo Izhaki,[7] Rabbi Shmuel ben Meir,[8] Rabbi Behor Shor,[9] Bahya ben Asher,[10] Rabbi Hizkiya bar Manoach,[11] Rabbi David Kimhi,[12] Rabbi Abra-

---

5. *Studies in Biblical Syntax* (Jerusalem: Magnes, 1994), 103.
6. Rasag, ninth century, Egypt and Babylon, who is considered to be the person who established biblical commentary.
7. Rashi, 1040–1105, Troyes, northern France.
8. Rashbam, Rashi's grandson, 1080–1169.
9. Twelfth century, France.
10. Thirteenth–fourteenth century, Saragossa, Spain.
11. Hazkuni, thirteenth century, France.
12. Radak, 1160–1236, Provencal.

ham Ibn Ezra,[13] Rabbi Moshe ben Nahman,[14] and Rabbi Ovadia Sforno.[15] It is interesting to note that Ibn Ezra, well-known for his systematic and highly analytical commentaries, does not relate to this important verse and that Rashbam, also known for his critical approach, relates to this verse only briefly. I will try to address all the questions that were mentioned.

First, let us look at the words—צדקה ומשפט, דרך יהוה, ביתו, ידעתיו—words that in our verse have multiple meanings.

1. ידעתיו

It is worth making some observations at the outset about translations, some that precede our commentators and may or may not have been known to them, and others that came much later. Onkelos,[16] the author of an Aramaic translation that would have been well-known to all later Jewish commentators, translates this word as אֲרֵי גְלֵי קֳדָמַי (Heb. הרי ידוע לפני) "because it is known to me/before me." Rasag translates as follows: וַאֲנָא אָעְלָם בְּאַנָּה סַיֲאָמֵר (Heb. ואני יודע שהוא יצווה) "and I know that he will command." The Septuagint translates this verse as: Ἤδειν γάρ ὅτι συντάξει "for I know that." The Vulgate likewise offers: scio enim quod praecepturus sit "for I know that he will command."

Modern translations vary immensely, as indicated by just three examples: John Skinner translates ידעתיו as "for I have known him"; Ephraim A. Speiser translates it as "singled him out"; and Robert Alter offers "I have embraced him."[17]

Isaac ben Judah Abrabanel,[18] who wandered from Portugal through Spain to Italy and is well-known for asking important questions, asks: מה ענין כי ידעתיו, אשר היקשו על כל המפרשים לישבו? "What is the issue with ידעתיו, that all commentators found it so hard to understand?"

The verb ידע in its different conjugations occurs 940 times in the Bible.

---

13. Raba, 1089–1164, Spain, North Africa, Egypt, Israel, Italy, France, England.
14. Ramban, also known as Nahmanides, 1194–1270; Gerona, Spain; Israel.
15. 1475–1550, Italy.
16. Circa third century. The official eastern (Babylonian) translation of the Pentateuch into Aramaic.
17. Skinner, *Genesis*, 304; Ephraim A. Speiser, *Genesis* (AB 1; New York: Doubleday, 1964), 132; Alter, *Genesis*, 80 .
18. 1437–1508, Portugal, Spain, Italy.

Abraham Even-Shoshan's concordance lists sixteen different meanings; 821 occurrences share the same meaning: "knowing intellectually."[19]

In Gen 18:19, the verb ידעתיו can be interpreted in more than one way. Let me list a few.

1.1. "To inform, to tell"

1.1.1. Rabbi Sa'adiyah Ga'on (Rasag)

כי ידעתיו והנני מודיעו שיצווה את

"because I have known him and I informed him that he will command"[20]

1.1.2. Rabbi Shmuel ben Meir (Rashbam)

ואני יודע שבניו ישמרו דרך ה' ויזכו להביא עליהם את אשר דיבר לאברהם...

"And I know that his sons (descendants) will keep the way of God and will have the privilege of bringing upon themselves what God said to Abraham ..."

However, his commentary may be understood here also in the sense of "having knowledge."

1.1.3. Rabbi David Kimhi (Radak)

כי ידעתיו שהוא ירא ממני ואוהב אותי ובדעתי שיהיו בניו כמותו ואודיענו...

"כי ידעתיו he is in awe of me and loves me. I intend for his children to develop in the same way. This is why I will inform him ..."

1.2. "To like, to love"

1.2.1. Rabbi Shelomo Izhaki (Rashi)

כי ידעתיו (ארי ידעתינה. התרגום מפרש) לשון חיבה כמו: "מודע

---

19. *A New Concordance of the Bible* (Jerusalem: Kiryat Sefer, 1988), 432–36.
20. If I do not mention the name of a translator, the translation is mine.

לאישה", "הלא בעז מֹדַעְתָּנוּ", "וָאֵדָעֲךָ בְשֵׁם". ואמנם עיקר לשון
כולם אינו אלא לשון ידיעה, שהמחבב את האדם מקרבו אצלו ויודעו
ומכירו.

"an expression denoting affection as in 'A kinsman on her husband's side,'[21] [and as in] 'our kinsman, Boaz,'[22] [and as in] 'I will know you by name.'[23] However, they all stem mainly from none other than ידיעה [knowing], because one who has affection for another relates to him more closely and knows him."[24]

So ידע, according to Rashi, implies not only cognition but also a closeness of relationship, as Nehama Leibowitz points out.[25]

1.2.2. Rabbi Hizkiya bar Manoach (Hazkuni)

לשון חיבה (לשון רש"י), כמו: "מודע לאישה", כלומר לגוי גדול יהיה
לפי שהוא חביב בעיני ועתיד להעמיד משפחות הרבה, ולפיכך נכון
להודיעו הדין שאני עושה בסדום.

This is "an expression denoting affection (Rashi's expression), as in 'A kinsman on her husband's side.'[26] That is, he will be a great nation, because he is beloved in my eyes, and he will raise many families. And so it is right to inform him of the judgment that I intend to carry out in Sodom."

So according to Hazkuni, the meaning of ידעתיו is "to like" as well as "to inform." This commentary is typical of Hazkuni, who often begins with Rashi and adds his own commentary.

---

21. Ruth 2:1.
22. Ruth 3:2.
23. Exod 33:17.
24. Avrohom Davis, *The Metsudah Chumash: Rashi, Genesis, A New Linear Translation* (trans. Avrohom Kleinkaufman; New York: Ktav, 1991), 183–84.
25. *Studies in Bereshit Genesis* (Jerusalem: World Zionist Organization Department for Torah Education and Culture, 1974), 167. See also 171 n. 3 concerning Martin Buber's idea of "know," based upon his book *Good and Evil: Two Interpretations* (New York: Charles Scribner & Sons, 1953), 55–56.
26. Ruth 2:1.

1.3. "To protect, to save"—ידיעה בו ממש

1.3.1. Rabbi Moshe ben Nahman (Ramban)

> ...והנכון בעיני כי היא ידיעה בו ממש ירמוז כי ידיעת השם שהיא השגחתו בעולם השפל היא לשמור הכללים וגם בני האדם מונחים בו למקרים עד בוא עת פקודתם, אבל בחסידיו ישום אליו לבו לדעת אותו בפרט, להיות שמירתו דבקה בו תמיד, לא תפרד הידיעה והז־כירה ממנו כלל, כטעם "לא־יגרע מצדיק עיניו", ובאו מזה פסוקים רבים כדכתיב "הנה עין יהוה אל־יראיו" וזולת זה.

> "... The correct interpretation appears to me to be that the word ידעתיו literally means 'knowing.' He is thus allowing that God's knowledge, which is synonymous with His Providence in the lower world, is to guard the species, and even the children of men are subject despite it to the circumstantial evil occurrences until the time of their visitation comes.[27] But as regards His pious, He directs His Providence to know each one individually so that His watch constantly attaches to him, His knowledge and remembrance of him never departs etc. [As it says: 'He withdraweth not his His eyes from the righteous' (Job 36:7). There are many verses on this theme, as it is written: 'Behold, the eye of the Eternal is toward them that fear Him,' (Psalms 33:18), and other verses besides."][28]

1.3.2. Bahya ben Asher

Bahya ben Asher mentions two options for interpreting the word ידעתיו. In one interpretation he follows in the footsteps of Ramban and interprets the verb as "to protect," "to save":

> או יהיה לשון השגחה, כי ידיעת הש"י את האדם היא השגחתו בו. וכשיאמר "כי ידעתיו", בא למעט שאר בני האדם שאינם צדיקים שאין ההשגחה בהם כמו בצדיקים, וצריך שתשכיל כי ההשגחה בעולם השפל במין האדם היא כללית ופרטית, ופסוק מלא הוא שמצינו "גדל העצה ורב העליליה אשר־עיניך פקחות על־כל־דרכי בני אדם לתת לאיש כדרכיו וכפרי מעלליו". ובשאר בעלי חיים היא כללית לא פרטית רק בכדי לקיים המין. וההשגחה הפרטית שבמין האדם

---

27. According to Jer 50:27: "Their day is come, The hour of their doom!"
28. Translation by Charles B. Chavel, *Ramban Commentary on the Torah, Genesis* (New York: Shilo, 1971), 242.

נחלקת לשני חלקים: השגחה בו לידע כל פרטי מעשיו ומחשבותיו, והשגחה בו להגן עליו ולהצילו מן המקרים. ההשגחה בו לידע כל פרטי מעשיו היא בכל אדם מישראל או מן האומות, כענין שכתוב: "היצר יחד לבם המבין אל-כל-מעשיהם". ההשגחה בו להציל מן המקרים אין זה בכל אדם, ואפילו בישראל, כי אם בצדיקים שבהם, שהקב"ה מציל את הצדיקים מן המקרים שושאר בני האדם נמסרים בידם, ולא יעזוב את חסידיו ולא יגרע מהם עיניו,[29] אלא השגחתו בצדיק תמיד, לא תפרד ממנו כלל, וזה לשון "כי ידעתיו" שההשגחה בו ובשאר הצדיקים להצילם ממקרי בני האדם.[30]

"Alternatively, the meaning of the word is that 'I have supervised him closely.' When God 'knows' a person this implies that He keeps careful track of all that this person does and He protects him. The words כי ידעתיו single out Abraham from other ordinary human beings who do not enjoy the constant supervision by God of what they do and what happens to them. The righteous enjoy this advantage over their secular-oriented fellow human beings. You should appreciate that God operates in this universe by means of both השגחה כללית and השגחה פרטית, 'supervision of a general kind' and 'supervision of a particular, personal kind.' We have a verse in Jeremiah 32:19 which spells this out. The text is: גדל העצה ורב העליליה אשר-עיניך פקחות על-כל-דרכי בני אדם לתת לאיש כדרכיו וגו' 'wondrous in purpose and mighty in deed, whose eyes observe all the ways of man, so as to repay every man according to his ways, and with proper fruit of his deeds!' Considering other living creatures, however, God's supervision of their fates is of a more general nature; it concerns itself only with preserving the respective species. The השגחה פרטית, personalized supervision of mankind, operates in the following manner. There is supervision in the sense that God is aware of all of man's action and thoughts; this extends both to Jews and to Gentiles alike. We know this from Psalm 33:15 היצר יחד לבם המבין אל-כל- מעשיהם 'He who fashions the hearts of them all, who discerns all their doings.' The supervision becomes manifest in God's protecting people against mishaps. This type of benevolent supervision does not extend to Gentiles and not even to all Israelites except the righteous among them. God saves the righteous from experiencing the kind of disasters which non-deserving people are prone to experience. This

---

29. According to Job 36:7.
30. Bahye ben Asher, *Commentary on the Torah, Genesis, 1* (Jerusalem: Mossad Ha'Rav Kook, 1981), 176.

is meant by the words כי ידעתיו in our verse (according to the view of Nachmanides)."[31]

So according to Bahya, there are two modes of divine supervision: (1) supervision in the sense that God is aware of the actions and thoughts of all people (Jews and non-Jews); and (2) supervision against errors and accidents (only the righteous among Jews and non-Jews).

1.4. "To raise, to elevate"

This is a suggestion that Ramban mentions and rejects:

ויתכן שיהיה ידעתיו, גדלתיו ורוממתיו, בעבור אשר יצוה את בניו אחריו לעשות את הישר לפני ולכך אשימנו לגוי גדול ועצום שיעבדוני וכמוהו "ידעתיך בשם", "מה־אדם ותדעהו".

"It is possible that the word ידעתיו means 'I have raised him and elevated Him so that he shall command his children after him to do that which is right before Me, and therefore I will make him a great and mighty nation so that he should serve Me. In a similar sense are the verses: 'I know thee (ידעתיך) by name'[32] (the sense would thus be: 'I have made thee great in name'); 'What is man, that Thou knowest him?'"[33]

1.5. "To bestow recognition"—לשון גדולה ומעלה: Bahya ben Asher

This is Bahya's other interpretation:

לשון גדולה ומעלה. מלשון "מה־אדם ותדעהו" וטעמו: מה אדם לפניך שתרבה לו גדולה.

"The root ידע is used here in the sense of bestowing recognition on someone, as in Psalm 144:3 מה־אדם ותדָעֵהו 'what is man that you should put him on a pedestal?'"[34]

---

31. This is according to the view of Ramban; Bahye ben Asher, *Torah Commentary* (trans. Eliyahu Munk; 7 vols.; Jerusalem: Lampda, 1998), 1:297–98.
32. Exod 33:12.
33. Ps 144:3; Chavel, *Ramban*, 242.
34. Ben Asher, *Torah Commentary*, 1:297.

1.6. "To admonish": Ovadia Sforno

כי ידעתיו — מוכיח במישור

"I admonish him with directions."[35]

For Sforno, God's knowledge of Abraham entails admonishment, as opposed to endearment.

Now let us look at the other words in our verse:

2. ביתו "His house/household"

Only Rashi and Radak relate to this term.

2.1. Rashi

על "בית אברהם" לא נאמר אלא "על אברהם". למדנו כל המעמיד בן צדיק כאילו אינו מת.

"It does not say 'upon the house of Abraham' but rather, 'upon Abraham.' We learned from this that he who produces a righteous son is considered as not having died.'"[36]

2.2. Radak

את בניו—ר"ל בני ביתו שאינם בניו להודיע כי חייב אדם להדריך בני ביתו אף על פי שאינם בניו בדרך ישרה ולהכריחם בזה אחר שהם בני ביתו ומשרתיו כמו שאמר דוד המלך "עיני בנאמני־ארץ לשבת עמדי הלך בדרך תמים הוא ישרתני. לא־ישב בקרב ביתי עשה רמיה וגו'". ונאמר על הרשע בהפך זה "משל מקשיב על־דבר־שקר כל משרתיו רשעים" על אברהם—ר"ל ועל זרעו אחריו.

את־בניו ואת־ביתו—both the members of his household who were not biologically related to him as well as his family, in order to teach us that a man is obliged to monitor the conduct of all members of his household and is responsible for their misconduct if he did not use his authority to put a stop to it. David spells out this responsibility

---

35. Obadiah ben Jacob Sforno, *Commentary on the Torah* (trans. Raphael Pelcovitz; New York: Mesorah, 1987), 87.

36. Based upon Gen. Rab. 49:4; *Midrash Bereshit Rabba* (ed. J. Theodor and Chanoch Albeck; Jerusalem: Wahrmann, 1965); Davis, *Metsudah Chumash*, 184.

of the head of the household in Ps 101:6–7 עיני בנאמני־ארץ לשבת עמדי הלך בדרך תמים הוא ישרתני. לא־ישב בקרב ביתי עשה רמיה 'My eyes on the trusty men of the land, to have them at my side. He who follows the way of the blameless shall be in my service. He who deals deceitfully shall not live in my house.' Concerning the wicked Solomon says in Prov 29:12: 'A ruler who listens to lies, all his servants become wicked.' על אברהם meaning on his descendants after him."

3. דרך יהוה "The way of God"

None of these commentators relates to this expression. It might be that the meaning of "the way of God" in this context is clear, namely, that דרך יהוה is to do justice and righteousness. Moses ben Maimon (Rambam)[37] sees it this way.[38]

4. צדקה ומשפט "Just and right/justice and righteousness"

The couplet of righteousness and justice, צדקה ומשפט, is a hendiadys, a figure of speech used for emphasis, typically transforming a noun plus an adjective into two nouns linked by a conjunction.[39] So משפט וצדקה and צדקה ומשפט mean the same thing.

The expression צדקה ומשפט occurs in the Bible twenty-six times, and in its reverse structure משפט וצדקה thirty-one times; they express the idea of social justice. Moshe Weinfeld claims that the concept of doing justice and righteousness in the literature of ancient Israel and the ancient Near East implies maintaining a just society so that equality and freedom prevail.[40]

Among all these commentators, only Ramban refers here to the expression צדקה ומשפט. In his commentary on verse 18, he writes:

---

37. Moses ben Maimon, 1138–1204, Cordova, Spain; Fostat, Egypt.

38. Moses Maimonides, *The Guide of the Perplexed* (trans. Shlomo Pines; Chicago: University of Chicago Press, 1963), 572.

39. "Sound and fury" gives a more striking image than "furious sound." Other examples include עני ואביון, חסד ואמת and many more.

40. Moshe Weinfeld, *Justice and Righteousness in Israel and in the Nations* (Jerusalem: Magnes, 1985), 2.

> כי ידעתי בו שהוא מכיר ויודע שאני ה' אוהב צדקה ומשפט, כלומר
> שאני עושה משפט רק בצדקה ולכך "יצוה את־בניו ואת־ביתו אחריו"
> לאחוז דרכו. והנה אם בדרך צדקה ומשפט יפטרו יפלל לפני להניחם
> וטוב הדבר, ואם חייבין הם לגמרי גם הוא יחפוץ במשפטם, ולכן ראוי
> שיבוא "בסוד יהוה"

"For I know that he recognizes and is cognizant that I the Eternal loveth righteousness and justice;[41] that is to say, that I do justice only with righteousness, and therefore *he will command his children and his household after him to follow in his path.* Now if it is possible in keeping with righteousness and justice, to free the cities from destruction, he will pray before Me to let them go, and it will be well and good. And if they are completely guilty, he too will want their judgment. Therefore, it is proper that he enter 'in the council of God.'"[42]

Not only does Ramban not relate to the notion of צדקה ומשפט as one expression, a hendiadys, but he breaks it into its components and claims that Abraham knows that God is doing justice only with righteousness. With this interpretation, he relates to righteousness as an adjective that describes divine justice.

5. למען "In order that"

5.1. Rashi

> כך הוא מצוה לבניו: שמרו דרך ה', כדי שיביא על אברהם וגו'
> "Thus he commands his children: 'Keep the way of God so that God will bring upon Abraham.'"[43]

According to Rashi, the words ושמרו דרך יהוה "keep the way of God," along with the continuation למען הביא יהוה על־אברהם "so that God will bring upon Abraham," are not God's words but rather Abraham's, who with these words commands his children to keep the way of God. Had they been God's words, they should have been written ... ושמרו דרכי ... למען אביא "and they would keep *my* way ... in order that *I* will bring...."

If these are Abraham's words, as Rashi is claiming, they should have been written למען הביא ה' עלי "so that God will bring upon me," not למען

---

41. See Ps 33:5.
42. Based upon Jer 23:18; Chavel, *Ramban*, 241.
43. Davis, *Metsudah Chumash*, 183.

הביא יהוה על־אברהם "so that God will bring upon Abraham." As Simcha Kogut writes in *Syntax and Exegesis*,[44] Rashi did not relate to this issue; that is, he did not deal with the moral difficulty that emerges here.

Behor Shor, Ramban, Radak, Hazkuni, and Bahya interpret למען as presenting a purpose. These examples are illustrative:

5.2. Ramban

... או יאמר שיצווה. וכן "למען ינוח שורך וחמרך" שינוח...
"... or the verse may be stating, I know that he will command, and in a similar sense is the verse 'so that thine ox and thine ass may have rest'[45] (למען ינוח), meaning that he may have rest."[46]

5.3. Radak

למען אשר יצוה את־בניו שישמרו דרך יהוה לעשות צדקה ומשפט— כי יאמר להם שמרו דרך ה' וייטב לכם ואם לא תשמרו יעשה עמכם בהפך וכל אשר דבר עלי לעשות טובה לי ולזרעי אחרי, לא יעשה אם לא תשמרו דרכו. ושמא תאמרו לא ישגיח במעשיכם, ראו מה עשה בסדום ועמורה לפי שהיו רשעים, ואם תאמרו מקרה היה כמו שאנו רואים מקומות נשקעים מפני הרעש, והנה הוא אמר אלי קודם שישחיתם שישחית סדום ועמורה בעבור מעשיהם הרעים.

"... so that Abraham will say to his children that if they practice and emulate God's ways by performing charitable deeds and at the same time endeavoring to make justice prevail, their lives will be successful because God will help them. They will then experience the fulfillment of all promises (conditional) which I, God, have made to him concerning his offspring. If they fail to emulate that lifestyle these promises are liable to remain unfulfilled."

5.4. Sforno

וכל זה אמר האל יתברך לעשות למען אשר יצוה אברהם למען אשר יצוה את־בניו. לבניו, בראותו גודל חסדיו גם לרשעים, ומשפטיו נגד הבלתי שבים. ושמרו... לעשות צדקה ומשפט למען הביא יהוה על־ אברהם את אשר־דבר עליו. והתכלית האחרון המכוון בזה מאת

---

44. Jerusalem: Magnes, 2002.
45. Exod 23:12.
46. Chavel, *Ramban*, 242.

האל יתברך היה להביא על אברהם את אשר דיבר באמרו: "להיות
לך לאלהים ולזרעך אחריך".

"All this (the blessings in the previous verse), God says that He will do—so that Abraham, observing the great loving-kindness (of God) even toward the wicked, and His justice against those who do not repent (will teach his children). ... The ultimate purpose intended by the Almighty was to bring upon Abraham that which He had spoken, when He said "to be a God to you and to your offspring after you."[47]

In Conclusion

It seems that God chose Abraham, as God says כי ידעתיו. The word ידעתיו is interpreted by different medieval Jewish commentators in various ways—"to inform," "to tell," "to like," "to love," "to protect," "to save," "to raise," "to elevate," "to bestow recognition," and "to admonish." All these commentators agree then that God is saying something very positive about Abraham.

Beyond this, the answers of these different commentators to the question of why God singled out Abraham from all other people depends on their interpretations of the words ידעתיו and למען. The word למען always indicates a relationship of cause and effect. In our verse it can be interpreted in two ways. If the word למען is being interpreted as a reason, then it implies that God chose Abraham because of what Abraham had done in the past, namely, commanding his children to keep the way of God. This interpretation fits with Rashi's interpretation of ידעתי as "I liked him" or "I loved him." If the word למען is interpreted as a goal or a purpose, as Behor Shor, Hazkuni, Radak, Ramban, and Sforno interpret it, then it implies that God chose Abraham because of what Abraham will do in the future: he will keep the way of God. This interpretation, which fits Onkelos's translation and other translations of the word ידעתיו as "to inform," "to bestow recognition," "to raise," "to guard," obviously differs from Rashi's and seems to fit better in the context. Sforno's commentary here is unique. He claims that God is extending his love even to the wicked. This fits with Sforno's general attitude toward human beings.

In any case, it is clear that Abraham and his children are those who are keeping "the way of the Lord," even though only Ramban among the commentators elaborated on the expression דרך יהוה. According to the

---

47. Gen 17:7; Sforno, *Commentary on the Torah*, 87.

structure of the verse, it seems that the meaning of דרך יהוה "the way of the Lord" is doing justice and righteousness. Ramban claims that דרך יהוה is doing justice with righteousness and that this may be what Moses meant when he said to the Lord הודעני נא את־דרכך ואדעך למען אמצא־חן בעיניך "let me know your ways, that I may know you and continue in your favor."[48]

Nehama Leibowitz sees keeping "the way of the Lord" as synonymous with doing righteousness and justice, and she proves this by comparing verse 19 with other biblical verses.[49]

Moshe Weinfeld makes two interesting points.[50] First, one cannot determine whether the expression of justice and righteousness applies to acts performed by the government (= monarchy) and its leaders or whether it means good deeds carried out by the individual. Second, there is a contrast between Abraham, who is doing righteousness and justice, and the people of Sodom and Gomorrah, who violated moral principles.

According to Rashi, Abraham is the one who is doing righteousness and justice, whereas according to Radak it is Abraham, his sons, and his progeny, representing the entire people of Israel who will descend from him, who will diligently perform acts of justice and righteousness.

Regarding the grammatical structure of the verse, Rashi sees the second למען, "in order that the Lord may bring about for Abraham what he has promised him," as independent of the first one. That is, God liked Abraham because Abraham commanded his children to keep God's way, so the reward that the Lord may bring about for Abraham (what he had promised him) will come automatically. According to Radak, Ramban, Behor Shor, Hazkuni, and Sforno, on the other hand, the second למען is a result of the first one.

It is interesting to note that William L. Holladay, in his claims that ידע in our verse means בחר "selected, chose."[51] So even though the verb בחר "chose" is not mentioned in Gen 18:19, it is clear that God chose Abraham to be the pillar of the world.[52] It would be interesting also to look at the

---

48. Exod 33:13; Jacob Tzevi Mecklenburg, *Ha'Ketav ve'ha'Kabbala*, I (Jerusalem: Lambda, 2001), 239.

49. Leibowitz, *Studies in Bereshit Genesis*, 169–70.

50. Weinfeld, *Justice and Righteousness*, 215.

51. *Concise Hebrew and Aramaic Lexicon of the Old Testament* (Leiden: Brill, 1971), 129. Thanks to Dr. Michael Avioz, who drew my attention to that interpretation.

52. See Exod. Rab. 2:6 and more; also Maimonides, *Guide of the Perplexed*, 516.

question of whether God chose Abraham, as Nehemiah says, because God found Abraham's heart true to him. But that must be a subject of another paper...

Bibliography

Alter, Robert. *Genesis*. New York: Norton, 1966.
Bahye Ben Asher. Commentary on the Torah, Genesis, 1. Jerusalem: Mossad Ha'Rav Kook, 1981.
———. *Torah Commentary, 1*. Translated by Eliyahu Munk. Jerusalem: Lampda, 1998.
Buber, Martin, *Good and Evil: Two Interpretation*. New York: Charles Scribner & Sons, 1953.
Carpenter, J. Estlin. *The Composition of the Hexateuch*. New York: Longmans, Green & Co., 1902.
Chavel, Charles B. *Ramban Cammentary on the Torah, Genesis*. New York: Shilo, 1971.
Davis, Avrohom. *The Metsudha Chumash: Rashi, Genesis, A New Linear Translation*. Translated by Avrohom Kleinkaufman.New York: Ktav, 1991.
Even-Shoshan, Abraham. *A New Concordance of the Bible*. Jerusalem: Kiryat Sefer, 1988.
Fassberg, Steven. *Studies in Biblical Syntax*. Jerusalem: Magnes, 1994.
Gunkel, Hermann. *Genesis*. Translated by Mark E. Biddle. Macon, Ga.: Mercer Universith Press, 1997.
Holladay, William L. *Concise Hebrew and Aramaic Lexicon of the Old Testament*. Leiden: Brill, 1971.
Kogut, Simcha. *Syntax and Exegesis*. Jerusalem: Magnes, 2002.
Leibowitz, Nehama. *Studies in Bereshit Genesis*. Jerusalem: World Zionist Organization Department for Torah Education and Culture, 1974.
Maimonides, Moses. *The Guide of the Perplexed*. Translated by Shlomo Pines. Chicago: University of Chicago Press, 1963.
Mecklenburg, Jacob Tzevi. *Ha'Ketav ve'ha'Kabbala, I*. Jerusalem: Lambda, 2001.
Sforno, Obadiah ben Jacob. *Commentary on the Torah*. Translated by Raphael Pelcovitz. New York: Mesorah, 1987.
Skinner, John. *Genesis*. ICC. Edinburgh: T&T Clark, 1980.
Speiser, Ephraim A. *Genesis*. AB 1. New York: Doubleday, 1964.
Theodor, J., and Chanoch Albeck, eds. *Midrash Bereshit Rabba*. Jerusalem: Wahrmann, 1965.
Wenham, Gordon. *Genesis 16–50*. WBC 2. Dallas: Word, 1994.
Weinfeld, Moshe. *Justice and Righteousness in Israel and in the Nations*. Jerusalem: Magnes, 1985.

Section 2
Justice by the Book

Outcry, Knowledge, and Judgment in Genesis 18–19

Ellen J. van Wolde

The reception history of the story of Sodom and Gomorrah keeps exerting its influence on the readings of Gen 18–19. In past and present studies the topics of hospitality, justice, Yhwh's righteousness, and, of course, homosexuality are addressed extensively and intensively, but—at least in my view—some important questions have never been posed. The first question is, *who* are those crying out for justice in Gen 18:20–21 and in Gen 19:13? And did their outcry brought about the expected results? If Lot was crying out for justice, why would he have done so, because none of the evil events had yet happened. If the men and women in Sodom were crying out for justice, and if this led to Yhwh's decision to send his messengers to the city to offer support, the final result is disastrous, because all inhabitants died out. If there were others who wanted help, who are they?

Another question reflects on the view that Gen 18–19 should be read in a juridical framework, and all kinds of linguistic and textual elements appear to confirm this explanation, but why then is the knowledge that the male inhabitants of Sodom are seeking in Gen 19:5 never interpreted within this juridical framework? And what does this knowledge tells us about Yhwh's role as a judge?

In order to answer these questions I will first concentrate on the outcry and on the juridical framework of Gen 18–19, then on the literary context of these chapters. Hopefully, in the end, a new picture will emerge of Gen 18–19.

This study is made in the memory of Dr. Ron Pirson, who originally organized the SBL session on Gen 18–19 with the intention to concentrate on topics of universality and particularity. His untimely death shocked us all. Yet, his final words, "Be of good hope," encourage us to this day.

1. Who Is Crying Out for Justice?

An element that in my view has not received sufficient attention is the outcry expressed by the nouns צעקה and זעקה in Gen 18:20–21 and 19:13. In order to clarify its meaning, a short study will be made of the biblical usages of the noun and verb forms.

Two introductory remarks to start with, the first regarding grammar, the second semantics. The word classes noun and verb refer in grammar to a distinction with regard to how an entity is expressed in language. Nouns profile an entity as a unity, as "something" or a "thing," and have therefore a nominal profile. Nouns enable their users to construe their perceptions, experiences, knowledge or ideas as a single meaning configuration in the mind. Verbs, on the other hand, put interconnections among conceived entities in profile, and this relational profile is of a temporal nature. Verbs enable their users to construe their perceptions, experiences, knowledge or ideas as a process and to follow its evolution through time. This means that the nouns צעקה and זעקה express an outcry as a unity or a single meaning configuration, whereas the verbs צעק and זעק express an outcry as a temporal process that spreads over a period of time. The second remark concerns semantics. The meaning of a word is paradigmatically determined by its place in the *language system* (described in the dictionary and encyclopaedia) and syntagmatically by its combination with other words in *language use*. Hence, to study the conceptual content of a word means to explain it paradigmatically and syntagmatically. The latter includes the study of the combinatory potential of a word or its valence structure. Each word has a valence or a disposition to combine with other words in that they can share meaning components. The combination of words in a text allows us to understand their grammatical disposition to combine with other language units. The composite textual meaning structure is built on the syntagmatic relations of the distinct components and their combinatory dispositions.[1] This being said, we can start our study of the usages in the Hebrew Bible of the nouns צעקה and זעקה and subsequently examine the verbs צעק and זעק (*qal*).

---

1. For an extensive study of these grammatical and semantic components of meaning and its consequences for biblical studies, see Ellen J. van Wolde, *Reframing Biblical Studies: When Language and Text Meet Culture, Cognition and Context* (Winona Lake, Ind.: Eisenbrauns, 2009).

The noun צעקה occurs twenty times and the noun זעקה eighteen times in the Hebrew Bible. It appears that the two terms for outcry are used interchangeably throughout the Hebrew Bible. The thirty-eight occurrences of the nouns צעקה and זעקה in the Hebrew Bible are:[2]

Gen 18:20	Then Yhwh said: "How great is the *outcry* of Sodom and Gomorrah"
Gen 18:21	[Yhwh to Abram] "I will go down to see whether **they** have done altogether according to the *outcry* that has come to me"
Gen 19:13	For we are about to destroy this place, because **their** *outcry* has become great before Yhwh
Gen 27:34	When Esau heard his father's words, **he** *cries out* a great and bitter *cry*
Exod 3:7	[Yhwh to Moses] "I have marked well the plight of my people in Egypt and have heeded **their** *outcry* because of their taskmasters"
Exod 3:9	Now the *cry* of **the Israelites** has reached me
Exod 11:6	And there shall be a loud *cry* in all the land of Egypt
Exod 12:30	And Pharaoh rose in the night ... because there was a loud *cry* in Egypt
Exod 22:22	[Yhwh to Moses] "You shall not ill-treat any widow or orphan ... I will heed **their** *outcry*"
1 Sam 4:14	And when Eli heard the sound of the *outcry* [of the city]
1 Sam 9:16	"For I [Yhwh] have taken note of my people, **their** *outcry* has come to me"
Isa 5:7	And he hoped for justice and there is injustice, [he hoped] for righteousness, but there is *outcry*

---

2. In this list, the biblical texts are presented in NJPS translation with the exception of "Lord," which is transliterated Yhwh. The subject of the noun of crying out is in bold font; the noun itself is printed in italics.

Isa 15:5	**They** raise a *cry* of anguish
Isa 15:8	Ah, the *cry* has compassed the country of Moab
Isa 65:19	Never again shall be heard there [= in Jerusalem] the sound of weeping and *wailing*
Jer 18:22	Let an *outcry* be heard from their houses
Jer 20:16	Let him hear *shrieks* in the morning
Jer 25:36	Hark, the *outcry* of the **shepherds**
Jer 48:3	Hark! An *outcry* from Horonaim, destruction and utter ruin
Jer 48:4	Moab is broken; the *cry* of **her young ones** is heard
Jer 48:5	On the descent to Horonaim a distressing *cry* of anguish is heard
Jer 48:34	There is an *outcry* from Heshbon to Elealeh
Jer 50:46	And an *outcry* is heard among the nations
Jer 51:54	Hark! An *outcry* from Babylon
Ezek 27:28	At the *outcry* of **your pilots** the billows shall heave
Zeph 1:10	In that day there shall be a loud *outcry* from the Fish Gate
Ps 9:13	For he [Yhwh] does not ignore the *cry* of **the afflicted**
Prov 21:13	Who stops his ears at the *cry* **of the wretched**
Job 16:18	Let there be no resting place for **my** *outcry*
Job 27:9	Will God hear **his** *cry*
Job 34:28	Thus he [God] lets the *cry* **of the poor** come before him
Job 34:28	He listens to the *cry* **of the needy**
Qoh 9:17	Words spoken softly by wise men are heeded sooner than the *scream* **of a lord** in [the manner of] the fools

Esth 4:1	**He** (Mordecai) went through the city, *crying out loudly* and bitterly
Esth 9:31	The obligations of the fasts with **their** *lamentations/ outcry*
Neh 5:1	There was a great *outcry* **by the common folk** and their wives against their brother Jews
Neh 5:6	It angered me very much to hear **their** *outcry* and these complaints
Neh 9:9	You heard **their** *cry* at the Sea of Reeds

An analysis of these occurrences of the nouns צעקה and זעקה show that (1) these nouns designate an "outcry *of* someone"; (2) these nouns are either used in the absolute state ("they raise a cry") or in the construct state with a pronominal suffix ("their cry") or without a pronominal suffix ("the outcry of"); when used in the construct state the subject takes up the position of *nomen rectum* while the nouns צעקה or זעקה take up the position of *nomen regens* ("the outcry of the city/the afflicted"); (3) in the vast majority of texts (34/38), the subject of this outcry is a plural entity, "they, the Israelites, the poor, the needy, the widow and orphan, the people";[3] (4) in the vast majority of texts (34/38), the subject of the outcry is either explicitly mentioned,[4] indicated by anaphoric links to previously mentioned subjects[5] or by locatives;[6] these occurrences make us think of an outcry in terms of peoples, social groups, inhabitants, or nations and

---

3. The singular uses are Gen 27:34: "Esau cries out [verb צעק] a loud cry [noun צעקה]"; Job 16:18: "my outcry"; Job 27:9: "his cry"; Esth 4:1: Mordecai "cries out [verb צעק] a loud cry [noun צעקה]." The word combination "cry out a cry" (verb plus noun) seems to be a fixed combination. So, only Job 16:18 and 27:9 stand out because of their irregular singular subject.

4. Exod 3:9: "the cry of the Israelites"; Jer 25:36: "the outcry of the shepherds"; Jer 48:4: "the cry of the young ones"; Ezek 27:28: "the outcry of your pilots"; Ps 9:13: "the cry of the afflicted"; Prov 21:23: "the outcry of the wretched"; Job 34:28: "the outcry of the poor, the cry of the needy"; Qoh 9:17: "the scream of a lord in the manner of fools"; Neh 5:1: "a great outcry by the common folk."

5. Exod 3:7; 22:21–22; 1 Sam 4:14; 9:16; Isa 15:5; Job 16:18; 27:9; Esth 9:31; Neh 5:6; 9:9.

6. Exod 11:6: "a loud cry in all the land of Egypt"; Exod 12:30: "because there was a loud cry in Egypt"; Isa 15:8: "the country of Moab"; Jer 48:3: "an outcry from Horonaim"; Jer 48:3: "an outcry from Heshbon to Elealeh"; Jer 49:21: "an outcry at the Sea of

indicate that the outcry entails the notion of a collective whose corporate identity is defined by need, destruction, and distress;[7] and (5) these nouns never mark the outcry as directed or addressed *against* someone or *against* people.

Based on these data we can draw the following conclusions of the *valence* structure and the *conceptual* structure of the nouns צעקה and זעקה. (1) Valence structure: the noun זעקה/צעקה is used by a COLLECTIVE {Explicit or Implicit Plural Subject} and NOT explicitly DIRECTED toward someone {Indirect Object}. (2) the noun זעקה/צעקה is NEVER used by a COLLECTIVE {Explicit or Implicit Plural Subject} in an orientation AGAINST SOMEONE {Indirect Object}. Conceptual structure: the nouns צעקה and זעקה designate (a) a collective raise of the voice (b) by peoples, social groups, inhabitants or nations (c) as a strong reaction of distress and need. As a noun the terms conceive of this outcry of distress as a single configuration or unity. The conceptualization of these nouns entails the notion of a collective whose corporate identity is defined by need, destruction or distress.

The verb צעק (*qal*) is used forty-eight times and the verb זעק (*qal*) sixty-one times in the Hebrew Bible. It appears that the two verbs for outcry are used interchangeably here and throughout the Hebrew Bible. The 109 occurrences of the verbs צעק and זעק in the Hebrew Bible are:

Gen 4:10   [YHWH to Esau] "What have you done? Listen, **your brother's blood** *cries out* to me from the ground!"

Gen 27:34   When Esau heard his father's words, **he** *cries out* a great and bitter *cry*, and said to his father: "Bless me too, Father!"

Gen 41:55   And when all the land of Egypt felt the hunger, **the people** *cried out* to Pharaoh for bread.

Exod 2:23   **The Israelites** were groaning under the bondage and *cried out*.

Reeds"; Jer 50:46: "an outcry among the nations"; Jer 51:54: "an outcry from Babylon"; Zeph 1:10: "an outcry from the Fish Gate"; Neh 9:9 "their cry at the Sea of Reeds."

7. In Isa 5:7: "there is outcry"; Isa 65:19: "never again shall be heard the sound of weeping and wailing"; Jer 18:22: "let an *outcry* be heard from their houses"; and Jer 20:16: "let him hear *shrieks* in the morning," the subject of the cry is not mentioned. Implied in these texts is, however, a plural not further identified subject, viz. the people who suffer from injustice.

Exod 5:8	That is why **they** *cry* "Let us go and sacrifice to our God!"
Exod 5:15	Then **the foremen** of the Israelites came to Pharaoh and *cried*
Exod 8:8	And **Moses** *cried out* to Y<small>HWH</small>
Exod 14:10	**The Israelites** *cried out* to Y<small>HWH</small>
Exod 14:15	[Y<small>HWH</small> to Moses] "Why do **you** *cry out* to me?"
Exod 15:25	So **he** (Moses) *cried out* to Y<small>HWH</small>
Exod 17:4	**Moses** *cried out* to Y<small>HWH</small>
Exod 22:22	[Y<small>HWH</small> to Moses,] "You shall not ill-treat any widow or orphan. If you do mistreat them, I will heed **their** *outcry* (n) as soon as **they** *cry out* to me"
Exod 22:26	[Y<small>HWH</small> to Moses] "Therefore, if **he** [someone's neighbour] *cries out* to me, I will pay heed, because I am compassionate"
Num 11:2	**The people** *cried out* to Moses
Num 12:13	**Moses** *cried out* to Y<small>HWH</small>
Num 20:16	**We** *cried to* Y<small>HWH</small> and he heard our plea
Deut 22:24	The girl because **she** did not *cry out* for help in the town.
Deut 22:27	Though the engaged **girl** *cried* for help, there was no one to answer her.
Deut 26:7	**We** *cried* to Y<small>HWH</small>
Josh 24:7	**They** *cried out* to Y<small>HWH</small>
Judg 3:9	**The Israelites** *cried out* to Y<small>HWH</small>
Judg 3:15	Then **the Israelites** *cried out* to Y<small>HWH</small>
Judg 4:3	**The Israelites** *cried out* to Y<small>HWH</small>
Judg 6:6	And **the Israelites** *cried out* to Y<small>HWH</small>
Judg 6:7	When **the Israelites** *cried* to Y<small>HWH</small> on account of Midian

Judg 10:10	Then **the Israelites** *cried out* to Y<small>HWH</small>
Judg 10:12	[Y<small>HWH</small> to the Israelites] "when **you** *cried out* to me"
Judg 10:14	[Y<small>HWH</small> to the Israelites] "Go *cry* to the gods you have chosen"
Judg 12:2	[Jephthah to Ephraimites] "**I** summoned/*cried out* you"
1 Sam 4:13	And **the whole city** *broke out in a cry*
1 Sam 5:10	**The Ekronites** *cried out*
1 Sam 7:8	[Philistines to Samuel] "Do not neglect us and do not refrain from *crying out* to Y<small>HWH</small> our God to save from the hands of the Philistines"
1 Sam 7:9	And **Samuel** *cried out* to Y<small>HWH</small>
1 Sam 8:18	[Samuel to Israelites] "The day will come when **you** *cry out* [to Y<small>HWH</small>] because of the king"
1 Sam 12:8	[Samuel to Israelites] "**your fathers** *cried out* to Y<small>HWH</small>"
1 Sam 12:10	**They** *cried* to Y<small>HWH</small>
1 Sam 15:11	**He** [Samuel] entreated/*cried out* to Y<small>HWH</small> all night long
1 Sam 28:12	Then **the woman** recognized Samuel, and she *shrieked* loudly
2 Sam 13:19	**She** [Tamar] walked away, *screaming* loudly as she went
2 Sam 19:5	The king covered his face and **the king** kept *crying aloud*
2 Sam 19:29	Mephiboshet to Saul] "What right have **I** to appeal/*cry out* further to Your Majesty?"
1 Kgs 20:39	As the king passed, **he** [the prophet] *cried out* to him [Y<small>HWH</small>]
1 Kgs 22:32	They turned upon him to attack him, and **Jehoshaphat** *cried out*

2 Kgs 4:1	A **certain woman** ... *cried out* to Elisha
2 Kgs 4:40	**They** began to *cry out*: "O man of God, there is death in the pot"
2 Kgs 6:5	And **he** *cried out*: "Alas, master, it was a borrowed one"
2 Kgs 6:26	Once, when the king of Israel was walking on the city wall, **a woman** *cried out* to him: "Help me, your majesty!"
2 Kgs 8:3	**The woman** went to the king to *cry out* to the king about (the loss of) her house and farm
2 Kgs 8:5	In came **the woman** whose son he had revived, *crying out* to the king about her house and farm
Isa 14:31	Howl, O gate; *cry out*, O **city**
Isa 15:4	**Heshbon and Elealeh** *cry out*
Isa 15:5	**My heart** *cries out* for Moab
Isa 19:20	So that when **they** *cry out* to Y HWH against oppressors
Isa 26:17	Like **a woman** with child approaching childbirth, writhing and *screaming* in her pangs
Isa 30:19	He will grant you His favor at the sound of **your** *cry*
Isa 33:7	Hark! **The Arielites** *cry* aloud!
Isa 42:2	**He** shall not *cry out* or shout aloud.
Isa 46:7	If **they** *cry out*, it does not answer
Isa 57:13	Shall not save you when **you** *cry out*
Isa 65:14	And **you** shall *cry out* in anguish
Jer 11:11	Then **they** will *cry out* to me [Y HWH], but I will not listen to them
Jer 11:12	And **the townsmen of Judah and the inhabitants of Jerusalem** will go and *cry out* to the gods to which they sacrifice
Jer 20:8	For every time I speak, **I** [Jeremiah] must *cry out*

Jer 22:20	Climb Lebanon and *cry out*
Jer 22:20	Raise your voice in Bashan, *cry out* from Abarim
Jer 25:34	Howl, **you shepherds**, and yell/*cry out*
Jer 30:15	Why *cry out* over your injury?
Jer 47:2	The towns and their inhabitants. **Men** shall *cry out*
Jer 48:20	Moab is shamed and dismayed; Howl and *cry aloud*!
Jer 48:31	Therefore I will howl for Moab, **I** will *cry out* for all Moab
Jer 49:3	*Cry out*, O daughters of Rabbah!
Ezek 9:8	**I** flung myself on my face and *cried out*, "Ah, Lord God!"
Ezek 11:13	**I** threw myself upon my face and *cried out* aloud, "Ah, Lord God!"
Ezek 21:17	*Cry* and wail, O mortal, for this shall befall My people
Ezek 27:30	**They** shall raise their voices over you and *cry out* bitterly
Hos 7:14	But **they** did not *cry out* to Me sincerely As they lay wailing
Hos 8:2	**Israel** *cries out* to Me, "O my God, we are devoted to You"
Joel 1:14	And *cry out* to Yhwh
Jonah 1:5	In their fright, **the sailors** *cried out*, each to his own god
Mic 3:4	Someday **they** shall *cry out* to Yhwh
Hab 1:2	How long, Yhwh, shall **I** *cry out* and You not listen
Hab 2:11	For **a stone** shall *cry out* from the wall
Ps 22:6	To You *they cried out* and they escaped
Ps 34:18	**They** *cry out*, and Yhwh hears

Ps 77:2	**I** *cry aloud* to God
Ps 88:2	O Yhwh, God of my deliverance, when **I** *cry out* in the night before you
Ps 107:6	In their adversity **they** *cried out* to Yhwh
Ps 107:13	In their adversity **they** *cried* to Yhwh
Ps 107:19	In their adversity **they** *cried* to Yhwh
Ps 107:28	In their adversity **they** *cried* to Yhwh
Ps 142:2	**I** *cry aloud* to Yhwh
Ps 142:6	So **I** *cry* to You, O Yhwh
Job 19:7	**I** *cry*, "Violence!" but am not answered
Job 31:38	If **my land** *cries out* against me (עָלַי)
Job 35:12	Then **they** *cry out*, but he [God] does not respond
Lam 2:18	**Their heart** *cried out* to Yhwh
Lam 3:8	And when **I** *cry* and plead, He shuts out my prayer
Esth 4:1	**He** (Mordecai) went through the city, *crying out* loudly and bitterly.
Neh 9:4	And *cried* in a loud voice to Yhwh their God
Neh 9:27	In **their** time of trouble **they** *cried* to you [Yhwh]
Neh 9:28	Again **they** *cried* to You, and You in heaven heard
1 Chr 5:20	For **they** *cried* to God in the battle
2 Chr 13:14	**They** *cried out* to Yhwh
2 Chr 18:31	**Jehoshaphat** *cried out* and Yhwh helped him
2 Chr 20:9	And **we** shall *cry out* to You in our distress
2 Chr 32:20	Then **King Hezekiah and the prophet Isaiah** son of Amoz prayed about this, and *cried out* to heaven.

An analysis of these occurrences of the verbs צעק and זעק show that: (1) these verbs designate the temporal process in which someone cries out; (2) the grammatical subject of these verbs is a person in the singular or in the plural and is clearly marked:⁸ the person who is crying out or the persons who are crying out are always mentioned; (3) the subject performing the action of crying out always directs it *to* someone who is explicitly mentioned; (4) in the majority of cases the outcry is addressed to Yhwh and the subject of the outcry are the Israelites; in cases where the outcry is addressed to a person, this person is hierarchically elevated (king, prophet, judge) and competent to judge and help; (5) the verbs never designate someone's crying out for help *against* someone else or directed *against* other people; and (6) the verbs conceive of the temporal process of crying out in terms of individuals, peoples or inhabitants of countries as directed towards Yhwh or the person in charge;⁹ this process includes the notion of need, destruction or distress.

Based on these data we can draw the following conclusions of the *valence* structure and the *conceptual* structure of the verbs צעק and זעק. Valence structure: (1) the verb זעק/צעק is used by an INDIVIDUAL OR A COLLECTIVE {Explicit Singular or Plural Subject} directed to Yhwh or to a SUPERIOR {Explicit Indirect Object with אל}. (2) the verb זעק/צעק is NOT USED by an individual or collective {Explicit Singular or Plural Subject} directed AGAINST SOMEONE {Indirect Object}. Conceptual structure: the verbs צעק and זעק designate (a) a raise of the voice (b) by an individual or by people (c) as a strong reaction of distress and need. As a verb the terms conceive of this outcry of distress as a temporal process. The conceptualization of these verbs entails the notion of an individual or of a collective whose (corporate) identity is defined by need, destruction, or distress.

---

8. A singular person occurs as subject in forty-three cases such as: Gen 4:10: "your brother's blood cries out to me"; Gen 27:34: "He (Esau) cries out"; Exod 8:8; 15:25; 17:4; Num 12:13: "Moses cried out to Yhwh"; Deut 22:24, 27: "the girl did (not) cry out for help"; 1 Sam 4:13: "the whole city broke out in a cry"; 1 Sam 7:8: people ask Samuel "do not refrain from *crying out to* Yhwh our God"; 1 Sam 10:17: "Samuel cried out to Yhwh in Mizpah"; 1 Kgs 20:30: "[the prophet] he cried out to him [Yhwh]"; 2 Kgs 2:12: "[Elisha] cried out"; 2 Kgs 4:14: "a certain woman cried out to Elisha"; 2 Kgs 8:3, 5: "the woman went to the king to cry out to the king"; Esth 4:1: "[Mordecai] went though the city crying out loudly." First person singular: Judg 12:2; Jer 20:8; 48:31; Pss 77:2; 142:2, 6; Job 19:7; Lam 3:8. For the plural subject, see below.

9. In other words, the verb זעק/צעק puts the interconnection among the conceived entity Israelites and Yhwh in profile and this relational profile is of a temporal nature, that is to say, we as readers follow the Israelites' crying out to Yhwh through time.

Wrapping up the results, this examination of all usages of the nouns צעקה and זעקה and the verbs צעק and זעק has demonstrated that the option that these terms designate a cry *against* someone is to be excluded. It is mainly the literary context and the interpretation of that context that brought biblical scholars to the conclusion that Gen 18:20–21 and 19:13 expresses the outcry *against* Sodom and Gomorrah. Therefore, the New Jewish Publication Society translation is wrong when it translates Gen 18:20 with "The *outrage* of Sodom and Gomorrah is so great, and their sin so grave" and Gen 19:13 with "For we are about to destroy this place, because the outcry *against* them before the Lord has become so great that the Lord has sent us to destroy it." Equally wrong are (among others) the English Standard Version (2007 updated) "Then the LORD said, 'Because the outcry *against* Sodom and Gomorrah is great and their sin is very grave'"; the New International Version (NIB and NIV) "Then the LORD said, 'The outcry *against* Sodom and Gomorrah is so great and their sin so grievous'"; the New Revised Standard Version "Then the LORD said, 'How great is the outcry *against* Sodom and Gomorrah and how very grave their sin!'"; Holman Christian Standard Bible (2004) "Then the LORD said, 'The outcry *against* Sodom and Gomorrah is immense, and their sin is extremely serious'"; the New Jerusalem Bible "Then Yahweh said, 'The outcry *against* Sodom and Gomorrah is so great and their sin is so grave.'" James Bruckner (see below in section 3) is also wrong when he renders Gen 18:20 "Then the Lord said: 'How great is the outcry *against* Sodom and Gomorrah, and how very grave their sin,'" and Gen 19:13 with "For we are about to destroy this place, because the outcry *against* its people has become great before the Lord."[10]

Instead we should read the outcry (צעקה in Gen 18:21 and 19:13, and זעקה in 18:20) as not directed against the inhabitants of Sodom and Gomorrah, but as uttered by them. The people of Sodom and Gomorrah are conceived as a collective whose corporate identity is defined by need and distress. However, their outcry is not directed to YHWH. Nevertheless YHWH is acting upon this request to lead an inquest. And who is he going to help? Only Lot and his family, although Lot did not ask for help. It seems like an excuse, a mere pretext to start the legal procedure. Most biblical scholars tend to read the story backwards: it is the lack of hospital-

---

10. James K. Bruckner, *Implied Law in the Abraham Narrative: A Literary and Theological Analysis* (JSOTSup 335; Sheffield: Sheffield Academic Press, 2001), 81.

ity or the sexual assault which they qualify as the Sodomites' crime in the first place. Yet, this crime has not yet been committed in the narrative of Gen 18.

2. Juridical Process and Its Terminology

In 1988 Richard Boyce published a study in which he examined the way legal processes are linguistically expressed in the Hebrew Bible.[11] Boyce offered an analysis of the function of the verbs צעק or זעק "cry out" and the nouns צעקה and זעקה "outcry" in four legal contexts: the cry of the legally marginal, the cry of the oppressed, the cry of the raped, and the cry of the blood.[12] These are all cries for help in a situation of need. In fact, every person who cries out intends to provoke a legal process, in which a human or divine judge offers justice. Boyce argues that the cry of the marginal or oppressed to the king is part of a legal process that is usually expressed in a fixed fivefold form.[13] It starts with the picture of the king sitting as a judge on the throne, continues with the appearance and approach of the marginal in which the appeal is expressed by the verbs צעק or זעק. The subsequent stages are marked by the king's inquest ("what is the trouble?") and a report of the result of the inquest. Finally, a statement about the king's judgment concludes the process. This fixed fivefold form is visible through the Hebrew Bible.

Six years later, Pietro Bovati published a monograph in which he first examined the vocabulary of the judgment in court and its procedures.[14] In the first part, Bovati shows that the legal process is expressed by terms derived from the root שפט.[15] The authority of judging is described by the noun שפט, "judge," and the act of judging is indicated by the verb שפט "to judge."[16] Those who exercise a judge's function are the elders (at the gates of the city), the priests (in the temple), the king (in the city gate or in the

---

11. Richard N. Boyce, *The Cry to God in the Old Testament* (SBLDS 103; Atlanta: Scholars Press, 1988).

12. Ibid., 25–46.

13. Ibid., 34–40.

14. Pietro Bovati, *Re-establishing Justice: Legal Terms, Concepts and Procedures in the Hebrew Bible* (trans. Michael J. Smith; JSOTSup 105; Sheffield: JSOT Press, 1994).

15. Ibid., 171–216.

16. Gen 18:25 uses the collocation עשה משפט as the equivalent of שפט, "to judge."

royal palace), or God. They do not only fulfil this function in someone's individual interest but in the general public interest. "Judging appears as the authoritative act of discerning, separating, deciding between what/whom is just and what/whom is unjust, between the innocent and the guilty."[17] The judgment itself is described by משפט, which might designate a procedural action, a sentence, a subjective law or an objective law.

In the second part, Bovati distinguishes the *inquiry phase* that relates to the origin and shape of the trial, the actual *trial phase* or the *debate*, and the *pronouncement and execution of a sentence*.[18] The *inquiry phase* itself consists of four stages that are expressed by a series of more or less equivalent verbs: (1) the initiative of summoning a trial; (2) the spatial positions of the individuals in the trial; (3) the preliminary investigation of the case; and (4) the result of the inquiry. A closer look at these stages and their terminology, which in general linguistics is usually called "prototypical scenario," is instructive for our study.[19]

(1) An important distinctive feature of the first stage of the inquiry phase is that the initiative by the parties at odds is generally expressed by verbs of motion, commonly by the verb בוא "go" (sometimes קום "arise," "stand up," or עלה, "rise") or by the verb נגש "draw near."[20] This initiative is then followed by the syntagm of the preposition אל "to" and the court of judgment, which might be the king, the elders, the priest, or the deity. It is concluded by its motivation, commonly indicated by the term למשפט

---

17. Bovati, *Re-establishing Justice*, 185.

18. Ibid., 217–56.

19. A prototypical scenario is defined as the pattern or chain of events that constitutes the content of an action, idea, or sentiment expressed by the same or a similar series of words. Such a scenario reflects the conventional behavioral sequences, emotions, actions, situations, or events in a culture as it is conceptually understood and formulated in language. In the field of biblical studies, this concept of prototypical scenario is explained and applied in Kjell Magne Yri, *My Father Taught Me How to Cry, but Now I Have Forgotten: The Semantics of Religious Concepts with an Emphasis on Meaning, Interpretation and Translatability* (Acta Humaniora; Faculty of Arts, University of Oslo 29; Oslo: Scandinavian University Press, 1998), and van Wolde, *Reframing*. In the here presented description of Bovati's work, the summaries at the end of each stage of the legal procedure in terms of a prototype are mine.

20. Bovati, *Re-establishing Justice*, 218–21. "It may be noted … that sometimes it is the one who claims to be in the right who takes the initiative in order to obtain satisfaction; but in other cases, both disputants simultaneously have recourse to the judge; in either case, however, the juridical structure set in motion always comprises three elements: the two parties and the judge" (218).

"for justice" or its equivalents. Hence, in its prototypical form the opening scene of a legal procedure can be summarized as: participant—go/draw near—to the king/deity—for judgment in court.

(2) The various individuals take up *bodily* positions. While the judge is "being seated" expressed by ישב, the people who come for judgment brought for the judge have to must stand up before the judge or take up their position before the judge. "By frequency, the verb עמד—usually with the preposition לפני—is the most important of these verbs of 'appearance' for judgment. Sometimes linked to verbs of motion (which emphasize the juridical initiative), it expresses the placement of the parties under the jurisdiction of the magistrate."[21] Hence, in its prototypical form the positioning scene of a legal procedure can be summarized as: participant—stands in front of the judge—judge is seated.

(3) The investigative stage of the trial is presented by a series of verbs. The inquest usually opens with one of the verbs of research: "explore," "investigate," "search," that is, בקש, דרש, or חקר. This is followed by either the verb ידע "know" or the verbs ידע and ראה "know" and "see." In poetic texts, another element is added, namely the verb בחן "search"; this verb does not occur in the Torah or in the Former Prophets.[22] Hence, in its prototypical form, the investigative stage of a legal procedure can be summarized as: judge investigates/explores—knows/knows and sees [—searches].

The verb ידע or the pair ידע and ראה is of nuclear importance, because in Israelite courts of law the stage of (logical) certainty based on sensory experience or some other kind of evidence is the only one that can guarantee correct juridical proceedings. This certainty may be gained from witnesses or acquired directly by the magistrate. It is only when the judge is in a position of "seeing" and "knowing" that it becomes possible to pronounce a sentence in harmony with the law.[23] Bovati's analysis of these series of investigative verbs shows that the verb ידע (or the word pair ידע and ראה) is the only element always present in the prototypical scenario or script of the juridical inquiry procedure. This element cannot be left out.

---

21. Ibid., 234.
22. Ibid., 244–47.
23. Ibid., 244 n. 47.

(4) The result or conclusion of the investigative stage is in Hebrew expressed by the verb מצא, "find," or by the concluding particle הנה or והנה.²⁴

> The link between verbs suggesting "research" (in particular דרש and בקש [Pi]) and the verb מצא is not of course exclusive to the sphere of the law court, but in this context the relationship becomes important to the extent that it shows the guilt (or otherwise) of a person, and consequently, the need (or otherwise) to proceed to sentence. ... When the guilt (or innocence) of an accused is discovered or established, the result reached is that of juridical certainty, which allows the passing of a verdict with confidence. This may be the reason why the "findings" after an inquiry are expressed in Hebrew by the same verb as means to "catch red-handed", "to catch in the act"; in fact, a similar juridical ability to proceed links the two situations.²⁵

Hence, in its prototypical form the concluding scene of the inquiry in the legal procedure can be summarized as: judge finds—with/without particle "behold."

Following these four stages that together form the investigative part of the law court proceedings comes the *debate* or *trial phase*, in which the two parties to the case, formally distinguished as accuser and accused, confront each other in front of a judge.²⁶ Each is granted the right to speak, and the alternation of speeches is expressed by rather generic *verba dicendi*, predominantly אמר, sometimes by ענה plus אמר. In this debate the act of complaint itself is expressed by the verbs צעק or זעק, קרא, and שוע (*piel*). Bovati shows that the main elements of the complaint syntagm are: the subject who takes the initiative, expressed by a verb of motion בוא or יצא, formulates his complaint to the tribunal (God or magistrate) expressed by the verb צעק or זעק, and gives the motive of the complaint, namely למשפט "for justice."²⁷

---

24. Ibid., 248–53.
25. Ibid., 248–49, where he also offers an inventory of the various expressions used with the verb מצא to describe the discovery of a crime, or more exactly of a criminal, in twenty-six biblical texts.
26. Ibid., 257–343.
27. Ibid., 314–15.

However, this "cry" is not just a personal outburst or a simple instinctive reaction to suffering: it is essentially addressed to someone (*'el...*) and demands to be heard in the name of right. ... In this way a complaint reveals another aspect of what constitutes it; it is a request for help addressed to an "authorized" person, juridically bound by the actual cry.[28]

The content of the complaint is that the victim of an injustice cries חמס "violence."[29] The term חמס has a definite juridical meaning, since it is one of the ways in which a crime or misdeed is specified. The primary content of a complaint is therefore the denunciation of a crime being committed.[30]

Hence, in its prototypical form the debate that follows upon the inquiry in the legal procedure can be summarized as: party goes in front of judge—cries "violence"—for justice.

After the inquiry phase and the trial or debate, the juridical procedure is brought to an end in the *sentence and execution*.[31] Verbs that express this jurisdiction are most commonly דין, שפט, or דבר in combination with משפט. These syntagms refer to the separation of the guilty from the innocent, an act that defines them juridically. Of particular importance, because of its appearance in legislative texts concerning the activity of judges, is the pairing of צדק (*hiphil*) "declare righteous" and רשע (*hiphil*) "condemn as guilty."[32] It is followed by the punishment and the application of the punishment. Hence, in its prototypical form the sentence in the law court procedure can be summarized as: judge/judges—declare righteous/condemn as guilty—punishment. Because of its great detail and explicative power the work of Bovati established itself as the standard point of reference for years to come.

3. The Juridical Framework of Genesis 18–19

James Bruckner built upon Bovati in his study of the implied law in the Abraham narrative in general and of the juridical framework and terminology of Gen 18–19 in particular. In surveying the long series of legal

---

28. Ibid., 317.
29. Cf. Hab 1:2–4; Job 19:7; Jer 20:8.
30. Bovati, *Re-establishing Justice*, 316–23.
31. Ibid., 344–87.
32. Ibid., 348–49.

terms in Gen 18–19, Bruckner demonstrates convincingly the juridical character of this text in a verse by verse analysis.³³

The phrase in Gen 18:19 "to keep the way of YHWH by doing righteousness and justice," contains the word דרך, "way," which is a common term sometimes used with משפט "justice" in a legal procedural sense. The complete syntagm for judging is עשה משפט וצדקה "doing righteousness and justice" and generally refers to uprightness in behaviour, but in some texts it is a reference to the administration of a just court procedure.

The words for "outcry," צעק and זעק, in Gen 18:20–21 and in 19:13 are technical terms for legal complaint requesting deliverance. The inquest itself, commonly expressed by the syntagm ראה+ירד, is present in Gen 18:21: "I must go down and see."

In Gen 18:22, "Abraham remained standing before YHWH," the syntagm of עמד "stand" and לפני "before" is the common word combination in biblical texts to describe the juridical position of those in trial.

In the phrase "Then Abraham came near" in Gen 18:23 the verb נגש "draw near" has special procedural value when it is used in the context of litigation.³⁴

Both in Gen 18:23 and 18:25 the triple usage of the opposition of the terms צדיק "innocent" and רשע "guilty" and the widespread usage of the term צדיק "innocent" in chapter 18 point to the core business of a trial, namely, to separate the guilty from the innocent.³⁵

With regard to Gen 18:25a, "to make a ruling like this" (מעשת כדבר הזה), Bruckner shows that whenever the word דבר is used with the language of judging (משפט) it is translated as "case," meaning "legal case," or "juridical decision," meaning "ruling."³⁶ In addition, the *hiphil* of the

---

33. Bruckner, *Implied Law*, 89–107.
34. Cf. Gen 44:18; Exod 24:14; Deut 25:1; 1 Sam 14:38; Isa 41:1.
35. However, Bruckner acknowledges that "a formal pronouncement of guilt in Genesis 19 is not made by means of this word pair. The narrative description of the behaviour of the men of Sodom functions to confirm the truth of the 'cry against' Sodom, resulting in a guilty verdict (19.13). Formal pronouncements in legal biblical contexts are usually declarations of innocence of the kind, 'You are innocent' (אתה צדיק)" (*Implied Law*, 98).
36. See ibid., 100: "There are only nine occurrences of the syntagma הדבר + משפט in the Hebrew Bible. In seven of them, the reference is to a legal case to be decided (Gen. 18.25; Deut. 1.17; 17.8, 9, 11; 2 Sam. 15.6; 2 Chron. 19.6). The two other occurrences of the syntagma, 2 Chron. 8.14 and Ezra 3.4, also have a legal context, referring to an ordinance (משפט) that has a specific duty (דבר)." (He adds in n. 73:

verb מות, "slay" or "put to death," is used to describe the official action of a court in meting out punishment.

With regard to Gen 18:25b, "shall not the judge ... make a just decision?" Bruckner shows that the syntagm שפט + משפט ("the judge" plus "a just judgment") occurs three times in the Hebrew Bible (Gen 18:25; Deut 17:9; 1 Kgs 3:28), where they are used in a technical sense to refer to the judge's just decision.

The syntagm יש + מצא ("here is" plus "find")—usually with the particle אם (either "if there is" or, as here, "if I find")—in Gen 18:26–29 "if I find ... suppose are found," is the typical biblical expression of the terms of a conclusion to the pretrial inquiry. It expresses legal findings.

In Gen 19:7, "I beg you, my brothers, do not act so wickedly" (אל־נא אחי תרעו), Lot articulates explicitly the notion that the intended action of the men of Sodom is wrong. The term רעע "wickedly" is not used in any technical way in legal contexts.

In the phrase "only do nothing to these men for they have come under the shelter of my roof" in Gen 19:8, the expression "shelter of my roof" is unique to this text. Lot discloses the obligation of hospitality and the implication is that those who have been welcomed in his house ought not be abused.

With regard to Gen 19:15, "get up, take your wife and your two daughters who are here," Bruckner notices that with the repeated imperatives in 19:12, 15, 17, 22 the messengers of Yhwh attempt to deliver Lot's family from the destruction of Sodom. These "royal" imperatives result in the saving of the innocent. That these words were not spoken to the other inhabitants of Sodom is equally a royal verdict.

In Gen 19:23, "the sun had risen on the earth," the sun's rising is one of the metaphors suggesting the advent of justice by right judgment.

This survey of the three works cited can be summarized as follows. Boyce examined the biblical usage of the verbs צעק and זעק "cry out" and showed its function in the fixed fivefold form or prototypical scenario, in which the cry of the marginal or oppressed to the king or deity is the opening part of the process of legal appeal. Bovati analyzed the linguistic expressions of the juridical inquiry procedure at large. He demonstrates that the investigative stage of this procedure is built upon a pattern of

---

"For the legal procedural use of עשה, see the commentary at 20.9b, 'You have done'. See also 18.21 and 20.10, where the verb עשה and the noun דבר are used together in a similar way.")

series of verbs, which starts with the verbs of movement (בוא "come," נגש "draw near") and of position-taking (עמד לפני "stand before," ישב "sit"), of inquiry (דרש, בקש, or חקר followed by "know" ידע or "know and see" ראה + ידע), and of the consequent proof-finding by the judge (מצא "find"). The subsequent debate stage is characterized by the verbs of speaking (אמר), the formulation of the complaint (צעק or זעק, קרא, and שוע [*piel*]) to the tribunal (God or magistrate) and the motive of the complaint (למשפט "for justice"). In the concluding stage of the legal process, the sentence and execution, two syntagms are essential: the making of the decision rendered by the verbs שפט, דין, or דבר in combination with משפט, and the pairing of the verbs צדק (*hiphil*) "declare righteous" and רשע (*hiphil*) "condemn as guilty." Finally, Bruckner's study of the juridical terminology and framework of Gen 18–19, demonstrated the widespread usage of the juridical terms in these chapters.[37]

4. What Do the Sodomites Want to Know?

Boyce, Bovati, and Bruckner outlined the juridical framework of Gen 18–20. However, it is remarkable that these authors exclude verses Gen 19:5 and 19:9 from their analysis of the judicial terminology.[38] Thus they fail to notice the legal components of the words of the townsmen of Sodom to Lot. My proposal is to include 19:5 and 19:9 in the legal investigation of Gen 18–19.

In the opening stage of the legal procedure, Bovati showed that the linguistic pattern is as follows: (1) the initiative of summoning a trial expressed by verbs of motion, commonly by the verb בוא "go," sometimes קום "arise," "stand up," or עלה, "rise," or by the verb נגש "draw near," and (2) the bodily positions of the involved parties and the movement of those coming forward for (לפני) judgment. This terminology is also noticeable in Gen 19:5, where the inhabitants of Sodom ask Lot to "bring out before us (הוציאם אלינו), the men that came to you in the night." Lot's reaction in Gen 19:6 stands, however, in sharp contrast to this request: he goes out

---

37. In my view, Bruckner made a better analysis of Gen 18 than of Gen 19. First, because Gen 18 does indeed contain the legal linguistic vocabulary Bovati examined, whereas Bruckner's analysis of Gen 19 does not contain these elements. And secondly, the phrases Bruckner does select in Gen 19 do not necessarily have a legal meaning, but could also have a more general meaning.

38. Bruckner just jumps over this passage at *Implied Law*, 103–6.

and closes the door behind him, and does not bring the foreigners forward for judgment for the inhabitants of Sodom.

The inquiry stage is, as Bovati demonstrated, characterized by the sequence of a verb of investigation (דרש, בקש, or חקר), followed by either the verb ידע "know" or the verbs ידע and ראה "know" and "see," in which the verb ידע or the pair ידע and ראה takes up a central position. The Sodomites' request in Gen 19:5, ונדעה אתם "so that we may know them," fits this inquiry scenario.

The legal process as such is, according to Bovati, always expressed by terms derived from the root שפט. Here again the behavior and evaluation by the men in Sodom in Gen 19:9 fits well. They protest against Lot's behavior: וישפט שפוט "A foreigner is acting as a judge?" The elders and other representatives of Sodom speak about who is to judge, Lot or they.

The result or conclusion of the investigative stage is commonly expressed by the verb מצא, "find" or by the concluding particle והנה/הנה or והנה ראה, "see and behold." The behavior of the foreigners hided by Lot in his house form a shrill contrast to this expected and correct behavior: they strike the inhabitants of Sodom with "blindness," so that they "were unable to find": וילאו למצא (Gen 19:11).

In the juridical framework of Gen 18–19 and according to the legal procedure as described by Bovati, the behavior of the inhabitants of Sodom appears to fit the ordinary juridical procedure: they want to know what the men who came in by night, and who are secretly staying in the house of the resident alien Lot, are planning to do here. Could they not be spies that threaten their security? Their logical and juridical reasoning fits the wider context, a situation of war and insecurity depicted earlier in Gen 14.

5. A Literary Reading of Genesis 19 in Its Juridical Framework

In an interesting analysis Lyn Bechtel pointed out that the characters in Gen 19 represent distinct groups: the outsiders, the insiders, and a marginal figure.[39] The divine messengers are the outsiders, or even spies, as is known to the readers only, sent out by Yhwh to see whether the sin of the Sodomites is as great as he has heard. Which sin? Nothing is clear yet. Yet, for the other characters in the story these messengers are merely rec-

---

39. Lyn Bechtel, "A Feminist Reading of Genesis 19.1–11," in *Genesis* (ed. Athalya Brenner; FCB 2/1; Sheffield: Sheffield Academic Press, 1998), 108–28.

ognizable as human beings. The second character is Lot, a resident alien in the city of Sodom, and as such a marginal figure, a representative of the outsiders, living inside. Remarkable, though, is that he, as a sojourner or *gēr* is sitting in the city gate, which does not only represent the value of the entrance to town, but also its administrative heart—the place where the male inhabitants discuss the city's legal, social, political, and religious matters. Resident aliens are not part of this administrative and juridical board. Finally, the third group introduced in verse 4 as "the men of the city, the men of Sodom, from young to old, all the people to the last men." They are the insiders, characterized as one group, the city's mature adults responsible for its administration, including its juridical and religious procedures. So far the story contains but groups—characters that are not defined as separate individuals, but as insiders, outsiders, and marginal people.[40] Only the marginal people, the outsiders sojourning in the land that is not theirs yet, are specified and identified by name: Lot, and in the previous chapter, Abraham. Their god has a name, too: Yhwh.

The messengers come to the city of Sodom by night. This differs greatly from their arrival at Abraham's place, because the three men visit Abraham "as the day grew hot." Their intentions are presumably not meant to be perceived in broad daylight. This is actually the starting point of the inquest by the inhabitants of Sodom. Where are the men that came to you by night? They use legal terminology: "bring," "before us," "so that we may know them," and the term ידע is crucial in this and any juridical inquest. The Sodomites are to judge whether these foreign men represent danger to the city or not. Nothing wrong so far.

Lot's reaction is astonishing. His behavior is, in the first place, secretive. He comes out of his house but closes the door behind him. He then asks the city's community not to do evil. I quote Bechtel:

> Then, as a response to this explosive situation, he offers his two daughters, who have not "known" (ידע) a man, to the townsmen who want to "know" the two men. Does Lot assume that the intentions of the men are sexual? Or does he just make a totally left field offer? The story does not say. But the apparent disregard for women in his offer violates the assumption of protection of women as the producers of life that characterizes ancient society. Next, Lot encourages the men to do with his

---

40. Ibid., 115.

daughters whatever is "good" in their eyes (v. 8), which would certainly not be to *rape* them![41]

Lot has an obligation to the community to protect his daughters, particularly in the light of the fact that they are betrothed to men of the community (v. 14). So he violates the rights of two males in this city's community.

The men of Sodom react furiously to Lot's offer. As Bechtel observes astutely, "The men of the city are responding to a threat to the community, not trying to fulfil their sexual needs. ... The townsmen's reaction to Lot's offer is central. They are offended and do not take Lot up on his sexual offer."[42] Now their attention tips over to Lot. Again they use legal terms: the verb נגש "draw near," as in "drawing near for judgment." First, they tell Lot to draw near because he is the person who brought the men in and whose offer brings the community in danger. He is to be questioned now. Consequently, they draw near the door, so that they will know what kind of men he is hiding in his house. The juridical terminology is obvious, as are the subsequent verses. Those who want to know and see (ידע and ראה) are now struck with blindness. They are rendered unable to know and see, to judge, or to act as judges. Even stronger, they are, from now on, denied the right to judge. Those who denied that Lot had a right to judge them find that they are struck blind. By whom? By the messengers of Yhwh, the one who is called by Abraham in Gen 18:25 the judge of the entire earth.

6. A Literary Reading of Genesis 19 in the Literary Context of Genesis 12–25

The story in Gen 18–19 functions in the wider literary context of the Abra(ha)m narrative, in which two strands are woven into one texture: Yhwh's promise to Abra(ha)m and his kinsmen who will inherit the land of Canaan,[43] and Abra(ha)m's relationship to the peoples or nations of the land.[44] In the latter strand, the city, king and inhabitants of Sodom are mentioned three times. The first time occurs in Gen 13 in which the separation between Abram and Lot is described: "Abram remained in the land of Canaan, while Lot settled in the cities of the Plain, pitching his

---

41. Ibid., 122.
42. Ibid., 124–25.
43. Gen 12:1–10; 15–17; 20–25.
44. Gen 12:11–14:24; 18–19.

tents near Sodom. Now the inhabitants of Sodom were very wicked sinners ליהוה" (Gen 13:12–13). No further explanation is given of the nature of their wickedness; it is just a comment.

It is in the context of war that the king of Sodom appears for the first time on stage in the book of Genesis, when he is mentioned as the leader of the four Canaanite city-state kings who fought against five invading foreign kings. This makes Sodom *the* representative of the Canaanite city-states. Genesis 14:11–12 indicates how "The invaders seized all wealth of Sodom and Gomorrah and all their provisions, and went their way. They also took Lot, the son of Abram's brother, and his possessions, and departed; for he had settled in Sodom." Abram and his allies were able to defeat the eastern invaders and to release Lot.

Genesis 14:13–24 offers an extensive report of the reception of the returning hero Abram by the kings of Sodom and Salem. The king of Salem is introduced by name, Melchizedek, and the narrator tells us that he brings Abram food and blessings. His words are extensively covered in a directly reported speech, in which Melchizedek attributes the victory to Abram's God, אל עליון El Elyon, God Most High, saying "Blessed be Abram of El Elyon, possessor of heaven and earth. And blessed be El Elyon, who has delivered your foes into your hand" (14:19). The king of Sodom, on the other hand, is not introduced by name, is not said to have given bread, and but a few of his words are reported in direct speech. The king of Sodom does not speak of God or El Elyon as the possessor of the world nor of his victory, but approaches Abram as the victorious combatant, saying "Give me the persons, and take the possessions for yourself" (14:21). It seems to be part of a negotiation, although Abram responds differently. He, too, refers to El Elyon as the possessor of heaven and earth, equalizing Yhwh with El Elyon, and says to the King of Sodom: "I lift up my hand to Yhwh, El Elyon who possesses heaven and earth. I will not take so much as a thread or a sandal strap of what is yours" (14:22). In other words, the defining feature of this El Elyon is, both according to Melchizedek and to Abram, that he is the most powerful deity, the possessor of the entire heaven and earth, and Abram apparently equalizes Yhwh with this El Elyon, God Most High. In Gen 18:25, furthermore, Abraham proclaims that Yhwh is the judge of all the earth. This Yhwh sends his messengers to Sodom and decides in the end for the purpose of destroying the town, so he does indeed turn out to be judge of Sodom and Gomorrah.

In all these chapters in Genesis only the perspective of Abraham and Lot is shared, and hardly that of the inhabitants of the land and their cities. It was demonstrated above that the cry out for help could not have been directed against the Sodomites, nor could they have direct their outcry to Yhwh whom they did not know. Nevertheless Yhwh initiates a legal inquest. The message is conveyed that it is Yhwh's right to start the inquest, as a powerful and righteous judge of all the earth, including the city of Sodom. The behavior of the townsmen of Sodom does not legitimize the deity's severe punishment or their total destruction. Their wish "to know" is completely regular. Yet what is at stake here is the right to judge. The insiders are denied the right to deal with administrative, social, legal, and religious matters in their city gates according to their own rules. Those who come from abroad, the Abra(ha)m family and their outsider God, are going to win: they are to judge, and they will make the rules. All textual characters, with the exception of the Sodomites, defend this view. The narrator seems to accept the ambiguity in Lot's offer of his two daughters and to confirm his interpretation of ידע in a sexual sense. The messengers share Yhwh's perspective; Abram shares it; the king of Salem shares El Elyon's perspective and acknowledges him as the rightful Most High deity. They all confirm Yhwh's right to act as a judge of the entire earth. The exceptions are the king of Sodom, who in Gen 14 does not speak of Yhwh, and the male inhabitants of Sodom who in Gen 19 wished to know the identity of the messengers of Yhwh and what they were planning to do. Their final reaction to Lot in 19:9 says it all: "Stand back! The fellow came here as an alien and he acts as the judge!" That's exactly the point: the outsiders and their God Yhwh have come to take over, because they consider their God to be the God Most High. It is from their perspective that the text is written. Since then all readers have interpreted the text through their eyes only and grew used to blame the men of Sodom for their unlawful behavior.

7. An Intertextual Reading of Genesis 19, Deuteronomy 32:8–9, and Psalm 82

Scholars have generally noted intertextual relationships between the various biblical references to El Elyon in Gen 14, Deut 32:8–9, and Ps 82. A short detour to these texts may help us to understand the wider background to Yhwh's behavior as judge in Gen 18–19.

The first text is Deut 32:8–9:

> When the Most High (Elyon) gave the nations their inheritance,

When he divided the sons of a human being,
He established the boundaries of peoples,
according to the number of the sons of God. (4QDeut^{q/j})
For the portion of Yhwh is his people,
Jacob, his inherited measure.

Emanuel Tov comments on Deut 32:8–9:

> In its probably original wording, as reflected in 4QDeut^q (and secondarily also in 4QDeut^j and LXX), the Song of Moses referred to an assembly of the Gods (cf. Psalm 82; 1 Kgs 22:19), in which "the Most High, *'Elyon*, fixed the boundaries of peoples according to the number of the sons of the God *El*." The next verse stresses that the Lord, יהוה, kept Israel for himself. ... It appears, however, that the scribe of an early text ... did not feel at ease with the possible polytheistic picture and replaced בני אל, "sons of El," with בני ישראל "sons of Israel," thus giving the text a different direction by the change of one word.[45]

In this picture El Elyon is the head god who oversees the division of the world into nations given to the various gods of the world, and in this scenario, Yhwh is one of the gods who receives his inheritance from El Elyon. Israel is his inheritance, whereas the other sons of El inherit the other nations.

A further step in the dynamics of Yhwh's relation to the nations is Ps 82. I follow Mark Smith in his literal translation and treatment of Ps 82.[46]

Narrative Statement about God (Elohim) in the Divine Assembly Headed by El/Elyon
1   Elohim stands (sg.) in the council of El
    Among the elohim he pronounces judgment:

God's Indictment of the Other Gods in the Assembly
2   "How long will you judge perversely,
    Show favour to the wicked?
3   Judge the wretched and the orphan,

---

45. Emanuel Tov, *Textual Criticism of the Hebrew Bible* (Minneapolis: Fortress; Assen: van Gorcum, 1992), 269.
46. Mark S. Smith, *God in Translation: Deities in Cross-Cultural Discourse in the Biblical World* (FAT 57; Tübingen: Mohr Siebeck 2008), 131–215.

>   Vindicate the lowly and the poor,
> 4 Rescue the wretched and the needy,
>   Save them from the hand of the wicked."
> 5 They neither know nor understand,
>   They go about in darkness,
>   All the foundations of the world totter.
> 6 "I had taken you for gods,
>   Sons of *Elyon*, all of you;
> 7 However, you shall die like a human,
>   Fall like one of the princes."

Command addressed to God
> 8 Arise, O Elohim (sg.), judge the earth,
>   For You inherit all the nations.

The juridical context of this psalm is visible in the verb שפט "judge," which is repeated four times. The contrast between the assembly of gods who are supposed to judge, to know and understand and to support the wretched and the needy (vv. 1–5) and the one and only God who is incited to stand up to judge the entire earth and all nations (v. 8) is the central topic of this psalm.

> The figure Elohim (God) indicts as mere mortals the other gods (*'elohim*, verse 1b and 6), whom he had thought were all sons of Elyon (verse 6). As the indictment indicates, the denounced figures were considered to be gods, all divine children of Elyon, but now they are to be viewed not as god but as dead like humans (verse 7). The psalm concludes (verse 8) with the human speaker calling on Elohim to "judge, rule" (less likely, to "prevail") and to assume all the nations his "inheritance."[47]

Elohim was originally seen as one of the members of the larger divine assembly of the gods, and verse 1 describes how he literally takes his place in the divine council or council of El, with all other gods or sons of the God Most High, El Elyon. Then Elohim realizes that the other gods have no knowledge or understanding whatsoever. They are not, therefore, able to judge properly. In fact, so he states, they are not proper deities and will

---

47. Ibid., 134.

die like human beings. Only Elohim is the righteous judge of the entire earth, and he will inherit all the nations.[48]

When we read Gen 18–19 against the background of Deut 32:8–9 and Ps 82, we can see Abram's proclamation in Gen 18:25 that Yhwh is the judge of all the earth and Yhwh's consequent behavior as judge of Sodom in a new light. It turns out that Gen 18–19 express in a narrative form what Ps 82 states explicitly. It is a testimony of the takeover by Yhwh who started as the judge and deity of one clan only, but ends here as the judge of the entire earth. Although the outcry was not directed against the inhabitants of Sodom (see section 1), this outcry is placed in a literary context that qualifies their behavior as sinful and functions as a pretext for Yhwh to act as judge. Although the Sodomites' wish to know the identity of the people that Lot hid in his house is legally justified (see section 4), the narrator confirms Lot's misunderstanding of the kind of knowledge they sought. In the end, all threads lead into a single network of meaning in which Yhwh is presented as the only rightful judge of the entire earth, including the Canaanites and among them, the Sodomites.

Bibliography

Bechtel, Lyn M. "A Feminist Reading of Genesis 19.1–11." Pages 108–28 in *Genesis*. Edited by Athalya Brenner. FCB 2/1. Sheffield: Sheffield Academic Press, 1998.

Bovati, Pietro. *Re-establishing Justice: Legal Terms, Concepts and Procedures in the Hebrew Bible*. Translated by Michael J. Smith. JSOTSup 105. Sheffield: JSOT Press, 1994.

Boyce, Richard N. *The Cry to God in the Old Testament*. SBLDS 103. Atlanta: Scholars Press, 1988.

Bruckner, James K. *Implied Law in the Abraham Narrative: A Literary and Theological Analysis*. JSOTSup 335. Sheffield: Sheffield Academic Press, 2001.

Smith, Mark S. *God in Translation: Deities in Cross-Cultural Discourse in the Biblical World*. FAT 57. Tübingen: Mohr Siebeck, 2008.

Tov, Emanuel. *Textual Criticism of the Hebrew Bible*. Minneapolis: Fortress; Assen: van Gorcum, 1992.

---

48. Cf. ibid., 139: "The operating assumption in Psalm 82 is that the other gods had been the gods of all the nations, but now in its final prophetic call, Elohim the god of Israel is to assume divine authority over all the nations. In short, Psalm 82 calls for an end to translatability. It is evident that Psalm 82 presupposes, even as it disputes, an older worldview of the nations each headed by its own national god. The translatability expressed in the worldview is acknowledged at the same time that it is being rejected."

Wolde, Ellen J. van. *Reframing Biblical Studies: When Language and Text Meet Culture, Cognition and Context*. Winona Lake, Ind.: Eisenbrauns, 2009.

Yri, Kjell Magne. *My Father Taught Me How to Cry, but Now I Have Forgotten: The Semantics of Religious Concepts with an Emphasis on Meaning, Interpretation and Translatability*. Acta Humaniora; Faculty of Arts, University of Oslo, vol. 29. Oslo: Scandinavian University Press, 1998.

Legal and Ethical Reflections on Genesis 18 and 19

Calum Carmichael

In this paper I shall first look at some prominent jurisprudential topics in Gen 18 and 19, turn to the topic of the threatened lineages of Abraham and Lot, and conclude by noting that certain biblical rules (in Lev 18:18–21 and Deut 23:2–6) critique the jeopardy that befell both lines.

Deuteronomy describes its laws as supremely wise and also proclaims their superior justness: "And who is a great nation that hath just statutes like this Torah?" (Deut 4:8). The statement contrasts Israel's laws with other countries' wisdom, but in a spirit that is at the same time nationalistic and universalistic. The foreign nations "shall hear all these statutes, and say, 'Surely this great nation is a wise and understanding people'" (Deut 4:6). The narratives in Gen 18 and 19 also combine nationalism and universalism and are, similar to the Levitical and Deuteronomic laws, much focused on justness.

The story of the destruction of Sodom and Gomorrah features implicit reflection on the communal principle of punishment: though some inhabitants of the city of Sodom are plainly innocent of iniquitous homosexual craving, they are nonetheless still treated as culpable. Abraham expresses opposition to the fundamentally unjust character of the principle. In opting to do so, however, he opposes it by substituting the magnificent but equally unjust principle of communal merit: the guilty are to go free because the community contains some innocent members. Thus Abraham says, "Peradventure there be fifty righteous within the city: wilt thou also destroy and not spare the place for the fifty righteous that are therein?" (Gen 18:24). The reason why the deity and Abraham proceed on the basis of the corporate principle is not because they fail to see that the only just approach is that of individual responsibility, that each person should be judged on his or her own merits or demerits. Rather, in the situation in Sodom where men are bent on abusing Lot's guests, there is recognition of political realities and the limitations they inevitably place on pursuing a just solution. In international affairs especially, the principle of individual responsibility is of little moment because of its impracticality. The only sensible procedure is to decide if there is a satisfactory minority with which a negotiated settling of matters might be possible. In this instance, it would be if ten innocent citizens of Sodom could be singled out (Gen 18:32). Ten are not found, however, and the entire city is wiped out.

The narrative also illuminates the contemporary interest in human rights. When Abraham wrests from God the promise that he will not destroy Sodom if some decent people can be found, there surfaces an elementary notion of fairness. As David Daube points out, in opposing God's application of the communal principle of responsibility, Abraham pursues his argument for the sake of heathens, that is, non-Israelites. Tellingly, Abraham reminds God of his position as "the judge of all the earth" (Gen 18:25). In Abraham's plea certain fundamental claims "have a knack of disregarding fortuitous barriers of race or culture" and those who plead as he did are pioneers possessing "the kind of minds that break through to the deepest concerns shared by all."[1]

The Sodom narrative also raises acutely the problem of the morality of punishment. Lot clearly offends by offering his two daughters to the mob for their sexual pleasure. He does so in order to protect his male guests. The daughters, in turn, manifestly abuse Lot when they get him drunk and have intercourse with him. The compiler of the stories in Gen 19 doubtless views what the daughters do to their father as paying him back in kind—via inappropriate nonconsensual sexual activity—for what he attempted to do to them. An inexorable law of mirroring retribution is seen to be at work. But the punishment also involves wrongdoing—a daughter should not compromise her father's sexual integrity even if he had set about compromising hers. Illustrated is the immorality of the kind expressed in statements such as "With the froward thou [God] will show thyself unsavoury"

---

1. David Daube, "Human Rights: The Rabbis, Philo, and Josephus," in *Ethics and Other Writings: Studies in Comparative Legal History* (ed. Calum Carmichael; vol. 4 of *Collected Works of David Daube*; Berkeley: Robbins Collection, School of Law, University of California, 2009), 281–99; also, *Law and Wisdom in the Bible: David Daube's Gifford Lectures* (ed. Calum Carmichael; 2 vols.; West Conshohocken, Pa.: Templeton Foundation Press, 2010), 2:28.

(2 Sam 22:27; Ps 18:26) and "Zeus fairly metes out unjust things to evildoers" (Aeschylus, *Suppliant Maidens*, 403). The problem is one that exercises contemporary legal philosophers.[2]

The matter is even more complicated. Extreme measures are necessary to cope with the two situations in question. Lot is bound to protect his guests and his daughters are obliged to perpetuate their father's line. A clash of values exists in each instance. Lot upholds the custom of treating a guest well but at the expense of violating the protection of a daughter's dignity. The women, in turn, affirm the importance of a father's lineage but at the cost of his honor (Gen 19:32). The narrator is plainly aware of the legal and ethical issues at stake. Universal rules, written or unwritten, have sometimes to be set aside and when that happens there exists a fundamental problem about the nature of justice. Any form of law is inherently indeterminate. A law can be both just and oppressive.[3] In the book of Numbers a progressive rule permits the daughters of Zelophehad to inherit in the absence of sons. Should they marry outside their tribe, however, a consequence is the wrong of unjust enrichment because their inherited property would unfairly become part of their husbands' tribal inheritance.[4] The transfer would be to the detriment of Zelophehad's Josephite tribe. A concession to the daughters made in the name of equity leads to a fresh injustice and a further balancing of rights is required. The extreme situations in the two Genesis narratives, when emotions are necessarily at their unreflective height, point to irresolvable conflicts between law and principle.

About biblical authors we can say, not that they were poor philosophers, but that they were not philosophers at all. Biblical legends are not philosophical tracts but nonetheless they exist to explain some prevailing state of affairs and to engage thought, the etiological aim often being a

---

2. "Whatever mechanism consequentialists endorse, they agree that the deliberate infliction of suffering involved in punishment is in itself an evil, justified only instrumentally by its good consequences" (David Dolinko, "Punishment," in *The Oxford Handbook of Philosophy of Criminal Law* [ed. J. Deigh and D. Dolinko; Oxford: Oxford University Press, 2011], 406).

3. See Walter Weyrauch, "The Experience of Lawlessness," *New Criminal Law Review* 10 (2007), 432 n. 41 (evaluating the role of unwritten law in a situation of anomie such as prevailed in postwar Frankfurt and Berlin in 1945).

4. "A benefit obtained from another, not intended as a gift and not legally justifiable" (*Dictionary of Modern Legal Usage* [ed. Brian Garner; Oxford: Oxford University Press, 1995], 901).

dominant one. An example is the way in which the destruction of the cities in the region of the Salt Sea is linked, as judged by the ancient narrator, to unacceptable human conduct. Homosexuality supposedly is the reason Sodom and Gomorrah are destroyed. The view appears to be that as a sterile activity not producing offspring, homosexuality matches the barren landscape in which the cities are located. The link explains the bewildering statement that "The men of Sodom compassed the house round, from young to old, the entire people from one end of the city to the other," seeking homosexual intercourse (Gen 19:4). At all times, homosexuality is a minority activity. Yet in this narrative, the entire population is involved, minus the women who, from the narrative's perspective, do not count. The attempt to explain the unfertile emptiness of the landscape determines that aspect of the narrative wherein all inhabitants, even those too young to be capable of sexual congress, are annihilated.

Religious belief and human progress can often be antithetical. Unsatisfactorily, the book of Job, like the two narratives in Gen 18 and 19, also falls back on affirming God's control of nature as paramount in assessing what goes on in the world. Second Esdras 4:2, picking up from the book of Job (38–41), has the angel Uriel tell the seer Salathiel: "Your understanding has utterly failed regarding this world, and do you think you can comprehend the way of the Most High?" Human beings embrace paramount principles of civilization and justice but their values wane before God who can behave as an absolute ruler acting arbitrarily.

The topic of sterility is a major feature of the narrative. Lot's wife looks back on the two cities and turns into a pillar of salt, a substance itself antithetical to fecundity (Gen 19:26). The significance of this development is that it triggers a problem with Lot's lineage because the family has no sons to carry on the line. Alert to the problem, Lot's daughters get their father drunk and become pregnant by him.[5] The narrative explains yet another

---

5. The focus, I think, is on preserving Lot's lineage, not on preserving life in the world at large. As Victor P. Hamilton points out, the daughters' plaint that there is no man on earth available to come in to them is "probably more hyperbolic than reflective of a response to a worldwide catastrophe." Zoar was spared from the catastrophe, and the term 'erets ("earth, land") in Gen 19:31 may have a more local geographical significance (Victor P. Hamilton, *The Book of Genesis: Chapters 18–50* [Grand Rapids: Eerdmans, 1995], 51). I also accept Hamilton's argument that the reference to Lot's sons-in-law has a future sense: "who were to marry his daughters" (Gen 19:14). That is, we should reject any suggestion that these sons-in-law are the husbands of other daughters of Lot (50).

aspect of the region's geography, namely, the close but separate location of Israel's kinspeople, the Moabites and the Ammonites. The children born of the two daughters' unions with Lot, who is Abraham's nephew, are their ancestors (Gen 19:36–38). The relationship between the two groups and Israel is, we shall note, the focus of two rules in Deut 23:2–6.

What occurs in Gen 19 illuminates the account in Gen 18 about the salvaging of Abraham's own endangered line of descent. The never-before-pregnant Sarah has become wholly sterile in old age. The narrative begins with a reference to the heat of the day—possibly an environmental condition reflecting the topic of Sarah's desiccated state at the time (Gen 18:1). Sarah learns that she will achieve the impossible and become pregnant, and she jests about again being able to experience sexual pleasure (Gen 18:12–15). Skepticism doubtless enters into her reaction. We recall that Lot's prospective sons-in-law consider the prediction of the city's demise to be but a jest. Both dismissive responses are tied to the problem of sterility. Sarah's laughter is directly linked to the reverse of her sterile condition. The sons-in-law's skepticism about a forthcoming disaster that will cause them to perish has the consequence that they will not experience sexual pleasure with Lot's daughters. The latter will then become sexually active with their father to overcome barrenness in his family (just as Sarah will become sexually active with her [half-]brother to overcome barrenness in his). The boldness of Lot's daughters has its counterpart in Sarah's situation when she audaciously gives voice to her anticipation of sexual pleasure. Both narratives are about exceptional births because of the extreme situations in which the women find themselves. (We might ask why prospective sons-in-law, not sons, play a role in the narrative. After all, they are unnecessary because the narrative's focus is on the threatened demise of Lot's lineage. The care with which one narrative is often made to balance with another may be a factor. Each account spells out why, despite the marital arrangements in place, potential loss of lineage looms for the two families.)

The women's boldness receives appraisal in biblical rules. An incest rule in Lev 18:7 targets a son's sexual involvement with a parent. That is surprising because we might expect the focus of the law to be on a parent with a child, not a child with a parent. The explanation is that this very first rule in the list of incest rules in Lev 18:7 responds to the two earliest instances of children compromising a parent sexually: Ham sees the nakedness of his drunken father (Gen 9:22–25) and the daughters of Lot lie with their drunken father (Gen 19:30–38). The Genesis narratives are foundational in the sense that their contents provide the subject matter for the nation's rules. Together, narratives and laws serve a universal need on the part of a collective to create a myth about its national origins and its distinctive legal order. The action of Lot's daughters with their father prompts a prohibition against the equivalent initiative, a son's sexual violation of his mother. Like other biblical rules, the male addressee (in most instances) incorporates the woman too and thus the rule includes an implicit prohibition against a daughter's sexual involvement with a parent.

Before turning to a rule about Sarah's boldness, I will highlight two other rules that focus on the Moabites and the Ammonites. A rule in Deut 23:2 bars someone born of an incestuous union from entering the ideal Israelite community that goes by the name of "the assembly of Yahweh" (*qahal yhwh*): "A bastard shall not enter into the assembly of Yahweh; even to his tenth generation shall he not enter." The idea of the assembly comes from Moses' farewell address in Deut 1–34 to the assembly of the sons of Israel. The association's makeup is thought to embody the ideal rules Moses addresses to the assembled Israelites and is modeled on Jacob's farewell address to his sons in Gen 49. Whereas Jacob (Israel) sought to exclude his son Levi from entering his assembly (*qahal*) because of Levi's (and Simeon's) hostile stance against the Hivites in Gen 34, Moses views Levi's fierce anti-Canaanite stance positively (Gen 49:5–7; Deut 33:8–11).[6] The assembly is to comprise those descendants of Jacob-Israel who observe all of Moses' laws and receive Yahweh's blessing of fruitfulness (Gen 35:9–12; Lev 18:2–4; Deut 28). The assembly's numbers, however, cannot be increased, for example, by fruit born of an incestuous union, a matter that comes up because of Lot's daughters' conduct with their father.

While Lot's descendants, the Moabites and the Ammonites, may dwell among the Israelites, the taint of their origin persists and denies them full privileges. The next law after the exclusion of one born of an incestuous union explicitly excludes these two ethnic groups: "An Ammonite or Moabite shall not enter into the assembly of Yahweh; even to their tenth generation. … Because they met you not with bread and with water in the way, when ye came forth out of Egypt; and because they hired against thee Balaam the son of Beor of Pethor of Mesopotamia, to curse thee. … Thou shalt not seek their peace nor their prosperity all thy days for ever" (Deut

---

6. For a fuller discussion of the nature of the assembly and the rules about it, see Calum Carmichael, *Law and Narrative in the Bible* (Ithaca, N.Y.: Cornell University Press, 1985), 225–34.

23:3–6). The underlying focus is again the topic of fecundity, the increase or decrease in Israel's numbers. The two groups are first judged negatively on the grounds of a universal law: not to feed an enemy in wilderness conditions is likely to bring about a reduction in his numbers due to starvation. It is not a crime against humanity on the scale of the Amalekites who attacked the Israelites when they were weak from hunger in the wilderness (Deut 25:17–19), but the failure constitutes passivity that is culpable. The fault comes to expression in wisdom circles: Prov 25:21 ("If thine enemy be hungry, give him bread to eat; and if he be thirsty, give him water to drink"); Job 22:7; 31:16, 17, 31. The other offense is that the king of Moab, fearing the great numbers of Israelites assembled before him—"Now shall this company [*qahal*] lick up all that are round about us, as the ox licketh up the grass of the field"—hired the Mesopotamian diviner Balaam to curse the Israelites in order to reduce their numbers (Num 22:4, 6). The gravity of the offense lies in the king's attempt to harness the power of the sacred, the curse, to dishonor a nation's progenitor, Jacob, and his offspring.

The extraordinary survival of Lot's and Abraham's lines is not, then, just a matter solely confined to the accounts in Gen 18 and 19. Further legal and ethical considerations of both a national and international character come into play in the form of biblical rules. I therefore turn back to Sarah's boldness when she hears that she will produce a child. Like the boldness of Lot's daughters' in producing theirs, Sarah's audacity receives attention in a rule in Lev 18:19 that bars sexual relations during a woman's menstrual period. The taboo will probably have been a familiar one before the lawgiver set it down. Why, then, is it committed to writing in Lev 18:19? A feature of legal and moral formulations at all times is how frequently an exceptional situation prompts the composition of a comprehensive rule that does not explicitly cite its idiosyncratic origin. Sarah's audacity in rejoicing openly at the prospect of sexual pleasure is an exceptional feature of the Genesis narrative. Another is that although she has long been postmenopausal and even before that had been barren, she will become fertile. Two sensational new things are then to happen to Sarah in her old age. She is to resume menstruation and she will experience sexual pleasure again. The two happenings, because of their miraculous character, overlap. Resumption of menstruation and anticipated sexual activity unexpectedly come together and Sarah's bold response to these developments raises the prospect of sexual intercourse coinciding with a menstrual period. The dramatic development in Gen 18 furnishes the opportunity for the lawgiver to oppose any such coming together in normal circumstances: "Thou shalt not approach unto a woman to uncover her nakedness, as long as she is put apart for her uncleanness" (Lev 18:19).[7]

Further considerations render this reading of the rule less speculative. The rule that precedes the one about intercourse during menstruation prohibits a polygamous marriage to two sisters while each is alive—"Neither shalt thou take a wife to her sister, to vex her, to uncover her nakedness, beside the other in her life time" (Lev 18:18)—and the rule that follows prohibits adultery—"Thou shalt not lie carnally with thy neighbor's wife, to defile thyself with her" (Lev 18:20). This sequence of rules (marriage to two sisters, sex during menstruation, and adultery) seems disjointed, but it is not. If we assume that the compiler of Genesis through 2 Kings integrates narratives and laws because he sets down laws in response to issues that arise in narratives detailing the nation's inception, the sequence becomes intelligible in light of a particular focus in the narrative history. Jacob's marriages to Leah and Rachel are under review in the rule against two sisters as cowives. The tension between the two women relates to their rivalry over sexual access to the husband Jacob: at this point in the story Leah has been denied access and Rachel needs it to overcome her barrenness (Gen 30:1–24). Rachel's remedy involves heightened sexuality in the form of the (presumably) aphrodisiac plants she acquires from Leah in return for Leah's spending a night with Jacob (Gen 30:14–16). As in the rule about menstruation, the rule responds to a situation in which not only fertility alone is the concern, but there is additionally focus on the woman's sexuality, on her openly expressed anticipation of intercourse. In each instance, the woman explicitly concentrates on the act of intercourse. This is unusual because delicacy of presentation tends to prevail when the subject of female sexuality arises. Style, molded by profound beliefs and feelings, usually contributes to guarded reporting of it.

Remarkably, Sarah's sexual history is again under review in the rule about adultery. The rule comes, seemingly randomly, after the rule about menstruation. But the sequence is not random. Immediately after the two interrelated stories about Sarah's barrenness and the destruction of Sodom and Gomorrah in Gen 18 and 19, we have the account in Gen 20 of how

---

7. While the ancients knew nothing about the ovum, they did recognize the link between menstruation and childbirth. The notices in 2 Sam 11:4, 5 about Bathsheba's cleansing herself after menstruation, which is followed by her conceiving David's child, serve to alert the reader that she is not pregnant by her husband Uriah.

Sarah comes very close to committing adultery with Abimelech, the king of Gerar. We recall that Abraham and Sarah feared that Abraham's life was in danger because a foreign male's interest in her might well lead to his taking her and killing Abraham. Before Sarah's anticipated sexual pleasure with her husband Abraham, she deceives the foreign monarch about her marital status. Her relationship to Abraham is given out as sister and brother. Sarah is taken into Abimelech's house and only divine intervention prevents him having intercourse with her: "And God said unto him in a dream, 'Yea, I know that thou didst this in the integrity of thy heart; for I also withheld thee from sinning against me: therefore suffered I thee not to touch her'" (Gen 20:6). Not until the following part of Gen 21 do we hear that sexual intercourse between Abraham and Sarah occurs and that she gives birth to Isaac. Her deceiving Abimelech accounts for the placement of the rule against adultery after the one about the onset of menstruation and the resumption of intercourse.[8] The adultery rule, like the two previous ones (accessing two sisters and entering a menstruating woman) is again a response to an exceptional, extreme situation in a narrative. It is all well and good for Sarah to help save her husband's life under threat in a foreign land. She must nevertheless refrain from engaging in

---

8. As we read the narratives Sarah goes from being an old woman to an attractive, presumably much younger woman when King Abimelech receives her at his court. To be sure, unlike the earlier reference to Sarah at the pharaoh's court in Gen 12:10–20 there is no reference to her beauty, a feature that presumably betokens her youth. The apparent awkwardness in the chronological narration of events appears to be of no significance either to the narrator or to the lawgiver. Their intent is not to provide historical narration of the kind we are familiar with for the past four hundred years (see J. G. A. Pocock, *The Ancient Constitution and the Feudal Law: A Study of English Historical Thought in the Seventeenth Century* [New York: Cambridge University Press, 1967], for the rise of modern historiography), but to convey information and ideas through the medium of storytelling and lawgiving (see Assnat Bartor, *Reading Law as Narrative: A Study in the Casuistic Laws of the Pentateuch* [SBLAIL 5; Atlanta: Society of Biblical Literature, 2010], for biblical laws also exhibiting features of storytelling). To deal with the problem of temporality in haggadic exposition the rabbis devised one of the thirty-two *Middoth*, the principles of interpretation compiled by Eliezer ben Jose Ha-gelili: "There is no before and after in Scripture." The ignoring of temporality in the narrative material has its parallel in the presentation of the laws: Moses goes back and forth over past, present, and future events in the history of the generations in laying out his rules (Sarah's sexual history, the experience of the oppression in Egypt, and a monarch's [Solomon] multiplying horses, silver, gold, and wives in the law in Deut 17:16, 17).

an adulterous relationship as a means of doing so.⁹ Once we observe the link between narrative and law, we can assess why a rule about adultery is set down at all. To record such a prohibition in writing is banal. Everyone knows that adultery is wrong but as a response to the story about the matriarch of the nation this particular rule becomes far more interesting.

I might add that the rule that follows the rule against adultery prohibits passing a child through fire to Molech by way of sacrificing him: "Thou shalt not let any of thy seed pass through the fire to Molech, neither shalt thou profane the name of thy God: I am Yahweh" (Lev 18:21). The narrative that follows the one about Isaac's birth tells how Abraham had to draw back at the last moment from offering his son by fire to God (Gen 22).¹⁰ (Like Agamemnon, who did not consult Clytemnestra about sacrificing their daughter Iphigenia, Abraham does not consult Sarah about sacrificing their son Isaac.) The sequence of four rules in Lev 18:18–21, like the sequence of the rules in Deut 23:2–6, furnishes an example in microcosm of how rules take up from problematical legal and ethical aspects of the narratives.

In conclusion, Israelite legal formulations of the kind we find in Lev 18:7, 18–21 and Deut 23:2–6 are crucial for a full comprehension of Gen 18 and 19, especially the jeopardy confronting Abraham's and Lot's lines. Abraham's line is compromised by Sarah's attitude to overcoming old age and by the circumstances she encounters in foreign terrain before becoming pregnant by Abraham. If certain rules are observed, comparable problems for future Israelites in less exceptional circumstances are seen to be surmountable. Lot's line is viewed as compromised from the beginning with enduring consequences for the national groups, the Moabites and the Ammonites. Although these groups can be tolerated as sometimes residing among the Israelites, when they do they are not to be admitted to the

---

9. David Daube once told me about an acquaintance of his in Freiburg who practiced psychoanalysis and whose wife was a very good-looking woman. When Hitler came to power, about thirty Jews were taken to concentration camps and her husband was one of them. She knew people who knew Hermann Goering well. They introduced her to him, she slept with him, and he released her husband. See Calum Carmichael, *Ideas and the Man: Remembering David Daube* (Studien zur europäischen Rechtsgeschichte 177; Frankfurt: Klostermann, 2004), 166, 167.

10. For a detailed analysis of this rule, see Calum Carmichael *Law, Legend, and Incest in the Bible: Leviticus 18–20* (Ithaca, N.Y.: Cornell University Press, 1997), 52–53.

august body that is Yahweh's assembly. The exclusion lies in their history when they acted against Israel's expansion.

BIBLIOGRAPHY

Bartor, Assnat. *Reading Law as Narrative: A Study in the Casuistic Laws of the Pentateuch* (SBLAIL 5; Atlanta: Society of Biblical Literature, 2010).
Carmichael, Calum. *Law and Narrative in the Bible*. Ithaca, N.Y.: Cornell University Press, 1985), 225–34.
———. *Law, Legend, and Incest in the Bible: Leviticus 18–20*. Ithaca, N.Y.: Cornell University Press, 1997.
———. *Ideas and the Man: Remembering David Daube*. Studien zur europäischen Rechtsgeschichte 177. Frankfurt: Klostermann, 2004.
Daube, David. "Human Rights: The Rabbis, Philo, and Josephus." Pages 281–99 in *Ethics and Other Writings: Studies in Comparative Legal History*. Edited by Calum Carmichael. Vol. 4 of *Collected Works of David Daube*. Berkeley: Robbins Collection, School of Law, University of California, 2009.
———. *Law and Wisdom in the Bible: David Daube's Gifford Lectures*. Edited by Calum Carmichael; 2 vols. West Conshohocken, Pa.: Templeton Foundation Press, 2010.
Dolinko, David. "Punishment." Pages 403–40 in *The Oxford Handbook of Philosophy of Criminal Law*. Edited by J. Deigh and D. Dolinko. Oxford: Oxford University Press, 2011.
Garner, Brian, ed. *Dictionary of Modern Legal Usage*. Oxford: Oxford University Press, 1995.
Hamilton, Victor P. *The Book of Genesis: Chapters 18–50*. Grand Rapids: Eerdmans, 1995.
Pocock, J. G. A. *The Ancient Constitution and the Feudal Law: A Study of English Historical Thought in the Seventeenth Century*. New York: Cambridge University Press, 1967.
Weyrauch, Walter. "The Experience of Lawlessness." *New Criminal Law Review* 10 (2007): 415–40.

Keeping the Way of Yhwh: Righteousness and Justice in Genesis 18–19

Megan Warner

In his book *Reading the Fractures of Genesis*, David M. Carr identifies the verse Gen 18:19 as one of a group of three late additions to the Abraham narratives.[1] The other two members of the group are Gen 22:15–18 and 26:3bβ–5. Carr describes these late additions as related, semi-Deuteronomistic, and intensely focused on the connection between Abraham's obedience and the covenant promises. In Gen 18:19, says Carr, as in the other two passages, the focus is on Abraham's obedience as a precondition for fulfillment of already-given promises. These three late additions are highly strategic, Carr argues, they change the theological import of the text in which they are placed and the ancestral history as a whole by establishing Abraham as an exemplar of obedience and by making the fulfillment of the covenant promises contingent upon Abraham's obedience.[2]

I am interested in how these three late additions "fit" in their host texts, and in this paper I ask how good a "fit" Gen 18:19 is in its context, which I take to be Gen 18–19. Are the themes of the verse evident in the surrounding text? Does the surrounding text support or undermine the explicit and implicit claims of the added text? And what conclusions might be drawn from the answers to these questions? Do they support Carr's conclusion that the added text establishes Abraham as obedient, and the covenant relationship as contingent upon Abraham's obedience?

I address these questions by means of a close reading of the literary context of Gen 18:19, namely, chapters 18 and 19. To that extent my interpretive method is narrative or literary. However, I also employ elements of

---

1. *Reading the Fractures of Genesis: Historical and Literary Approaches* (Louisville: Westminster John Knox, 1996), 153–61.
2. Ibid., 160–61.

historical-critical method, asking how the addition might be reflective of the cultural and political circumstances of fifth-century Yehud, the likely historical context of the final editing of the book of Genesis.[3] To that end, I work on the basis that a fifth-century editor would have assumed a familiarity with earlier legal traditions on the part of fifth-century readers, and would have expected such readers to bring that background knowledge to bear in their reading of any given narrative, so that use in that narrative of distinctive words, phrases or themes could have been expected to bring to mind the legal provisions or principles with which they were associated.[4]

THE LATE ADDITION

Beginning by looking closely at Gen 18:19, we find that three elements can be identified: (1) Abraham has been known (ידע) by YHWH;[5] (2) *in*

---

3. Mark G. Brett, *Genesis: Procreation and the Politics of Identity* (London: Routledge, 2000), 4, citing Rainer Albertz, *History of Israelite Religion in the Old Testament Period* (2 vols.; London: SCM, 1994), vol. 1. See also Thomas Römer, "The Exodus Narrative According to the Priestly Document" in *The Strata of the Priestly Writings: Contemporary Debate and Future Directions* (ed. Sarah Shectman and Joel S. Baden; Zürich: Theologischer Verlag, 2009), 157.

4. I assume, further, that contemporary readers cannot know the full extent of the late redaction(s) of the text. Some late additions are substantial and can be identified with relative certainty using indicators such as those identified by Carr. However, other editorial activity may have included the addition, or substitution, of single words. Some of this more subtle editorial activity may be guessed at by close reading of text together with other texts with which resonances are noted. For a detailed exploration of these ideas see Gershon Hepner, *Legal Friction: Law, Narrative and Identity Politics in Biblical Israel* (New York: Lang, 2010). See also Megan Warner, "Genesis 20–22:19: Abraham's Test of Allegiance," 53 *ABR* (2005): 13–30.

5. The verb ידע, where it appears in Gen 18:19 (ידעתיו), has often been translated "chosen." Claus Westermann, *Genesis 12–36* (trans. John J. Scullion; Minneapolis: Augsburg, 1985), 288, notes that Gen 18:19 is the only place in the patriarchal writings where ידע is used with the sense "chosen." That it should be translated with this sense is, I believe, unfortunate for two reasons. First, it is suggestive of a Deuteronomic "election" of Abraham not otherwise made explicit in the book of Genesis. (The verb בחר [to choose] appears in Gen only twice [Gen 6:2 and 13:11] and on neither occasion is the choice one that is exercised by YHWH. See further Joel S. Kaminsky, *Yet I Loved Jacob: Reclaiming the Biblical Concept of Election* [Nashville: Abingdon, 2007], 40, 102.) Conversely, the concept of a person significant to Israel's history being "known" to YHWH is not novel: YHWH also "knew" Moses (Exod 33:12, 17; Deut 34:10), David (2 Sam 7:20), and Jeremiah (Jer 1:5). In Amos 3:2, Amos tells Israel on YHWH's behalf,

order that he will teach/order his sons and his household to keep the way of Yhwh by doing righteousness and justice;[6] and (3) *in order that* Yhwh will give to Abraham what he had promised to him.

There is something a little circular about this progression, but the effect of the verse is to place the doing of righteousness and justice at the very center of Yhwh's motivation for honoring the covenant promises. There is also a sense in which Abraham, in being known as "teacher" of Yhwh's way, is made the source of the practice of doing righteousness and justice. Further, by highlighting Abraham's "knownness" the verse implies

---

"You only have I known of all the families of the earth." Secondly, the verb ידע is a significant one for the host narrative, which exploits an ambiguity between its judicial and sexual meanings. The use of ידע in the added verse speaks to the wordplay in the host text and it seems desirable that this interplay should be reflected in translation. See Lyn Bechtel, "A Feminist Reading of Genesis 19.1–11" in *Genesis* (ed. Athalya Brenner; FCB 2/1; Sheffield: Sheffield Academic Press, 1998), 108–28; and Ellen van Wolde's paper in this volume.

6. This is the semi-Deuteronomistic aspect of the verse noted by Carr, who observes, at 160, that "it describes Abraham as fulfilling the programmatic Deuteronomistic stipulation to teach children righteousness" (see Deut 6:1–3, 20–25). Carr notes a significant difference between that stipulation and the formula used here—rather than "decrees and commandments" (Deut 6:2) Abraham is instructed to teach the keeping of "justice and righteousness," and Carr states that this "grounds Yhwh's relationship with Israel in an ancestral righteousness that long predates the all-important Deuteronomistic law." (In fact the concepts of justice and righteousness do appear associated in one verse in Deuteronomy, namely, 33:21, but they are most commonly found associated in the prophetic books, especially Isaiah, Jeremiah, Ezekiel, and Amos, in a formulaic manner referring primarily to social justice, and also in royal contexts; see Richard G. Smith, *The Fate of Justice and Righteousness during David's Reign: Re-reading the Court History and Its Ethics according to 2 Samuel 8:15-20:26* [New York: T&T Clark, 2009].) There is a further significant difference between the Deuteronomistic stipulation and the adaption of it in Gen 18:19 not noted by Carr. In Deut 6:1–2 Moses announces that he has been instructed to teach Israel, in order that "you and your children and your children's children" (אתה ובנך ובן־בנך) might fear Yhwh and keep his decrees and commandments." Gen 18:19 introduces a small but significant gloss—Yhwh states that he has known Abraham in order that he might charge "his children *and his household* after him" (את־בניו ואת־ביתו אחריו) to keep the way of Yhwh by doing righteousness and justice. Space does not allow for a full discussion of the significance of this gloss, except to observe that, given the description in the immediately preceding chapter of the circumcision of members of Abraham's household other than those standing within the covenant relationship (Gen 17:23–27), this formulation of the intended group of students does not fit comfortably with the elements characteristic of Deuteronomistic literature listed by Carr at 157.

that the quality of Abraham's own observance made him, if not an ideal, then at least an appropriate person to teach the righteousness and justice of Yhwh.

So how good is the "fit" between this verse and its host text?

My answer is twofold: the "fit" is good to the extent that the principal theme of 18:19, doing righteousness and justice, is also a principal theme of chapters 18 and 19; however, the fit is poor in the sense that the implication to be drawn from Gen 18:19 about Abraham's own doing of righteousness and justice is not matched by the host text, which paints a mixed picture of Abraham's conduct in this regard.

A Good Fit

Let's begin with the sense in which the "fit" is good, a shared focus on the theme of doing righteousness and justice. Both chapters 18 and 19 include a "hospitality" narrative and a "Sodom" narrative. I will consider the Sodom narratives first.

The scene set in 18:22–33 is a court of law. Abraham is legal counsel for the defendant, the city of Sodom, and Yhwh is judge. The language used confirms these roles. Pietro Bovati demonstrates that within the Hebrew Bible judicial-inquiry procedure is indicated by the presence of four elements: an initial verb of crying out, a verb of movement toward the judging authority, an inquest in which the verb ידע (to know) plays a crucial role and a conclusion employing the verbs ראה (to see) or מצא (to find).[7] All four elements are present in chapter 18. First, in 18:20 (and also 18:21) Yhwh remarks on the outcry of Sodom (זעקת סדם). Second, in 18:23 Abraham draws near (נגש) to Yhwh before beginning his advocacy.[8] Third, Yhwh announces that he must go down and see (ראה) the situation for himself and that having done this he will know (ידע). Fourthly, in the course of his advocacy on behalf of Sodom, Abraham repeatedly refers to the numbers of innocent persons who might be found (מצא) in

---

7. Pietro Bovati, *Re-establishing Justice: Legal Terms, Concepts and Procedures in the Hebrew Bible* (trans. Michael J. Smith; Sheffield: Sheffield Academic Press, 1994). I am indebted to Ellen van Wolde for bringing this to my attention. See her paper elsewhere in this volume.

8. *HALOT* (2:670) also identifies this as a legal term, signifying the plaintiff's approach to the judge.

Sodom. In addition, in Gen 18:25 Abraham calls Yhwh "the judge (שפט) of all the earth."⁹

In Gen 19 a second judicial procedure is established. This time Lot is judge and the men of Sodom are self-appointed prosecutors of Lot's visitors for crimes unknown. The men of Sodom surround Lot's house and call (קרא) to Lot demanding that he bring out the visitors that they might know (ידע) them.¹⁰ In 19:9 the men of Sodom instruct Lot to "come near!" (נגש), and in verse 10 they themselves draw near (נגש) to Lot's door. But the men are struck with blindness, so they cannot see and are unable to find (מצא) the door. This time the men of Sodom call Lot judge (שפט).

Also in chapter 19 the consequences of the judicial procedure begun in chapter 18 are played out when judgment is executed against Sodom and Gomorrah. Yhwh rains sulfur and fire on those cities from heaven and they are overthrown. However, Yhwh shows mercy to Lot and his family, giving them the opportunity to flee Sodom before the destruction.

In short, the Sodom narratives in chapters 18 and 19 describe two separate legal proceedings, tracing the events of both trials and the execution of judgment against the unsuccessful defendant in the first. These passages are concerned with legal justice.

The hospitality narratives in chapters 18 and 19 are concerned with righteousness. They feature a case study about the offering of hospitality to

---

9. Again, *HALOT* (4:1624) identifies this as an essentially legal term.

10. Traditionally, interpreters of Gen 19 have interpreted the demand of the men of Sodom to know (ידע) the visitors as being a demand to know them sexually, i.e., to rape them. There is another way to interpret the demand—the men of Sodom wish to judge the mysterious visitors (just as Yhwh wished to judge the men of Sodom). Their grievance against Lot is that he, an alien himself, has usurped them in their judicial intentions, and this grievance is expressly stated: "This fellow came here as an alien, and he would play the judge!" (Gen 19:9). Lot's response to the men's demands, a plea not to act so wickedly, and an offer of his two betrothed daughters who have not known (ידע) a man, suggests that he, at least, understood the meaning of the men's demands to be sexual. Lyn Bechtel, in "A Feminist Reading of Genesis 19.1–11," in *Genesis* (ed. Athalya Brenner; FCB 2/1; Sheffield: Sheffield Academic Press, 1998), has argued persuasively that the intentions of the men of Sodom were judicial rather than sexual/criminal. Bechtel suggests that Lot's offer of his daughters is not supposed to be taken seriously by the men of Sodom but rather is designed to defuse a tense situation. While finding Bechtel's analysis persuasive, and noting the clear evidence within the text that it intends to depict judicial proceedings in the way described, I would nevertheless suggest that a degree of fluidity between the sexual and the judicial imbues the text's use of the verb ידע throughout chs. 18 and 19.

strangers. In chapter 18 Abraham offers hospitality to three visitors. Many scholars have written about the extent and quality of Abraham's hospitality, with the general consensus being that it was more than adequate. For example, Gunkel has described it as "extravagant," and Weston Fields has described Abraham as the "ideal host."[11] Abraham is "rewarded" for his hospitality with the promise of a son. The opening of chapter 19 sees Lot also offering hospitality to strangers. It is arguable that Lot is "rewarded" for his hospitality by being saved from the destruction of Sodom.[12]

Many of the events of chapter 18 are repeated in chapter 19, but sometimes in ways that are exaggerated or grotesque. That is the case here. In offering his hospitality Lot goes to the extraordinary length of trying to protect his visitors by offering the baying crowd his two virgin daughters. Although Thomas Bolin has expressly doubted that this offer could be classed as "hospitality," it can be seen as a caricatured offer of hospitality, exaggerated and grotesque and designed to stand in contrast with the exaggerated and grotesque lack of hospitality shown to the strangers by the men of Sodom.[13]

A Poor Fit

So, Gen 18 and 19 are concerned with questions of justice and righteousness, the principal theme of Gen 18:19. So far the "fit" is good. But what about the portrayal of Abraham's obedience?

To this point the portrayal of Abraham is flattering. As I have mentioned, the consensus is that Abraham's exercise of hospitality was at least adequate and probably extravagant. And his advocacy on behalf of Sodom could be judged admirable for its altruism.[14] However, there is something else happening in this text that disturbs the picture.

---

11. Hermann Gunkel, *Genesis* (trans. Mark E. Biddle; Macon, Ga.: Mercer University Press, 1997), 193; Weston W. Fields, *Sodom and Gomorrah: History and Motive in Biblical Narrative* (Sheffield: Sheffield Academic Press, 1997).

12. Cf. Gen 19:29 (also thought to be late), which attributes Lot's rescue to Yhwh's remembrance of Abraham.

13. Thomas M. Bolin, "The Role of Exchange in Ancient Mediterranean Religion and Its Implications for Reading Genesis 18-19," *JSOT* 29 (2004): 49.

14. The text does not indicate explicitly that Abraham was motivated in his advocacy by the presence in Sodom of the family of Lot, although Gen 14 might suggest such a motivation.

The problem arises in relation to the promise of a son to Abraham and Sarah. Sarah's response to the promise is laughter. Several features of the story suggest that Sarah's laughter is significant. First, every character apart from Abraham comments on it. Yhwh asks Abraham, "Why did Sarah laugh?" Sarah says, "No, I did not laugh," and Yhwh says, "No, but you did laugh."[15] Second, laughter had been Abraham's response also when he made the same promise in chapter 17. Third, Isaac's name is built on the root "to laugh" (צחק). Fourth, the text says that the fiancés of Lot's daughters, when told of the impending danger to Sodom, considered Lot to be joking (כמצחק). Finally, Gen 18:12 says of Sarah's laughter that she laughed inwardly, literally "in her inward parts" (בקרבה). This unusual construction is used again in 18:24, when Abraham speaks of the innocent ones who may be found in the inward parts of Sodom.

So Sarah's laughter is important. But what happens next is the really crucial thing. In Gen 18:15 Sarah denies her laughter. The Hebrew root for the verb "to deny," כחש, is rare and does not appear in Genesis outside this verse.[16] The use of this unusual root, I suggest, directs the attention of the reader familiar with the pentateuchal legal material to Lev 5:20–26, where כחש appears in two consecutive verses, 5:21 and 22. Leviticus 5:20–26 sets out the penalty for sacrilege against oaths. The passage provides that when a person deceives (כחש) a neighbor in the matter of a deposit, and swears falsely regarding the deception, then when the person realizes her guilt she must restore the thing deposited to its owner and add one-fifth to it. In addition, she should have the priest bring a guilt offering, of a ram without blemish, from the flock, to Yhwh. By these means the guilt may be forgiven.

At first sight this law about the penalty for sacrilege appears to have little or nothing to do with Sarah's denial of her laughter in Gen 18:15, but on closer inspection something very intriguing becomes apparent. If one were to consider the promised son, Isaac, as a "deposit," then one would see that that Isaac's fate is played out in accordance with the requirements of Lev 5:20–26. In Gen 22 Abraham obeys Yhwh's demand that he sacrifice (or restore) Isaac—literally, "give him back." At the last moment the sacrifice (or restoration) of Isaac is not required and Yhwh "provides" a

---

15. In fact, the text of v. 15 is ambiguous. It might equally be Yhwh or Abraham who speaks.

16. This suggests the possibility that the word was a redactional addition.

ram to be sacrificed in Isaac's place.[17] The Hebrew word, איל, is the same in both places.

Is there any justification for considering Isaac a "deposit"? Gershon Hepner, who also recognizes the intertextual allusion that I suggest here, notes that Gen 21:1 says that Yhwh "visited" Sarah.[18] The verb is פקד. The noun formed from that root is פקדון, or "deposit." From this verbal resonance, Hepner concludes that Isaac is a deposit, and that his fate is played out as stipulated in Lev 5:20–26.[19]

---

17. The conversation between Abraham and Isaac on the way to Moriah (Gen 22:7–8) indicates that Yhwh's provision of a ram was at odds with their mutual expectation that a lamb was the appropriate sacrificial animal.

18. "Jacob's Oath Causes Rachel's Death: Reflecting the Law in Lev. 5:4–6," *ZABR* 8 (2002): 131–65; *Legal Friction* 285.

19. One possible objection to the interpretation I am proposing is that the text does not indicate that Sarah swore an oath. Jacob Milgrom, *Leviticus* (Minneapolis: Fortress, 2004), 61, notes some dispute about whether the swearing of an oath was understood to be a necessary element of the offense described in Lev 5:20–26. Milgrom himself takes the view that swearing an oath is a necessary element of the offense; however, he notes that a majority of "the ancients" were of the view that the offense was complete upon the denial. Milgrom maintains that the offense had two necessary steps: the deception of a human neighbor in which Yhwh was then made complicit by the invocation of his name in an oath. If Milgrom is right, and an oath is required, that is not of itself a fatal objection to the interpretation I propose. The situation in which Sarah and Abraham find themselves is rather different from the normal state of affairs envisaged by Leviticus. In the general run of things the world of humans and the divine are clearly separate. At any given moment a person can say whether she is conversing with another human being or with God. That is not the case in Gen 18. The text of Gen 18 is ambiguous not only about the number of visitors to appear before Abraham at Mamre, but also about their nature. It refers variously to "the men" or "three men" (18:2, 16, 22) and Yhwh (18:1, 13, 17, 20, 22, 26, 33). The impact of this ambiguity, in the context of Sarah's laughter and her denial of it, is, I suggest, unusual. With her single denial, whether she knows it or not, Sarah is setting out to deceive both her human neighbor and Yhwh at the same time. In these circumstances, I suggest, the element of sacrilege can be understood to be present without the formal swearing of an oath. (It is further worth observing that an "H" equivalent to P's provisions, Num 5:5–8, has no requirement for the swearing of an oath; see Milgrom, *Leviticus 1–16: A New Translation with Introduction and Commentary* [AB 3; New York: Doubleday, 1991], 13; and Israel Knohl, *The Sanctuary of Silence: The Priestly Torah and the Holiness School* [Minneapolis: Fortress, 1995], 114.) Note further that, because the provisions of Leviticus were designed to accommodate a sophisticated sacrificial apparatus not in existence during Abraham's lifetime, it would be unrealistic to expect the Genesis narrative to comply exactly with the stipulations of the Levitical

There are, in addition, further verbal resonances not noted by Hepner. Lev 7:1–6 sets out the "instructions" (תורה) for the making of a guilt offering (אשם) pursuant to Lev 5:26, and there are significant resonances between those instructions and the narrative of Abraham's actions in Gen 22. Abraham binds Isaac at the place (מקום) that Elohim had shown him (Gen 22:9; Lev 7:2) and prepares to slaughter (שחט) him (Gen 22:10; Lev 7:2) on the altar (המזבח; Gen 22:9; Lev 7:2, 5) before offering him as a burnt offering (עלה; Gen 22:13; Lev 7:2). Following the first speech of the angel in Gen 22:12, Abraham offers instead a ram (איל; Gen 22:13; Lev 5:25) that he sees caught in a thicket. Note that in Gen 26:5 Abraham is explicitly said to have followed Yhwh's instructions (תורה).

How does Sarah's breach of the laws concerning sacrilege against oaths relate to Abraham's obedience and suitability as a teacher of justice and righteousness? First, it can be demonstrated that the text builds a subtle case for Abraham's responsibility for Sarah's sacrilege. In 18:9 the visitors ask Abraham, "Where is Sarah, your wife?" The syntax of this question mirrors exactly the question of Yhwh to Cain in Gen 4:9, "Where is Abel, your brother?" Further, in Gen 18:13 Yhwh asks not Sarah, but Abraham, why Sarah laughed. This question not only suggests Abraham's responsibility for Sarah's laughter but also reminds the reader of Abraham's own laughter in chapter 17.[20] Finally, in chapter 22, it is to Abraham that the duty of "returning" Isaac eventually falls.

In any event, regardless of who is ultimately responsible for Sarah's denial, the reality was that the punishment for it would be felt equally by Sarah and Abraham. Their son would have to be returned to his "owner," Yhwh, and therefore lost to both parents. The punishment for Sarah's breach would be visited on innocent and guilty alike.

This, of course, was also the situation of the people of Sodom. The text gives no explanation for Abraham's decision to advocate on behalf of the innocent of Sodom and it is tempting to interpret it as a further example of

---

guilt offering. Therefore neither Sarah nor Abraham approaches a priest with a ram. However, see the body of the text for details of verbal resonances between Gen 22 and instructions for the making of guilt offerings found in Lev 7.

20. In light of Abraham's own laughter (and his apparent failure to mention to Sarah the promise made in Gen 17:16), his failure to speak up in Sarah's support in this situation does not portray him in a particularly positive light. Note the ambiguity in Gen 18:15 by which it might have been Abraham who said to Sarah "No, but you did laugh." If it was indeed Abraham who spoke then his behavior is even less impressive.

Abraham's righteousness.[21] Viewed in the light of Sarah's act of sacrilege, however, Abraham's championing of the innocent of Sodom looks different. It is difficult to avoid the conclusion that in seeking justice for the innocent of Sodom, Abraham is also seeking justice for himself, indirectly asking Yhwh to forgo his rights to Isaac. Abraham's use, in 18:24, of the unusual construction בקרבה, which reminds the reader of Sarah's laughter in 18:12 where the construction is also used, strengthens this sense that Abraham's advocacy is not entirely altruistic, but is prompted by a healthy dose of self-interest.

There is a further parallel to note before moving to some conclusions. In this reading the wife of the patriarch falls short in some way in both chapters 18 and 19. Sarah falls foul of the legal prohibition of sacrilege against oaths and her punishment is the loss of her son. Lot's wife turns back toward Sodom and is turned into a pillar of salt.[22] In both cases the punishment impacts not only the guilty but also the innocent and issues of collective justice arise.

Some Conclusions

So, how good is the "fit" between Gen 18:19 and its host text, chapters 18 and 19? This discussion indicates that the "fit" is poor in the sense that chapters 18 and 19 do not consistently support the implication of Gen 18:19 that Abraham was, if not an ideal, then at least an appropriate person to teach the keeping of the way of Yhwh by doing righteousness and justice. Abraham's record, as presented by chapters 18 and 19, is mixed. His hospitality to the visitors was excellent; however, he was, to a greater or lesser extent, implicated in Sarah's act of sacrilege. Further, the fact of Abraham's liability to punishment following Sarah's sacrilege shines a less-than-positive light on Abraham's advocacy for Sodom, suggesting a motivation of self-interest rather than altruism.

The implication of Gen 18:19, that Yhwh chose Abraham to be a teacher of justice and righteousness because of the strength of his own record in those areas, is not borne out by the surrounding text. In fact, I

---

21. See n. 14 above.

22. The phrase "pillar of salt" is not used elsewhere in the Hebrew Scriptures. However, "salt" plays a role in the Priestly understanding of covenant. Num 18:19 speaks of a "covenant of salt," and in Lev 2:13 the Israelites are exhorted not to leave meat undressed by the "salt of the covenant."

would argue that it is actively subverted, so that the implicit assertion of Abraham's obedience in 18:19 is made to stand in uncomfortable contrast with the mixed and even murky portrayal of Abraham's character in the surrounding text.

If this is the case, then Carr's conclusion about the significance of Gen 18:19 and the other late additions—that they are intensely focused on Abraham's obedience and make the fulfillment of the covenant promises contingent upon it—is undermined.

Why insert a piece of text claiming for Abraham a particular relationship with righteousness and justice into a text that undermines the claim by demonstrating a different relationship?

One answer could be that the result is to convey a sophisticated and nuanced overall understanding of the covenant relationship. The implication of Gen 18:19 that Abraham was consistently righteous and just in his dealings invites the reader to focus on those areas in which his behavior was neither righteous nor just. What were the consequences of that behavior for the divine covenant? Abraham's character, as depicted in Gen 18–19, could be thought to be like that of the Israelites—generally faithful to the requirements of the law and focused on the standards of Yhwh, but regularly falling short of those requirements and standards. If that were the case, then the effect of the insertion of 18:19 into Gen 18–19 is to reassure the people that a failure to maintain the demands of the covenant to the letter would not result in the withdrawal of the covenant relationship.[23] As a flawed model Abraham could be thought to provide a more helpful yardstick than he could have done as a consistent one, and Gen 18:19's statement of the covenant equation becomes richer and more nuanced, I suggest, when stated in the context of narrative of Abraham's own mixed record.

Universalism and Particularism at Sodom and Gomorrah

The theme of these collected essays, universalism and particularism at Sodom and Gomorrah, calls for a consideration of these findings against the historical and political context of fifth-century Yehud. To that end, there are three further observations to make. Perhaps the most striking element of this reading, when considered in the light of fifth-century concerns, is

---

23. Such reassurance resonates, for example, with the theological underpinnings of the covenant as presented by the Holiness Code (Lev 26:44–45).

that Sarah is depicted as having committed sacrilege (מעל). The books of Ezra and Nehemiah indicate that the most contentious social and religious issue in fifth-century Yehud was intermarriage with foreigners. In Ezra 9:2, 4 and 10:6 intermarriage with foreigners is described as sacrilege (מעל). In light of that description it is intriguing that Sarah, the appropriate wife *par excellence* (i.e. the "elect," as opposed to the "diselect" Hagar)[24] should be depicted as guilty of sacrilege. That this should be so, and that Abraham should be depicted as bearing some degree of responsibility for making the appropriate reparations, does not sit well with majority religious views of the time. It is unlikely in the extreme that a Deuteronomistic redactor should have wished to promote such an idea.

Second, there is a theological tension in chapters 18 and 19 that has received little attention from commentators. Abraham refers to Yhwh, in Gen 18:25, as "the judge of all the earth." In the same way, the chapter presents the city of Sodom as being subject to Yhwh's jurisdiction and his laws, so that the behavior of its citizens is properly measurable against Yhwh's laws and standards. Neither of these things seems strange to the twenty-first-century reader. But do these ideas sit comfortably with fifth-century understandings?[25] There can be little doubt that in the schema of the story the people of Sodom were not included in the divine covenant. On what basis, then, was it appropriate for their behavior to be measured against Yhwh's laws and standards? And what jurisdiction did Yhwh have to enter and execute judgment against the city? The prevailing theology of the time, with its concern for the distinctiveness of the covenant relationship, does not offer any simple answers to these questions, which suggest rather Priestly concepts such as those underlying the Noahic covenant (Gen 9:8–17) and "There shall be one law for the native and for the alien who resides among you." (Exod 12:49; Lev 24:22; Num 9:14).

The third observation I would make is that the kind of nuanced statement of the covenant equation that I have suggested is the product of the insertion of Gen 18:19 into Gen 18–19 is unlikely to have been the goal of fifth-century editors from the Deuteronomistic school. The covenantal

---

24. For the concepts of the "elect" and "diselect," see R. Christopher Heard, *Dynamics of Diselection: Ambiguity in Genesis 12–36 and Ethnic Boundaries in Postexilic Judah* (SemeiaSt 39; Atlanta: Society of Biblical Literature, 2001). See also Kaminsky, *Yet I Loved Jacob*, 111–36.

25. For a helpful general discussion, see Mark G. Brett, *Decolonizing God: The Bible in the Tides of Empire* (Sheffield: Sheffield Phoenix, 2008), 112–31.

understanding evident in the book of Deuteronomy favors clarity over nuance. Here obedience is rewarded with blessings and disobedience with curses.[26] Such a covenant understanding requires an unambiguous model. The insertion of Gen 18:19 in this narrative does not have the effect of presenting Abraham as a model of that type.

Even on the basis of these brief observations it is apparent there must be doubt as to whether the identification of Deuteronomistic elements within Gen 18:19 necessarily implies the hand of a Deuteronomistic editor.[27] This exploration of a late-added text in its narrative context indicates, to the contrary, that a non-Deuteronomistic editor, likely from a Priestly school, deliberately adopting Deuteronomistic language and themes with the intention of displacing and subverting them, is the better hypothesis.

Bibliography

Albertz, Rainer. *History of Israelite Religion in the Old Testament Period*. 2 vols. London: SCM, 1994, vol. 1.
Bechtel, Lyn M. "A Feminist Reading of Genesis 19.1–11." Pages 108–28 in *Genesis*. Edited by Athalya Brenner. FCB 2/1. Sheffield: Sheffield Academic Press, 1998.
Bolin, Thomas M. "The Role of Exchange in Ancient Mediterranean Religion and Its Implications for Reading Genesis 18–19." *JSOT* 29 (2004): 37–56.
Bovati, Pietro. *Re-establishing Justice: Legal Terms, Concepts and Procedures in the Hebrew Bible*. Translated by Michael J. Smith; Sheffield: Sheffield Academic Press, 1994.
Brett, Mark G. *Decolonizing God: The Bible in the Tides of Empire*. Sheffield: Sheffield Phoenix, 2008.
———. *Genesis: Procreation and the Politics of Identity*. London: Routledge, 2000.
Carr, David M. *Reading the Fractures of Genesis: Historical and Literary Approaches*. Louisville: Westminster John Knox, 1996.
Fields, Weston W. *Sodom and Gomorrah: History and Motive in Biblical Narrative*. Sheffield: Sheffield Academic Press, 1997.

---

26. Kaminsky, *Yet I Loved Jacob*, 102: "In some senses the blessings and curses found in Deut. 28 reflect the two potential outcomes of Israel's election, blessing for obedience and curse for disobedience, with no real middle ground." Compare Lev 26, and especially vv. 40–45, with their reassurance that Yhwh will not utterly destroy Yhwh's people, or beak the covenant with them.

27. Carr himself does not make this leap. In a discussion of the other two late additions, Gen 22:15–18 and 26:3bβ–5, he posits "an author/reviser who creatively revised and extended the non-P Genesis tradition, while working in a context where Deuteronomistic themes and language are 'in the air'" (*Reading the Fractures*, 159).

Gunkel, Hermann. *Genesis*. Translated by Mark E. Biddle. Macon, Ga.: Mercer University Press, 1997.
Heard, R. Christopher. *Dynamics of Diselection: Ambiguity in Genesis 12–36 and Ethnic Boundaries in Post-exilic Judah*. SemeiaSt 39. Atlanta: Society of Biblical Literature, 2001.
Hepner, Gershon. *Legal Friction: Law, Narrative and Identity Politics in Biblical Israel*. New York: Lang, 2010.
———. "Jacob's Oath Causes Rachel's Death: Reflecting the Law in Lev. 5:4–6." *ZABR* 8 (2002): 131–65.
Kaminsky, Joel S. *Yet I Loved Jacob: Reclaiming the Biblical Concept of Election*. Nashville: Abingdon, 2007.
Knohl, Israel. *The Sanctuary of Silence: The Priestly Torah and the Holiness School*. Minneapolis: Fortress, 1995.
Milgrom, Jacob. *Leviticus*. Minneapolis: Fortress, 2004.
———. *Leviticus 1–16: A New Translation with Introduction and Commentary*. AB 3. New York: Doubleday, 1991.
Römer, Thomas. "The Exodus Narrative according to the Priestly Document." Pages 157–74 in *The Strata of the Priestly Writings: Contemporary Debate and Future Directions*. Edited by Sarah Shectman and Joel S. Baden. Zürick: Theologischer Verlag, 2009.
Smith, Richard G. *The Fate of Justice and Righteousness during David's Reign: Re-reading the Court History and Its Ethics according to 2 Samuel 8:15–20:26*. New York: T&T Clark, 2009.
Warner, Megan. "Genesis 20–22:19: Abraham's Test of Allegiance." 53 *ABR* (2005): 13–30.
Westermann, Claus. *Genesis 12–36*. Translated by John J. Scullion. Minneapolis: Augsburg, 1985.

Section 3
The Ethics of Hospitality

Was Lot a Good Host? Was Lot Saved from Sodom as a Reward for His Hospitality?*

Yitzhak (Itzik) Peleg

1. Introduction

Was Lot a good host? Was it his exemplary hospitality that secured his escape from Sodom? In order to evaluate Lot as a host, we must apply a close reading to the account of his hospitality in Gen 19:1–29.[1] Yet this reading, while a necessary condition, is not in itself enough. The narrator apparently wishes to remind us of at least two other stories of hospitality.[2]

---

* This essay is based on a paper that I presented at the SBL International Meeting in Edinburgh, July 2006. I would like to thank Dr. Nancy Rosenfeld for her help in preparing this version.

1. A new episode, occurring in a different location, begins in v. 30: "Lot went up from Zoar, and settled in the hill country with his two daughters; for he was afraid to dwell in Zoar: and he and his two daughters lived in a cave"; a second sign of the new division is the use of the verb ישב, which also opens both the story of the hospitality in v. 1, "as Lot was sitting in the gate of Sodom," and the new story, which takes place in a mountain cave, in v. 30. The story of Lot's hospitality and its reward (19:1–29) is one of four interconnected stories in chs. 18–19. Unless otherwise stated, all citations of the Hebrew Bible are taken from *The New JPS Translation* (Philadelphia: Jewish Publication Society, 1985). Biblical citations are from Genesis, unless otherwise noted.

2. A comparison of Lot's story with that of the concubine in Gibeah (Judg 19) is not part of the framework of this article. This article focuses on the host and his reward, while in the story of the concubine there is no mention of any reward received by the hosts. The two stories can usefully be compared as examples of the "measure for measure" principle, while focusing on punishment. For a discussion of the sin of the men of Sodom and their punishment, see Claus Westermann, *Genesis 12–36: A Commentary* (trans. John J. Scullion; Minneapolis: Augsburg, 1995), 297.

Yairah Amit, *The Book of Judges* [Hebrew] (Miqra le-Yisrael; Jerusalem: Magnes, 1999), 287–94, notes: "In order to emphasize the negative hospitality in *Gibeah*, the

The first, adjoining Lot's story,[3] tells of Abraham and the three guests (ch. 18); the second tells of Rahab and the two spies (Josh 2). What can we learn from this double comparison? Why is it important to compare Lot as a host simultaneously both with Abraham and with Rahab?[4] In this essay I demonstrate how this double analogy enables us to answer the two opening questions: Was Lot a good host in the eyes of the narrator? Was Lot saved from the destruction of Sodom as a reward for his hospitality?[5]

2. Lot's Hospitality: A Close Reading of Genesis 19:1–5[6]

From the story's outset we sense that Lot is an exemplary host. Sitting at

---

composer uses the 4-5 pattern as well as systematic hints at other descriptions of hospitality in the Torah, of which the most outstanding is the story of Sodom and Gomorrah. ... This comparison points to the text's intention to show the similarities between the men of *Gibeah* and the men of Sodom and Gomorrah; while the father of the concubine in Bethlehem and the old man from Mt. Ephraim are heroes of the patriarchal period. Because of the similar plot framework, most of the similar threads are pulled from the story of *Gibeah* in the direction of the story of Lot and the angels. ... The reader of the story of the rape in *Gibeah*, who is already familiar with the story of Sodom and Gomorrah, connects the two: *Gibeah* sounds like Sodom. ...The story of the concubine from Gibeah is dependent on the story of Sodom. To the extent that the events in *Gibeah* recall the events in Sodom, the city's sin—and the sin of those trying to cover it up—becomes greater and greater."

3. In addition to the adjacency of the stories of Abraham (Gen 18) and Lot (Gen 19) and their common theme of hospitality, the family relationship of the two provides a reason for comparison. For a discussion of the latter see Moshe Garsiel, *I Samuel: Literary Study of Systems of Comparison, Analogies and Parallels* [Hebrew] (Ramat Gan: Revivim, 1983), 17–18. Garsiel argues that the comparison between characters (whether real or imaginary) is strengthened when they are connected by a basic relationship (e.g., siblings, parent and child, leader and one who is to inherit the latter's leadership).

4. Yair Zakovitch, *Readings in the Land of Mirrors* [Hebrew] (Tel Aviv: HaKibbutz Hameuhad, 1992), 82, suggests: "The story of Rahab is a reflection of a previous story: Gen 19. A comparison of the two dwarfs both Joshua's spies and the woman who 'settles accounts' by enabling them to escape. ... Rahab is not a host, but rather a prostitute who makes an income by welcoming visitors—such as the spies—who choose to come to her house." Yet even if we accept the distinction between host and prostitute, we cannot help but compare Rahab and Lot as hosts.

5. On the basis of the text it can be claimed that Lot was saved by God's mercy (v. 16: "in the LORD's mercy on him") and/or because of his family relationship with Abraham (v. 29).

6. Talia Rudin-O'Brasky, *From the Patriarchs in Hebron and Sodom (Genesis*

the city gate, Lot sees the approaching visitors; he does not wait for them to come to him, but rather rises, goes to them, and bows low: "He rose to greet them, and bowing low with his face toward the ground" (19:1). Lot then invites the visitors to be his guests, specifically to enter his house, bathe, and spend the night (v. 2). But the visitors at first refuse: "No, we will spend the night in the square" (v. 2). Lot, however, does not accept this refusal and begs the guests to accept his hospitality. The narrator, apparently eager to show the hero at his best as a host, emphasizes that he pleaded with the visitors to stay, even though he did not know their identity: "But he urged them strongly" ויפצר־בם מאד (v. 3). This reading reflects what may be the Bible's ultimate form of universalism—hospitality, the willingness to be generous to others (the other), and to welcome them into one's own space. At last the guests accept the invitation.

A careful reading reveals that Lot, the host, does even more for his guests than he had at first promised. In his original invitation he said nothing of a tasty meal, which might have tempted hungry visitors to stay. Yet once they come in he prepares them a feast (v. 3). Thus far, the initiative has been Lot's.

The hero's hospitality is impressive and the scene is serene. Yet suddenly the calm is broken and the plot changes direction: "They had not yet lain down, when the townspeople, the men of Sodom, young and old ... gathered (surrounded) about the house" (v. 4). Why is Lot's house surrounded by the men of Sodom? What do they want from him? The motive is undoubtedly connected with the visitors. The story continues: "And they called unto Lot, and said unto him, 'Where [are] the men which

---

18–19) [Hebrew] (Jerusalem: Hotsa'at Simor, 1982), 105, points out an ancient parallel to the story of Sodom: the myth of the elderly couple Philemon and Baucis. In Ovid's version (*Metam.* 8.611–724), the gods Jupiter and Mercury, disguised as humans, visit a village in Phrygia. The only ones willing to host them are the old couple, who go out of their way to welcome them. The narrator details the efforts taken by the old people to entertain their visitors, whose divine identities were of course not known to them. Eventually the gods reveal themselves to the elderly couple, after deciding to destroy the whole village. Philemon and Baucis are taken to a nearby mountainside, from which they see that the whole village has been destroyed, all its inhabitants killed, and the land turned into a swamp. Only their house remains. The house is turned into a temple and the old couple are appointed its keepers. According to Rudin-O'Brasky, "Ovid's story provides authentification for the mythological roots of the story of Sodom."

came in to thee this night? Bring them out unto us, *that we may know them* [ונדעה אתם]'" (v. 5).[7]

What do they want "to know"? What is the meaning of the expression "that we may know them" (v. 5)? In the Bible the verb "to know" (ידע)[8] bears both cognitive and sexual[9] meanings. Thus we must ask whether the men of Sodom wanted to know the visitors carnally, or intellectually,[10] that is, to know who they are, to determine their identity.

---

7. As in KJV. The NKJV adds: "that we may know them [carnally]." The NJPS has: "And they shouted to Lot and said to him: 'Where are the men who came to you tonight? Bring them out to us, that we may be intimate with him.'"

8. Knowledge has many meanings, but here I focus on two. One is intellectual: the ability to distinguish between good and evil, or as the serpent says to the woman, "But God knows that as soon as you eat of it your eyes will be opened, and you will be like divine beings (others: God) who *know* good and evil" (Gen 3:5). The latter receives a divine seal of approval at the end of the chapter. "And the LORD God said, 'Now that the man has become like one of Us, knowing good and evil'" (3:22). The other aspect of knowledge is sexual, as it appears at the beginning of the next chapter: "Now the man *knew* his wife and she conceived and bore Cain" (4:1), in which we learn that Adam did something to Eve which caused her to become pregnant. This action is described by "to know." See Itzik Peleg, "A Time to Know the Biblical Text" [Hebrew], *Al Haperek 19, Bible Teaching Journal* (2002): 176–89.

9. For discussions of the verb "to know," see Meir Malul, *Knowledge, Control and Sex* (Tel Aviv: Archaeological Center Publication, 2002), 233. Concerning the conceptual juxtaposition of eating and sex, see 294. Malul notes other locations of ידע in its sexual sense: Gen 4:17, 25; 19:5, 8; 24:16; 38:26; Num 31:17; 18:35; Judg 11:39; 19:22, 25; 21:11–12; 1 Sam 1:19; 1 Kgs 1:4; see also Malul's "A Holistic-Integrative Approach to the Study of Biblical Culture," *Shnaton* 14 (2004) [Hebrew]: 143: "At the center of my research is the clear overlap of three semantic fields which superficially seem to have nothing in common: cognitive knowledge, control, sex. The central question is how to explain this overlapping, at least linguistically, of cognitive knowledge and sexual knowledge."

10. See Radak, in Menachem Cohen, ed., *The Crown: Mikra'ot Gedolot according to the Crown of Aram Tsoba* [Hebrew] (Ramat Gan: Bar Ilan University, 1991), 171: "As to the words 'and we shall know them,' Who are they, and how is it that strangers did not fear coming to our city, i.e., they wanted to kill the guests as in Judg 19:2." Radak adds that others argue: "Homosexual intercourse." I had the privilege of discussing this very point at the SBL 2004 conference in Groningen with the late Dr. Ron Pirson, who offered a number of observations on the subject that are central to my argument. The idea of having a seminar focusing on Gen 18–19 was raised there by Ron for the first time.

In his interpretation of the expression "that we may know them" (v. 5), the medieval Jewish commentator Rashi[11] argues that "Homosexual intercourse may be described as 'knowing a man'" (v. 8). Rashi herein opts for the erotic sense of the word "know" as used by Lot (in v. 8). The refusal of the men of Sodom to accept Lot's "generous" offer of his daughters' sexual services supports the assumption that they wanted to know the (male) visitors sexually.[12] Rashi's interpretation is further supported when the men of Sodom ask: "Where are the men who have come to you this night?."[13] In a way similar to the verb "to know" (ידע), the use of the verb "to come" (בוא) in the Bible can bear a sexual connotation. In verse 31, for example, in the story of Lot and his daughters in the cave, it is written: "And the firstborn said unto the younger: 'Our father is old, and there is not a man in the earth to come in untous after the manner of all the earth'" (KJV); later on, the older daughter comes to her father and lies with him. In another case (Gen 39:17), when Potiphar's wife protests to her household that Joseph "came in unto me" (בא־אלי, KJV), she means that her husband's servant wanted "to lie with her." In other words, to "come to" can mean the same as "lie with."

While it is highly likely that the men of Sodom wished to have homosexual intercourse with the visitors, it is possible that they were angry at Lot for suspecting them of sexual intentions which they did not, in fact, have. Yet whether they simply wished to know the strangers' identity ("Are they with us or against us?" Josh 5:13), or did indeed lust after the visitors, the gross, violent behavior of all the men of Sodom, from young to old, illuminates and emphasizes Lot's nobility as a host. The men of Sodom wished to harm the visitors, while Lot wished to protect them.

---

11. See Rashi in Cohen, *Mikra'ot Gedolot,* 170.

12. Though it may also suggest that they were not interested in sex at all. Indeed, this is more plausible, since it is more likely that the men were accustomed to sex with men and women than that they were exclusively homosexual.

13. Why is the expression "came to you" used, rather than "came to your house"? There is, moreover, a sense of over-definition in the report of the visitors' agreement. It would have been enough to say "and they turned aside to his house." Why was it found necessary to note that "they turned aside to his house and came to his house"? It is not clear: Did they come to his house, as would an ordinary guest? Or did they intend to come to him, i.e., to have sex with him? This ambiguity allows the reader to pursue the story from two viewpoints: from that of the men of the city, the visitors intended to have a sexual relationship with Lot; while from the viewpoint of the narrator, the visitors merely intended to stay at Lot's house, and had no sexual intentions.

3. Lot as a Host: A Close Reading of Genesis 19:5–9; Lot as Opposed to the Men of Sodom:[14] A Story Based on the Principle of Reward

Let us turn now to further evidence for the cumulative impression of the hero as an exemplary host. When the men of Sodom ask Lot to bring his guests out to them, Lot endangers himself[15] by going outside and shutting the door after him. The door symbolizes the wall separating not only the men of the city from Lot's guests but the moral distance between the men of Sodom and Lot himself. Lot appeals to the men in a discourse of politeness and tolerance (v. 7). The men of the city, however, "drew near to break the door" (v. 9).

Another literary tool that distinguishes Lot from the men of the city is the repeated use of the verb "urged" (ויפצר). This verb, which appears twice in the story of Lot's hospitality, hints at an oppositional relationship between the two descriptions. When the strangers at first refuse Lot's generous invitation, we learn: "And he urged them greatly" (v. 3). The same verb is used to describe the response of the men of Sodom to Lot's refusal to allow the mob to enter his house: "And they pressed sore [urged; ויפצרו] upon the man, even Lot" (v. 9). The implicit aggression in the latter becomes explicit when the men of Sodom attempt to break down the door.[16]

Why was it so important for the narrator to lead the reader to draw a comparison between Lot and the men of the city? The contrasting behavior of Lot and of the men of Sodom is meant, on the one hand, to justify the punishment of the people of Sodom by showing the contrast between

---

14. See Nahum Sarna, *Understanding Genesis* (New York: Jewish Theological Seminary of America, 1966), 150. Sarna discusses the comparison of Lot with the men of Sodom on the basis of the role of hospitality in the ancient Near East as "a sacred duty." The host was obligated to defend his guests, even if called upon to risk his own life in order to do so. This is, of course, what Lot did.

15. See Westermann, *Genesis 12–36*, 301; Rudin-O'Brasky, *From the Patriarchs*, 106, notes that the second part of the story of Lot's hospitality (vv. 4–11) "tells of the danger which the host takes upon himself in his attempt to save himself from the men of Sodom." The extent of the danger is shown by the fact that only the intervention of the guests, who pull their host inside, saves Lot. Thus the guests save Lot twice: once from the men of the city and then from the destruction of the city.

16. See BDB 823, for ויפצר ("push, press"). Regarding v. 9: "physically," see also 2 Sam 13:27: ויפרץ־בו.

their behavior[17] and that of Lot, and on the other hand, to explain Lot's reward as the result of the nobility of his behavior as a host. Lot, the main character in the story of his hospitality, appears to be an exemplary host whose behavior is rewarded when his guests save his life (19:10–22). The story of Lot's hospitality is thus built on the principle of "measure for measure": Lot is saved from the destruction visited on Sodom as a reward for protecting his guests, while the men of Sodom are punished for their evil.

Let us admit that the story does not contain an explicit statement of a cause-and-effect connection between Lot's hospitality and his salvation from the destruction of Sodom.[18] The explicit connection is between the actions of the men of Sodom and their punishment (e.g., v. 13). Moreover, the connection between the "measure for measure" principle and Lot's salvation is weakened by the words of the visitors: "in the LORD's *mercy* on him" (19:16). Was Lot saved as a reward for his hospitality? Or perhaps the Deity simply had mercy on him? In his explication of this verse the medieval Spanish Jewish commentator Nahmanides argues: "He was not saved in his own right, but because God pitied him, because of God's mercy.[19] He was brought out quickly, in order not to allow time for God to become angry" (see Num 17:11).[20] Yet despite Nahmanides's convincing argument, a comparison with the story of Rahab and the spies (Josh 2) will strengthen my claim that the story of Lot's hospitality is based on the "measure for measure" principle, and that his salvation represents the working out of this principle.

---

17. Lot's righteousness and his reward, vis-à-vis the evil of the men of Sodom and their punishment, is a reflection of Noah's righteousness and reward vis-à-vis the evil of his fellowmen. "Noah was a righteous man, he was blameless in his age" (Gen 6:9). Lot is not actually called "righteous," but his righteousness is certainly hinted at.

18. In a comparison of Lot and Abraham as hosts, Frank Polak, *Biblical Narrative: Aspects of Art and Design* [Hebrew] (Jerusalem: Mosad Biyalik, 1994), 196, discusses the stories' common structure of reward and punishment, and the suggestion that Lot was saved as a reward for his hospitality: "Both Abraham and Lot receive their guests nobly (18:3–8; 19:1–3) and are rewarded. Abram and Sarai are promised by God, against all probability, that they will have a child (18:9–14), and Lot and his household are saved by the angels from the destruction of Sodom (19:12–25)."

19. See Isa 63:7–10.

20. See Nahmanides and Radak in Cohen, *Mikra'ot Gedolot*, 175; the phrase "by God's mercy upon him" is explicated: "For Abraham's sake they hastened to bring him out and save him"; and this although "him" refers to Lot, while Abraham is not mentioned in the story.

4. A Comparison of Lot and Rahab as Hosts, Based upon the "Measure for Measure" Principle

Zakovitch has charted the similarities between the two stories:[21]

	Genesis 19	Joshua 2 (+ 6:17, 22–23)[22]
The two visitors are called "people"/"men" and "angels"	"Where are *the men* [האנשים] who came to you tonight"? (v. 5); "The two *angels* [שני המלאכים] arrived in Sodom in the evening" (v. 1).	"*Some men* [אנשים] have come here" (v.2); "For she had hidden the messengers [את־המלאכים], that Joshua sent to spy out Jericho" (6:25).[23]
The visitors are on a mission; use of verb "to send," שלח	Visitors to Lot: "The LORD *has sent us* [וישלחנו] to destroy it" (v. 13).	"Joshua son of Nun secretly *sent* [וישלח] two spies" (v. 1).

---

21. See Zakovitch, *Readings*, 83. I should like to thank Dr. Itamar Kislev for calling my attention to the common fate of Sodom and Jericho, as well as their geographical proximity. The latter supports the validity of a comparison of the two hospitality stories.

22. According to Zakovitch, *Readings*, 83, "The story of Rahab also sends tendrils in the direction of Joshua 6. ... It is clear, moreover, that whoever added the verses on Rahab to Joshua 6 (verses 17b, 22–23, 25) was aware of the connections to Genesis 19, and assimilated this addition in the spirit of Genesis 19."

23. It is worth noting that the messengers in the story of Rahab, unlike those in Lot's story, are men of flesh and blood. Their similarity to Lot's guests lies in their role as guests.

Time of the visitors' arrival in the city	"The two angels arrived in Sodom *in the evening* [בערב]" (v. 1).	The king of Jericho is told: "Some men have come here *tonight* [הלילה]" (v. 2).
Did the visitors come to the host's house or to him?	"*entered his house* [ויבאו אל־ביתו]" (v. 3); "Where are the men *who came to you* [אשר־באו אליך] tonight?" (v. 5).	"and they *came to the house* of a harlot [ויבאו בית־אשה זונה] named Rahab" (v. 1); "Produce the men *who came to you* [הבאים אליך]" (v. 3).[24]
The men of the city demand that the guests be brought out of the host's house	"bring them out [הוציאם] to us" (v. 5).	"Bring forth [הוציאי] the men that are come to you" (v. 3).
Closing of the door/gate	"shut *the door* behind him" (v. 6); "and shut the door" (v.10).	"when *the gate* was about to be closed" (v. 5); "then *the gate* was shut behind them" (v. 7).
The host endangers himself in order to protect his guests	"Look I have two daughters who have not known man. Let	The liar: "The woman however had taken the two men …" (vv. 4–5).

24. Note the double meanings of "come to my house" and "come to me." The verb "come" (בוא) acts as a keyword in the story (Josh 2:1, 2, 3 [3x], 4), in much the same way as do the verbs "to lie with" (שכב) and "to know" (ידע)—all of which intertwine and enrich the story. As do occurrences of other words in the Bible, these three verbs both describe ordinary daily activities and bear sexual connotations. The reader cannot be sure which of the two meanings is intended by the narrator. The narrator often seems to enjoy basing his story on the tension between the two meanings.

	me bring them out to you … but do not do anything to these men, since they have come under the shelter of my roof" (v. 8).	
Those who are saved escape/flee to a mountainside/the hills	"flee *to the hills* [ההרה] lest you be swept away" (v.17); "I cannot flee *to the hills* [ההרה]" (v. 19).	Rahab to the king's men: "Make *for the hills* [ההרה] so that the pursuers may not come upon you" (v. 16).

We note a clear literary link between the story of Lot and the story of Rahab in the phrase "before they lay down," טרם ישכבו which only appears twice in the Bible: Gen 19:4 טרם ישכבו (Lot) and Josh 2:8 והמה טרם ישכבון (Rahab). The rarity of this phrase points to the narrator's (or redactor's) intention of encouraging the reader to compare the two.

In the light of the similarities, it is worth noting the differences. From the hosts' point of view: while Rahab does not invite the visitors to her house—they come of their own initiative—Lot urges his visitors to accept his hospitality. Rahab knows the identity of her guests; Lot has no idea of the identity of his guests. Rahab makes a clear request of her guests: "Now since I have shown loyalty [חסד] to you swear to me by the Lord that you in turn will show loyalty [חסד] to my family" (v. 12), while Lot asks nothing for himself. This is the main difference: Rahab plays host to her visitors, or rather assists them in escaping, in return for helping her and her family to escape with their lives ("Only Rahab the harlot is to be spared and all who are with her in the house because she hid the messengers we sent"; Josh 6:17). Lot, on the other hand, who did not know his guests' identity, asks nothing from them in return for his generous, unselfish hospitality.

Keeping Rahab's behavior in mind, Lot's actions are highly admirable. Let us, too, recall that Rahab's story is an example of the "measure for measure" principle,[25] or more exactly, of "grace for grace [חסד]," as is made

---

25. See Yitzhak (Itzik) Peleg, "The Measure-for-Measure Principle via Word-for-Word" [Hebrew], *Beit Mikra* 44 Quarterly (1999): 357–60.

explicit in verse 12. The analogy to Rahab's story emphasizes Lot's nobility, indeed his greatness, as a host, as one who does good for its own sake, rather than for a possible reward.[26] The differences between the stories unite to form our central message:[27] Lot was a better host than Rahab.[28]

In the story of Lot we discern two stages: in the first we witness Lot's exemplary hospitality, in which the host both initiates the visit and protects his guests (vv. 1–10). In the second stage, the guests take the initiative into their own hands,[29] protect Lot and his family, and save them from the destruction of Sodom. The measure-for-measure principle is indicated when we note that each of the stages contains the same number of verses: in the first stage, the story of Lot's hospitality (vv. 1–11), and in the second stage, in which the guests save Lot and his family and then destroy the city (vv. 11–22). Eventually Lot is taken out of the city and finds refuge in Zoar, in which "the sun was risen upon the earth" (v. 23). The story began with sunrise (v. 1), and now the sun rises once again: a new day begins. Lot is saved, while the men of the city are punished when God rains sulphur and brimstone on Sodom (v. 24).

Yet in verse 24 there is a reversal, not only of the identity of the heroes, but vis-à-vis the story's message. It is not the guests (v. 13), but rather God who destroys the city,[30] and in place of Lot, whose story begins "in the

---

26. See Zakovitch, *Readings*, 85: "Lot is an excellent host; even though he is unaware of his guests' identity, he endangers his life in order to protect them."

27. According to Zakovitch, "Sometimes the biblical narrator fashions the character and his actions as the antithesis of another character. ... the reflection reverses the traits of the original story; and now the reader who notes the intentional connection between the two—original and reflection, the more recent figure and its antecedent—will evaluate the hero in the light of the parallel character" ("The Reflected Story: An Additional Dimension for Evaluating Biblical Characters" [Hebrew], *Tarbiz* 54 [1985]: 165).

28. Zakovitch, *Readings*, 82: "The comparison between these stories dwarfs Joshua's spies and the 'account-keeping' woman who helps them escape." Those of us attempting to evaluate Lot as a host find this comparison complimentary towards Lot.

29. See Rudin-O'Brasky, *From the Patriarchs*, 111: "In this story the miraculous action is reversed. The initiative is taken away from Lot, the exemplary host, and the visitors carry out their mission."

30. Regarding the question of who destroyed the city, God or the people, see Rudin-O'Brasky, *From the Patriarchs*, 119: "According to J's editorial intention, in which miraculous acts are executed by God (see 18:10–13), God—not the people—destroys Sodom and its surroundings (19:13); it seems that there is a polemic between Gen 19:24, 'The LORD rained upon Sodom and Gomorrah sulfurous fire from the LORD out of heaven,' and Gen 19:13, 'For *we* are about to destroy this place.'"

evening" (v. 1), we have his uncle Abraham "in the morning" (19:27–28).[31] The epitome of this change, in regard to the question of why Lot was saved, is reached in v. 29; the latter deserves special attention.

5. "And God Remembered Abraham" (v. 29): A Reversal in Understanding the Story

Toward the end of the story, as Sodom is overturned, our understanding of the story and its meaning is reversed. It suddenly seems that Lot was saved, not as a reward for his hospitality, but rather because of his family relationship with Abraham (v. 29). This option is perhaps the ultimate form of particularism: a person's destiny is shaped by the family to which he belongs. How can we explain the tension between verse 29 and the story of Lot's hospitality until this point? Does this tension stem from the need to relate to chapter 18? Is the story in its current form drawn from a variety of sources?[32] I shall offer a different solution, a synchronic one.

Let us clarify the tension/difference. In verse 29 we suddenly discover another possible justification for Lot's salvation: "Thus it was that when God destroyed the cities of the Plain and annihilated the cities where Lot

---

31. See Westermann, *Genesis 12–36*, 307–8: "The man, Abraham, is the subject; and so the narrative of the destruction of Sodom, 19:1–26, which does not mention him, is linked with the figure of Abraham. That is to say, this conclusion was not an original part of the narrative. This suggests that it should be ascribed to the author who attached Gen. 13:18–19 to a narrative cycle, i.e, to the Yahwist. However, the relative sentence (v. 27b), 'where he had stood in the presence of Yahweh,' seems to be against this, apparently referring back to 18:17–33, or following immediately on it or in any case presupposing it. … But this is very unlike it because 19:27–28 bears a completely different stamp from 18:17–33. It can just as well refer back to 18:16b before v. 17–33 were added."

32. Supporters of the source hypothesis (e.g., Skinner, von Rad, Speiser) who attribute chs. 18–19 to J, and attribute v. 29 to P; the different sources thus explain the tension between v. 29 and the story up until that point. Verse 27: "Next morning Abraham hurried to the place where he had stood before the LORD" takes us back to 18:16 (See, for example, 18:22: "The men went on from there to Sodom while Abraham remained standing before the LORD." See John Skinner, *A Critical and Exegetical Commentary on Genesis* (ICC; Edinburgh: T&T Clark, 1930), 298, 306, 310; Gerhard von Rad, *Genesis, A Commentary* (trans. J. H. Marks; London: SCM, 1961), 217; in his discussion of v. 29, Ephraim A. Speiser (*Genesis* [AB 1; Garden City, N.Y.: Doubleday, 1964]) notes: "P's one-sentence summary of the episode (29)—unmistakable in its wording, style, and approach—is an example of scholastic succinctness at its best" (143).

dwelt, *God was mindful of Abraham* and removed Lot from the midst of the upheaval" (19:29).[33] In other words, Lot is saved, not as a reward for his good deeds as a host, but rather as a reward for his uncle Abraham's good deeds. Verse 29 contains two intertwined statements: first, that while God was destroying the cities of the plains he remembered Abraham, and, second, that he "sent Lot out of the midst of the overthrow." We must therefore ask: How are these two statements connected? Do we have a statement of the chronological order of the occurrences? Or is this a cause-and-effect connection,[34] that is, *because* God remembered Abraham, he saved Lot? After all, within the story's context we would logically expect to learn that "God remembered Lot," and therefore rewarded him.

Moreover, when it is written that "God remembered Abraham," *what* he remembered is not clear.[35] Does the narrator (or editor) mean that at the last moment God recalled Lot's and Abraham's family connection and therefore saved Lot? If so, the idea that Lot was saved as a reward loses credibility. According to Sarna's interpretation,[36] Lot was saved for Abraham's sake and not for his own. Von Rad relates verse 29 to the priestly

---

33. According to Westermann (*Genesis 12–36*, 308), v. 29 deals with the overthrow of the cities of the plains and Lot's rescue in the light of the P source. He argues that the phrase "and God remembered Abraham" is an exact parallel to "and God remembered Noah" in Gen 8:1: "The author is no longer interested in the destination of a city in the distant past, nor even in the fate of Lot as such. The only thing that is important for him is the relationship between God and Abraham which was the object of ch. 17. For Abraham's sake God rescued his relative from that ancient catastrophe."

34. See, for example, Shimeon Bar-Efrat's definitions in *The Art of Narration in the Bible* [Hebrew] (4th ed.; Tel Aviv: Sifriyat Po'alim, 1993), 146–47.

35. The fact that what the Deity remembered is not specified has enabled much fruitful filling-in of gaps. Thus Rashi in Cohen, *Mikra'ot Gedolot*, 176, following Genesis Rabbah, suggests that God remembers Lot's behavior—which is not detailed in the Bible—when Abraham went down to Egypt: "Why is Abraham remembered? Did God recall that Lot—who knew that Sarah was Abraham's wife—heard Abraham tell the Egyptians that Sarah was his sister and kept silent? Perhaps because Lot pitied Abraham, God pitied Lot." Rashi fills in the gaps in the story via midrash, since the text does not provide specific information. Nahmanides (in Cohen, *Mikra'ot Gedolot*, 179) refers to Lot's accompanying Abraham to the land, and notes that had it not been for Abraham, Lot would have remained in Haran and not reached Sodom at all ("Had it not been for Abraham, he would have remained in his homeland, and would have avoided the evil which came upon him for Abraham's sake; the latter had followed God's commandment; for this reason Abraham pursued the angels").

36. See Sarna, *Understanding Genesis*, 150.

source (P).³⁷ He poses the following question, but does not provide an answer: According to P, does Abraham debate with God in chapter 18 for Lot's sake? Perhaps the Deity recalls his debate with Abraham in chapter 18,³⁸ in which Abraham accuses him: "Will you also destroy the righteous with the wicked?" (v. 23). In other words, God accepts Abraham's argument and destroys the wicked of Sodom and Gomorrah, while allowing Lot, who was not evil, to escape. If this interpretation is accepted, there has been no reversal here. Although God recalls Abraham's righteousness, Lot's righteousness, too, is noted, and he is saved for his own sake. In any case, while the narrator does not specify what God remembered, we are told that he remembered Abraham; we are not told that he remembered Lot, and this is despite the likelihood, in the context of the story, that God would have remembered Lot.

Verse 29 opens a window through which we view God's direct role (rather than that of his angels) in the destruction of Sodom and the rescue of Lot. Is verse 29 therefore meant to push aside the assumption that Lot was saved because he was an exemplary host? At this point in our reading are we intended to understand that our positive impression of Lot was mistaken? If so, should we reread the story of Lot's hospitality and search out faults in his behavior as a host?³⁹

---

37. See von Rad, *Genesis*, 217: "Verse 29 belongs to the P source, which contains an abstract of the whole event in one sentence, in a typical Priestly formulation. He does not intend to tell a story, the details of which are presumably familiar, but rather to describe the Deity's part. Thus God is the subject of both parts of the sentence: That God 'remembered' Lot for Abraham's sake is a conception which is not emphasized in the Yahwistic narrative. Did P think of Abraham's conversation with God as intercession for Lot?"

38. It is worth noting the use of the verb "to destroy" (שחת) (18:28, 31, 32; 19:13, 14) and the repeated use of the verb "to sweep (away)" (תספה) (18:23, 24; 19:15, 17).

39. It is reasonable to claim that Lot's offer of his virgin daughters' sexual services to the men of the city in order to protect his guests was an act of abandonment. Sarna, *Understanding Genesis*, 150, notes that for the modern reader, Lot's willingness to abandon his daughters to the men of Sodom is incomprehensible, even though we know that in those days daughters were seen as their fathers' property: "At any rate, it is to be noted that the salvation of Lot, unlike that of Noah, is not attributed to his righteousness. The Bible underlines this fact by reporting that it was due to 'the Lord's mercy on him' (19:16) and that 'when God destroyed the cities of the Plain … God was mindful of Abraham.'" We shall return to this point later. At any rate, we are still left with the sense that Lot was an exemplary host, although a failure as a father to his daughters. The story of Lot and his daughters at the end of the chapter (vv. 30–38) is

I should like to suggest that verse 29 functions as a "reversal ending,"[40] or perhaps as a "reversal verse." The reversal ending is a familiar literary device, recently explicated by Yairah Amit,[41] whose purpose is to cause the reader to entertain the possibility of a different understanding of the story. The reversal ending results from tension between the story's ending and what is told prior to the ending; this tension creates in the reader the need to reread the story in the light of the "reversal."

It is my suggestion that the "reversal verse" (19:29), which returns Abraham to centerstage, reminds us that Abraham—rather than Lot—is the central figure of the stories of the patriarchs in Genesis. Therefore the story of Lot's hospitality must be seen in a wider context, in the framework of the stories of the patriarchs. This wider context, as well as Lot's family position as Abraham's nephew, returns Lot to his "natural" size as a secondary figure in the stories of the patriarchs.

Before setting out to trace Lot's relationship to Abraham in the wider context, let us first follow in the Deity's footsteps ("and God remembered Abraham," 19:29) by recalling the description of Abraham as a host in chapter 18.

6. Who Was the Better Host: Lot or Abraham?

The validity of a comparison between Lot's hospitality and Abraham's hospitality receives support from a number of directions. First, the stories appear in tandem. Second, the plot, which describes the journey of the visitors from Abraham's tent to Lot's house as a continuum whose aim is the destruction of the sinful Sodom, justifies a view of chapters 18–19 as a single literary unit; this, too, encourages comparison. The story of Lot's hospitality begins with the words "And there came the two angels [שני המלאכים] to Sodom" (19:1). The presence of the word "the" in "the two angels" recalls the story of Abraham's hospitality, in which we learn that "the men set out from there looked down toward Sodom, Abraham walk-

---

outside of the boundaries of this essay, although undoubtedly a case of the "measure for measure" principle. The story of the concubine from Gibeah and her bitter fate (Judg 19) shows us what would have happened to Lot's daughters, had the angels not acted.

40. In v. 30 a new episode, in a new place—a cave—clearly begins; see n. 1 above.

41. See Yairah Amit, "Endings—Especially Reversal Endings," *Scriptura* 87 (2004): 213–26.

ing with them to see them off. ... 'The men went on from there to Sodom'" (18:16, 22). Moreover, the family relationship of Lot with Abraham encourages a comparison. A literary comparison is furthermore encouraged by "wash your feet" in Gen 18:4 and 19:2; these are the only two appearances of the latter in the Bible.[42] Neither of them knew the identity of the visitors (which reflects universalism). The following chart will clarify the similarities and differences between the two stories:

Abraham as a Host: Genesis 18	Lot as a Host: Genesis 19
	v. 1: "The two angels arrived in Sodom
v. 1: "he was sitting at the entrance of the tent as the day grew hot (כחם היום).	in the evening (בערב), as Lot was sitting in the gate of Sodom.
v. 2: Looking up he saw (וירא) three men...	When Lot saw (וירא) them,
He ran (וירץ) from the entrance of the tent	He rose (ויקם) to greet them
and, bowing to the ground (וישתחו ארצה),	and, bowing low with his face to the ground (וישתחו אפים ארצה),
v. 3-4: he said, 'My lords, if it please you do not pass. ... Let a little water be brought; bathe your feet (ורחצו רגליכם) ...	v. 2: he said, 'Please, my lords, turn aside to your servant's house ... and bathe your feet (ורחצו רגליכם)...'
	But they said, 'No, we will spend the night in the square.'
	v. 3: But he urged them strongly ...

---

42. See Garsiel, *I Samuel*, 17–18.

vv. 5–8: And let me fetch a morsel of bread that you may refresh yourselves, then go on seein that you have come your servent's way. ... Abraham hastened into the tent to Sarah and said: quick three seabs of choice flour, knead and make cakes. Then Abraham ran to the herd, took a calf, tender and choice and gave it to the servant boy. ... He took curds and milk and the calf that had been prepared and set these before them and he waited on them under the tree	He prepared a feast for them and baked unleavened bread,
as they ate (ויאכלו).	And they ate (ויאכלו).
	v. 4: They had not yet lay down, when the townspeople, the men of Sodom, young and old ... gathered (surrounded) about the house.
v. 9: They said to him, 'Where (איה) is your wife Sarah?'"	v. 5: And they shouted ... 'Where (איה) are the men who came to you...'"

By focusing on the differences I shall be able to emphasize the message borne by the comparison.

Rashi, who noted that the phrase "wash your feet" (18:4; 19:2) appears in both stories, emphasizes the differences in the order of the acts:

> "spend the night and bathe your feet": do people usually stay the night and then wash their feet (18:4)? But this is what Lot said: "when the men of Sodom see that the guests have already washed their feet, they will surely say that the guests must have been here two or three days, and I

haven't yet announced their coming; it would be best, therefore, for their feet to remain dusty, so that the men of Sodom will think that they have just arrived, and haven't yet washed" (see Gen. Rab. 50:4).[43]

The different order of the acts in the two stories, therefore, stems from the different situations. The significant difference between the two hosts is revealed in their responses to the first appearance of the visitors. When Abraham sees the latter he does not hesitate, but rather runs toward them[44] ("he ran to meet them from the tent door"), lest they pass by without entering his tent. Lot, on the other hand, merely stands up ("he rose up to meet them"). In comparison with Abraham, Lot's response seems somewhat pale, lacking enthusiasm and determination. Yet without this comparison to Abraham, Lot's response would not be problematic; after all, both hosts bowed down before the visitors and invited them into their homes.

Moreover, it seems at times that Lot was trying harder than Abraham. Not only did he urge the strangers to be his guests; he "pressed upon them greatly." On the other hand it may be that the visitors' initial refusal of Lot's hospitality ("Nay; but we will abide in the street all night," KJV) led him to pressure them to stay with him. In any case, at this point Lot's hospitality is impressive, even in comparison with Abraham.

In contrast, Lot's efforts for his guests are described in a laconic five words (in Hebrew): "He prepared a feast for them and baked unleavened bread" ויעש להם משתה ומצות אפה, while a description of Abraham's hostly efforts takes three verses (18:6–8).[45] If we add the multiplicity of verbs[46] applied to Abraham, we indeed are impressed by his activity and determination in comparison with Lot's activity, which is less impressive.

---

43. See Rashi in Cohen, *Mikra'ot Gedolot*, 170.

44. Abraham "runs toward them," as does the servant who runs toward Rebecca at the well in Gen 24:16: "The servant ran toward her and said, 'Please let me sip a little water from your jar'"; Rebecca's brother Laban, too, runs toward Jacob in Gen 29:13: "On hearing the news of his sister's son Jacob, Laban ran to greet him"; and Esau runs toward Jacob in 33:4 "Esau ran to greet him."

45. Although the description of Lot's hospitality is laconic, Rudin-O'Brasky's suggestion is credible (*From the Patriarchs*, 108): "The shortness of this description is not meant to diminish Lot in comparison with his uncle, since the narrator emphasizes Lot's concern for his guests and his efforts to save them from the men of the city (vv. 4–11)."

46. For a multiplicity of verbs as signifying tension, emotion, and determination, see Bar-Efrat, *Art of Narration*, 26–27.

In other words, despite evidence of Lot's excellence as a host, the final accounting leaves us with the impression that Abraham—not Lot—is the perfect host.

At this point in our discussion we see that a comparison with Abraham (beginning with the reference to the latter in 19:29, including the description of his hospitality in 18:1–16) diminishes[47] our positive view of Lot as a host. This conclusion is strengthened by following the description of Lot's relationship with his uncle Abraham from its beginning. Throughout the stories of the patriarchs Lot appears as a figure secondary[48] to Abraham, whose literary purpose is to strengthen the latter, or simply as a dependent of his uncle. We shall now provide evidence for this claim.

7. Lot as a Secondary Figure to Abraham throughout the Stories of the Patriarchs[49]

Let us now examine the contribution made to the story of Lot's hospitality

---

47. Rudin-O'Brasky, *From the Patriarchs*, 108, adds another criterion to the comparison between the two: "the description of Lot's preparation of food and drink is limited to half a verse (3b). The enthusiasm with which Abraham's preparation of a meal is described is lacking in chapter 19." However, Rudin-O'Brasky does not see this as diminishing the image of Lot.

Later on, in the comparison between Lot and Rahab as hosts, the narrator places a high value on Lot's hospitality. Yet in a comparison with Abraham's hospitality, Abraham, as it were, wins. Lot's problem is not with his actual behavior as a host, but with being compared to his uncle.

48. See Uriel Simon, "Secondary Figures in the Biblical Story" [Hebrew], in *Reading Prophetic Narratives* (Jerusalem: Mosad Byalik; Ramat-Gan: Hotsa'at Universitat Bar-Ilan, 1997), 323, 324. There is a reversal in the hospitality story in ch. 19: Lot is the central figure, while Abraham is the secondary figure.

49. See Yair Zakovitch, *An Introduction to Inner-biblical Interpretation* [Hebrew] (Even Yehuda: Rekhes Hotsa'ah le-Or Proyektim Hinukhiyim, 1992), 47: "even though the reader is sure that he has discovered the truth of the story from beginning to end, he still must answer the following: Is the story an independent literary unit, which can and must be interpreted without reference to its literary environment, or was the story composed as part of a wider context, which both illuminates, and is illuminated by, the story?" The question raised by Zakovitch—whether the story stands on its own or is dependent on its context—is extremely important, although any answer can only be based on speculation; for this reason I prefer to approach the story synchronically rather than diachronically. Thus this discussion of Lot's hospitality views the latter in ever-widening circles, beginning with adjacent stories and moving on to the broader context of the patriarchal stories.

by viewing Lot as a secondary character and Abraham as a main figure.[50] In his discussion of the role of the secondary character in interpreting the biblical text, Simon argues that this figure serves as a means to morally evaluate the main character. Simon notes that this moral evaluation is hardly ever couched in explicit words, but is rather expressed in deeds and rewards.[51] Weinfeld, on the other hand, describes Lot as "dependent" on Abraham: "Lot appears in the Stories of the patriarchs as helpless, permanently dependent upon others; without Abraham's help he would simply disappear. Lot is dependent on his uncle, who takes care of him."[52]

I prefer to define the secondary character, Lot, as one whose purpose is to enhance Abraham, the main character. It is important to note that Lot does not appear in a negative light; he simply emphasizes Abraham as an exemplary figure. In other words, rather than focusing on Lot negatively, the story focuses on Abraham's noble qualities.

We shall now survey the events in the lives of Lot and Abraham[53] in the order in which they occur in the stories of the patriarchs, in order to exemplify the above.

(1) We first hear of Lot in 11:27, in which Lot appears as the grandson of Terah, Abraham's father. "Now this is the line of Terah, Terah begot Abram, Nahor and Haran, and Haran begot Lot" (11:27). Haran, Lot's father, had died in Ur (v. 28); but the text does not relate the circumstances of Haran's death,[54] nor the fact that Lot is an orphan. Nothing is told of any

---

50. Rudin-O'Brasky, *From the Patriarchs*, 16, notes that in the complete literary cycle of which Gen 18–19 forms a part, "Abraham appears as the main hero, following divine commands, while Lot appears as a passive companion." In n. 6, Rudin-O'Brasky suggests that "the Midrash has already noted that 'Lot went with him,' 'Lot accompanied him'" (Gen. Rab. 39:13).

51. See Simon, "Secondary Figures," 323.

52. Moshe Weinfeld, *Encyclopedia of the World of the Bible: Genesis* [Hebrew] (Ramat Gan: Revivim, 1982), 127.

53. See Rudin-O'Brasky, *From the Patriarchs*, 16–27.

54. See Yair Zakovitch, "The Exodus from Ur of the Chaldeans: A Chapter in Literary Archaeology," in *Ki Baruch Hu: Ancient Near Eastern, Biblical, and Judaic Studies in Honor of Baruch A. Levine* (ed. R. Chazan, W. W. Hallo, and L. H. Schiffman; Winona Lake, Ind.: Eisenbrauns, 1999), 429–39. Zakovitch argues that the circumstances of Haran's death as told in the book of Jubilees are not a midrashic "'filling in of gaps,' but rather represent a prepriestly tradition which was removed from Genesis but continued orally" (434, 438). In Jubilees we learn that "At night Abram set fire to the house of idols and burned everything that was in the house; nobody in the house knew. The people awoke during the night and tried to save their idols from the

sorrow which Lot may have felt. We later learn that Terah took responsibility for his grandson:[55] "Terah took his son Abram, his grandson Lot of Haran and his daughter in law Sarai, the wife of his son Abram, and they set out together from Ur of the Chaldeans for the land of Canaan, but when they had come as far as Haran they settled there" (11:31).

(2) We first hear of Lot's connection to Abraham in the description of their departure from Haran: "The LORD said to Abram, 'Go forth from your native land and from your father's house to the land that I will show you'" (12:1-4). In other words, Abraham continues in the path of Terah, his father, by taking responsibility—a sort of custody—for Lot.

The Deity commanded Abraham—not Lot—"Go forth from your native land," but Lot went with him to the land of Canaan. The following verse emphasizes this motif: Abraham takes his wife and his nephew Lot: "Abram took his wife Sarai and his brother's son Lot and all the wealth that they had amassed, and the persons that they had acquired in Haran, and they set out for the land of Canaan, when they arrived in the land of Canaan" (12:5). Here, too, Lot appears passive, one who is taken from place to place.

(3) We then learn of the famine which led Abraham and his wife to go down into Egypt (12:10-20). Lot is not mentioned,[56] as might be expected vis-à-vis a secondary character in the Bible.[57] At this point it is not clear whether Lot, too, went down into Egypt.[58]

---

flames. Haran hurried to save them from the fire. He was burned, and died in Ur of the Chaldees before his father Terah, and was buried in Ur. Terah and his sons left Ur for Lebanon and Canaan" (12:12-15). See Yitzhak (Itzik) Peleg, "'I Am the Lord Who Brought You Out from Ur of the Chaldeans': Who Brought Abraham Out?" [Hebrew] *Mo'ed* 17 (2007): 26-28.

55. If we accept Zakovitch's approach ("Exodus from Ur"), a tragic connection between Terah, Abraham, and Lot is revealed. This connection may provide an additional explanation for Abraham's fatherly relationship with his nephew Lot, as well as for Abraham's feelings of guilt (although Abraham did not intentionally cause Haran's death). This provides a psychological explanation for the sense of responsibility toward Lot that accompanied Abraham throughout his life. Is the description of Lot as Abraham's nephew in the story of their journey to Canaan (in 12:5) merely informative, or is it meant to express Abraham's feelings of guilt?

56. See Rudin-O'Brasky, *From the Patriarchs*, 17: "Lot is not mentioned at all; not even as a passive traveling-companion of Abraham."

57. See Simon, "Secondary Figures," 320.

58. In the words of the Samaritan version of the Pentateuch and the Septuagint:

(4) On their return, however, we learn that Lot came back with Abraham from Egypt to the Negev: "From Egypt Abram went up into the Negeb with his wife and all that he possessed, together with Lot" (13:1). The phrase "and Lot with him" emphasizes Lot's status as a secondary figure. If Lot returned with Abraham from Egypt (13:1), he had of course been with his uncle all along, as we conclude after the fact.

(5) As the story unfolds, we learn that Lot returns from Egypt "rich in cattle"; the latter fact is connected to a discussion of Abraham's riches: "Now Abram was very rich in cattle, silver and gold" (13:2), and regarding Lot it says: "Lot, who went with Abram, also had flocks and herds and tents" (v. 5).[59] This short description of Lot contains every possible sign of the secondary character: "Lot, too [וגם], went with Abraham"; that is, Lot does not make the journey alone but rather accompanies his uncle.

(5.1) The same verse then tells us that Lot had "sheep and cattle and tents," although in contrast to Abraham he is not described as "very rich" (13:2). It seems that the *vav* with which this verse opens prepares us for a disagreement between the two: "so that the land could not support them staying together for their possessions were so great that they could not remain together" (13:6). And the problem is quickly revealed: "And there was quarreling between the herdsmen of Abram's cattle and those of Lot's cattle" (v. 7). Note, however, that the quarrel is not between Lot and Abraham, but rather between their shepherds.

(5.2) In the dialogue between Abraham and Lot, Abraham takes the initiative. Abraham nobly offers his nephew first choice, even at the price of giving up parts of the land which had been promised him by God: "Abram said to Lot, 'Let there be no strife between you and me ... for we are kinsmen ... let us separate'" (13:8–9). The fact that Lot does not

---

"Lot with him" in 12:20 (also in 13:1). Rudin-O'Brasky argues that "there is an intentional expansion here" (*From the Patriarchs*, 18 n. 7). See also Skinner, *Genesis*, 250.

59. Nechama Leibowitz argues that the word order is not coincidental: "When they departed from Haran, he was part of a family whose possessions were held in common. When they departed Egypt, they returned as two families. Lot is not mentioned immediately following Sarah, as one who joins the family group, but rather as an independent unit." As proof Leibowitz offers the following: "Lot, who went with Abram" (13:5); moreover, with the support of the sages she notes that Lot is said to "go with Abraham," rather than to "go on his way." The latter discernment, in my view, borders on the midrashic. See *Studies of Genesis according to Early and Later Interpreters* [Hebrew] (Jerusalem: World Zionist Congress, 1977), 88–90.

answer again depicts him as passive, as a secondary figure, although not in a negative light.

(6) Years later Lot becomes a prisoner of war, together with all his possessions (14:12–16). Here, too, Lot is shown as a passive figure. Lot is presented as Abraham's brother[60] or nephew. Again, the family relationship and Abraham's concern for Lot form a thread running through the story (e.g., 13:8: "for we be brethren").

(7) In chapter 19 there is a sudden change in Lot's character: he is active; he is more than merely Abraham's brother or nephew. Indeed, he is the main character. The story of Lot as a host opens with "And there came the two angels to Sodom in the evening as Lot was sitting in the gate of Sodom. When Lot saw them he rose to greet them, and bowing low with his face toward the ground" (19:1), and focuses exclusively on Lot; Abraham is not even mentioned until v. 29. Note the multiple verbs used to describe Lot. There are seven verbs in the first three verses. In v. 29 Abraham reappears; this is the last time that Lot and Abraham appear together in the story.[61]

(8) The story of Lot and his daughters at the end of chapter 19 does not fall within the framework of this essay. We will note, however, that once again Lot appears passive—even helpless in the hands of his daughters, and lacking in self-control.[62] The scene in the cave ends the biblical story of Lot; we are not even told of his death.

---

60. Lot is not Abraham's brother, but rather his brother's son. Is the reference to Lot as Abraham's brother an example of metonymy, shorthand for "his brother's son"? In any case the family relationship, whether "son of" or "nephew of," is repeatedly mentioned. For more on the usage of "brother" as "nephew, relative" in the Bible, see BDB, 26, 2.

61. In *That's Not What the Good Book Says* [Hebrew] (Tel Aviv: Yediot Aharonot, 2004), 135, Zakovitch and Shinan draw an analogy between the story of Haran's death by fire in Ur and Lot's rescue from the flames which consumed Sodom: "We note an echo of the story of Haran's son, Lot. Haran was consumed by fire because he sinned, while Lot, who did not sin, does not perish in the flames ('The LORD rained upon Sodom and Gomorrah sulfurous *fire* from the LORD out of heaven'—19:24), but is rather saved by God's messengers." This discernment can be employed in an additional way: if we accept Zakovitch and Shinan's suggestion, we have an example of the "measure for measure" principle vis-à-vis the complex relationship between Abraham and Lot. Abraham, who did not save his brother from the fire which he—Abraham—may have set, now saves his brother's son from the flames. The circle is closed; Abraham has achieved closure for his guilt over his brother's death.

62. Rudin-O'Brasky, *From the Patriarchs*, 24.

With the exception of the story of Lot's hospitality in chapter 19, in all of the above Lot serves as a secondary figure. As Simon suggests: "Generally speaking, we learn only as much about the secondary biblical character as is needed to move the plot forward, or to illuminate the main character; we are not given information relating to the secondary character alone."[63]

Let us now draw a connection between the relationship between Lot and Abraham throughout the stories of the patriarchs and 19:29. We have seen that there are two readings of God's remembering of Abraham: verse 29 may be a "reversal verse" in which Lot is saved because Abraham is his uncle (which reflects particularism). This implies that God saved Lot, not as a reward for the latter's exemplary hospitality, but rather because he was Abraham's nephew. On the other hand, if God remembered that he had promised Abraham not to destroy the righteous with the wicked (18:3), we can conclude that Lot was saved as a reward for his righteous behavior as a host. Although the Deity may have remembered Lot's hospitality because Lot was Abraham's nephew, in this reading Lot appears as a righteous man. If we accept the validity of this reading, Lot was indeed saved because of his righteousness. The phrase "and God remembered Abraham" is not clear, perhaps intentionally so. It is this lack of clarity which makes the two readings possible. Abraham remains the hero of the stories of the patriarchs, but Lot, too, has his hour of glory as the hero of chapter 19. In other words, Lot is the main character in the story of his hospitality, but remains a secondary figure in the rest of the stories of the patriarchs.

8. Terah and Lot: The Secondary Figures in Abraham's Life

Throughout the stories of the patriarchs Abraham appears as a main figure, while the surrounding characters serve as secondary figures. Terah, too, appears as a figure secondary in importance to his son Abraham. This is first seen in the depiction of Terah's departure from Ur (11:31). In this verse three generations meet in order to depart for the promised land: Terah, his son Abraham and his grandson Lot. Although Terah is said to be the initiator, and in this may be seen as a main character, it is Abraham who is mentioned repeatedly; Terah, in other words, is important as "Abraham's father."[64]

---

63. Simon, "Secondary Figures," 320.

64. The description of Terah's departure contains two hints at the secondary nature of the character. The phrase "Abram's father" (11:31) is repeated twice more,

Moreover, the description of Terah's departure from Ur (11:31) is contrasted with the depiction of Abram's departure from Haran (12:5). A comparison of these two departures[65] serves to illuminate the positive image (or perhaps positive deeds) of Abraham when compared to the deeds of his father, although this is not stated explicitly. This comparison enables the reader to evaluate Abraham's actions, and to conclude that Abraham succeeded in achieving that which his father did not—or could not—achieve. The impression created by Abraham's going up to the land is enhanced against the background of Terah's story; the latter invested great efforts in journeying toward the land, but eventually "dwelt" in Haran (11:31).

It is ironic that the father serves as a secondary character whose role is to ennoble his son. Yet it is important to note that rather than intending to minimize the father's importance, the narrator uses him to enlarge, as it were, the character of the son. In any case, Terah the father and Lot the nephew are costars, while Abraham is the star.

Let us now return to the story of Lot's hospitality and ask what we have learned from this broad survey of Lot as a figure secondary to Abraham in the stories of the patriarchs: in contrast to all of the other events in which both Abraham and Lot are involved, and in which Lot serves merely as a secondary character, in the story of his hospitality in chapter 19 Lot is indeed the main character. This seems to be the one and only opportunity to understand Lot in depth. Simultaneously, the lack of detail vis-à-vis Lot in the rest of the stories of the patriarchs—both before and after the story of his hospitality—is not meant to cast aspersions on him, but rather emphasizes his role as a character secondary to Abraham (as was Terah) in the stories of the patriarchs.

---

thus serving as a *leitwort* whose repetition causes us to be aware of its importance. In this case, our attention is called to the fact that Terah is Abraham's father; the figure of Terah is thereby minimized in comparison to that of Abraham. The second hint— "they went forth with them" ויצאו אתם—is linguistically problematic: Who went out with whom? Did Terah join the departure of the members of his household, or did they depart with him? The latter sounds more probable; yet both of these hints dwarf Terah in comparison to his son Abraham. Let us note, however, that the intention herein seems less to dwarf Terah's image and more to ennoble that of Abraham, the main character.

65. See Itzik Peleg, "Abraham: The First 'Zionist' and the First '*yored*,'" *Al Haperek* 14 (1998): 25–31; and Peleg, "I Am the Lord," 22–40.

The story of Lot in chapter 19 shows him as a warm, good person. Unlike the men of his city, he is shown to be a host who is willing to sacrifice all that is dear to him in order to protect his guests. This positive view of Lot is supported, moreover, by a comparison with the story of Rahab's hospitality.

9. In Conclusion: Was Lot a Good Host? Was Lot Saved from Sodom as a Reward for His Hospitality??

Having completed this journey through the story of Lot's hospitality, I conclude that, although at first glance the story of Lot's hospitality in chapter 19 seems to present Lot as a hero, an exemplary host who is rewarded "measure for measure" by being allowed to escape from Sodom, by the end of the story we must conclude that he was saved because Abraham was his uncle (19:29). This reading of 19:29 leads the reader to return Lot to his position as a secondary figure in the stories of the patriarchs. We thus return to our questions: Why was Lot saved? As a reward for his exemplary hospitality? Because the Deity is a merciful God? Or because he is Abraham's nephew? The answer is that the three possibilities are interconnected, and do not stand in opposition to one another. Lot was saved as a reward for his hospitality, because the Deity is indeed a merciful God (v. 15), and because he is a member of Abraham's family (v. 29). The comparison of Lot's hospitality (ch. 19) with Abraham's hospitality (ch. 18) does not serve to dwarf the character of Lot, but rather to ennoble the character of Abraham, the main character of the stories of the patriarchs.

Moreover, a comparison of Lot's hospitality with Rahab's hospitality leads us to conclude that Lot was the better host. This comparison supports the conclusion that Lot's rescue is based on the "measure for measure" principle; that is, Lot is saved from Sodom as a reward for his exemplary hospitality. The comparison of Lot and Rahab, in which Lot appears as a noble host, balances the less positive picture which might result from the comparison of Lot's hospitality with Abraham's hospitality.

The answer to the question of whether Lot was an exemplary host is, therefore: yes and no. It depends with whom he is compared. In comparison with Rahab, the answer is: yes, he was an exemplary host. In comparison with Abraham the answer may appear negative. Yet Lot was raised by Abraham, and may have learned the duties of a host from his uncle. It is thus not surprising that while Lot was an excellent host, Abraham was better.

Bibliography

Amit, Yairah. *The Book of Judges* [Hebrew]. Miqra le-Yisrael; Jerusalem: Magnes, 1999.
———. "Endings—Especially Reversal Endings." *Scriptura* 87 (2004): 213–26.
Bar-Efrat, Shimeon, *The Art of Narration in the Bible* [Hebrew]. 4th ed. Tel Aviv: Sifriyat Po'alim, 1993.
Cohen, Menachem, ed. *The Crown: Mikra'ot Gedolot according to the Crown of Aram Tsoba* [Hebrew]. Ramat Gan: Bar Ilan University, 1991.
Garsiel, Moshe. *I Samuel: Literary Study of Systems of Comparison, Analogies and Parallels* [Hebrew]. Ramat Gan: Revivim, 1983.
Leibowitz, Nechama. *Studies of Genesis according to Early and Later Interpreters* [Hebrew]. Jerusalem: World Zionist Congress, 1977.
Malul, Meir. *Knowledge, Control and Sex*. Tel Aviv: Archaeological Center Publication, 2002.
Peleg, (Itzik) Yitzhak. "Abraham: The First 'Zionist' and the First '*yored*.'" *Al Haperek* 14 (1998): 25–31.
———. "'I Am the Lord Who Brought You Out from Ur of the Chaldeans': Who Brought Abraham Out?" [Hebrew]. *Mo'ed* 17 (2007): 22–41.
———. "The Measure-for-Measure Principle via Word-for-Word" [Hebrew]. *Beit Mikra* 44 (1999): 357–60.
———. "A Time to Know the Biblical Text" [Hebrew]. *Al Haperek19* (2002): 176–89.
Polak, Frank. *Biblical Narrative: Aspects of Art and Design*. Jerusalem: Mosad Biyalik, 1994.
Rad, Gerhard von. *Genesis, A Commentary*. Translated by J. H. Marks. London: SCM, 1961.
Rudin-O'Brasky, Talia. *From the Patriarchs in Hebron and Sodom (Genesis 18–19)* [Hebrew]. Jerusalem: Hotsa'at Simor, 1982.
Sarna, Nahum. *Understanding Genesis*. New York: Jewish Theological Seminary of America, 1966.
Simon, Uriel. "Secondary Figures in the Biblical Story" [Hebrew]. Pages 317–24 in *Reading Prophetic Narratives*. Jerusalem: Mosad Byalik; Ramat-Gan: Hotsa'at Universitat Bar-Ilan, 1997.
Skinner, John. *A Critical and Exegetical Commentary on Genesis*. ICC. Edinburgh:T&T Clark, 1930.
Speiser, Ephraim A. *Genesis*. AB 1. Garden City, N.Y.: Doubleday, 1964.
Weinfeld, Moshe. *Encyclopedia of the World of the Bible: Genesis* [Hebrew]. Ramat Gan: Revivim, 1982.
Westermann, Claus. *Genesis 12–36: A Commentary*. Translated by John J. Scullion. Minneapolis: Augsburg, 1995.
Zakovitch, Yair. "The Exodus from Ur of the Chaldeans: A Chapter in Literary Archaeology." Pages 429–39 in *Ki Baruch Hu: Ancient Near Eastern, Biblical, and Judaic Studies in Honor of Baruch A. Levine*. Edited by R. Chazan, W. W. Hallo, and L. H. Schiffman. Winona Lake, Ind.: Eisenbrauns, 1999.
———. *An Introduction to Inner-Biblical Interpretation* [Hebrew]. Even Yehuda: Rekhes Hotsa'ah le-Or Proyektim Hinukhiyim, 1992.

———. *Readings in the Land of Mirrors* [Hebrew]. Tel Aviv: HaKibbutz Hameuhad, 1992.

———. "The Reflected Story: An Additional Dimension for Evaluating Biblical Characters" [Hebrew]. *Tarbiz* 54 (1985): 165–76.

Zakovitch, Yair, and Avigdor Shinan. *That's Not What the Good Book Says* [Hebrew]. Tel Aviv: Yediot Aharonot, 2004.

Hospitality Compared: Abraham and Lot as Hosts

Jonathan D. Safren

1. Introduction

Ever since Second Temple times, Abraham has been held out as a paragon of virtue.[1] The Mishnah conceives of Abraham as having successfully passed ten tests of his righteousness and loyalty to God,[2] tests which qualified him for being chosen by God to be the father of the chosen people and worthy of the divine promise of inheriting the land of Canaan.

By comparison, Lot has come off a poor second place. Weinfeld, who lists Lot's shortcomings,[3] calls him "a helpless character, always dependent on outside aid, and who, if it had not been for Abraham, would have van-

---

1. See, e.g., Isa 52:1–2; 2 Esd 3:13; 7:36; Sir 44:19–20; Pr. Man. 1:7; 1 Macc 2:52; 2 Macc 1:2. English translations of biblical verses are generally according to the NJPS, but changes have been introduced where deemed necessary.

2. M. 'Abot 5:3. The belief that Abraham had been tested several times was already extant in late Second Temple times; see Jdt 8:26: "Remember what things he did to Abraham."

The ten trials are detailed in 'Abot R. Nat. A 33, "Ten Trials"; B 36, "Ten Trials" (Solomon Schechter, ed., *Avot de-Rabi Natan* [New York: Bet ha-Midrash le-Rabanim be-Amerikah, 1997], 94–95; and see now Hans-Jürgen Becker, ed., *Avot de-Rabbi Natan: Synoptische Edition beider Versionen* [Tübingen: Mohr Siebeck, 2006], 238–39, 378). Each version of the 'Avot presents a different arrangement of the trials; the order followed here is according to the exposition by Umberto Cassuto, *A Commentary on the Book of Genesis: From Noah to Abraham* (trans. Israel Abrahams; 2 vols.; Jerusalem: Magnes, 1964), 2:294–96; Hebrew orig.: Moshe David Cassuto, *A Commentary on the Book of Genesis: From Noah to Abraham* (2 vols.; Jerusalem: Magnes, 1949), 2:201–2.

3. Moshe Weinfeld, "The Figure of Lot" [Hebrew], in *Genesis* (ed. Moshe Weinfeld; Olam haTanakh; Tel-Aviv: Revivim 1993), 127.

ished from the world."[4] When their shepherds quarrel, it is Abraham who gives in to Lot and lets him have first choice over whatever portion of the land he desires.[5] And Lot makes a very bad choice—the Jordan Plain and Sodom (Gen. 13:10).[6] When Lot is captured in the War of the Kings, it is Abraham who comes to his aid.[7] Finally, when God overturns Sodom and Lot is about to perish, it is only because of Abraham that he is saved (Gen 19:29).[8] When the men of Sodom assail Lot, the angels put him inside the house and thus avert a tragedy (19:10). When the city is about to be destroyed and Lot hesitates, the angels take him and his family by the hand and lead them outside the city (19:15-16), an ironic sidelight, writes von Rad, to a man who, only a short time earlier, had tried to protect his heavenly guests.[9]

---

4. Ibid.

5. This is the third of the "Ten Tests" (Cassuto, *Genesis*, 2:295).

6. Speiser takes a very negative view of Lot's behavior: "By taking advantage of his uncle's kindness and staking out the Plain for himself (xii 10f.), Lot became an unwitting accessory to Sodom's guilt" (Ephraim A. Speiser, *Genesis* [AB 1; Garden City, N.Y.: Doubleday, 1964], 142). Bowie even calls Lot a "mean man" (Walter Russell Bowie, "The Book of Genesis: Exposition," *IB* 1:506-7). Hermann Gunkel takes a somewhat less derogatory view, writing that Lot, the younger of the two, should have given first choice to his elder, Abraham, and, as a result of not doing so, "If Lot then receives the worse portion in the end ... it is his own fault" (*Genesis* [3rd ed.; Göttingen: Vandenhoeck & Ruprecht, 1910], 174; see the translation by Mark E. Biddle in Gunkel, *Genesis* [Macon, Ga.: Mercer University Press, 1997], 174; subsequent page references are to the German edition). Rashi does not place any blame on Lot, either for the quarrel that developed or for Lot's having first choice, but he does say that Lot, knowing that the men of Sodom were evil, shouldn't have gone there in the first place; Rashi on Gen 13:7 (Menahem Cohen, ed., *Mikra'ot Gedolot haKeter* [Hebrew] [9 vols.; Ramat Gan, Bar-Ilan University, 1992-2007], 1a:128; references to Rashi throughout are from this edition); Shamai Gelander's appraisal of the situation is even more favorable toward Lot: "Abraham left the choice to Lot not only out of generosity, but also because, at this point, Abraham had no inclination at all towards settling in any particular place. Lot's choice is described as most natural and logical" (*Studies in the Book of Genesis* [Hebrew] [3 vols.; Ra'anana: Open University, 2009], 2:95). Lot's only fault, in comparison with Abraham, writes Gelander, is that "He sees the present and not what lies in store."

7. Abraham's fourth trial; Cassuto, *Genesis*, 2:295.

8. Abraham's seventh trial; Cassuto, *Genesis*, 2:295.

9. To Gerhard von Rad this seems "almost a bit comic" (*Das erste Buch Mose* [9th ed.; ATD 2/4; Göttingen: Vandenhoeck & Ruprecht, 1972)], 172).

This last of Lot's foibles is described in the final chapter of a narrative unit that includes Gen 18–19.[10] Though scholarly opinions have been divided as to the origins of the various sections of the narrative,[11] these will be treated as they stand today: as integral parts of one unified narrative.[12]

Genesis 18 begins with a depiction of Abraham's hospitality toward three "men," who are in reality angels (vv. 1–8), and the angels' announcement that Sarah will conceive and bear a son (vv. 9–15).[13] Abraham's

---

10. On Gen 18–19, see Talia Rudin-O'Brasky, *The Patriarchs in Hebron and Sodom (Genesis 18–19)* [Hebrew] (Jerusalem: Hotsa'at Simor, 1982); Nachman Levine, "Sarah/Sodom: Birth, Destruction, and Synchronic Transaction," *JSOT* 31 (2006): 131–46; Yitzhak (Itzik) Peleg, "Was Lot a Good Host?" [Hebrew] *Mo'ed* 18 (2008): 22–41.

11. Gunkel, *Genesis*, 193, 201, 206, regards both chapters as J compositions combined by a redactorial J hand (J^r). John Skinner (*A Critical and Exegetical Commentary on Genesis* [2nd ed.; ICC; Edinburgh: T&T Clark, 1930], 298, 306) regards 18:17–19:38 as later Yahwistic expansions of a primary J narrative. Cuthbert A. Simpson ("The Book of Genesis: Exegesis," *IB* 1:626) writes that the narrative was originally "non-Yahwist." Von Rad (*Das erste Buch Mose*, 160) claims that "many traditions are reflected which were originally independent of one another, yet the inner unity here is such that the seams, which can still be recognized, seem to be integral paragraphs of the whole." Claus Westermann (*Genesis* [3 vols.; BK 1; Neukirchen-Vluyn: Neukirchener, 1981], 2:331–32) considers Gen 18–19 a large narrative complex, in which 18:1b–6, not an original part of the narrative, serves as the introduction to not only 18:1–16a but to the whole narrative complex. Nahum M. Sarna regards each of these chapters as a "unity" or "an integral unit," while not expressing an opinion about the pericope as a whole (*Genesis* [JPSTC; Philadelphia: Jewish Publication Society, 1989], 134).

12. With Rudin-O'Brasky, *The Patriarchs in Hebron and Sodom*, 14, who, while not ignoring the "diachronic" approach taken by earlier scholars, chooses to "adopt the synchronic approach in the analysis of the passage, thus enabling the understanding of the narrative in its present context alone."

13. The motif of a mortal entertaining strangers, unaware that they are divine, is a common one in ancient literature; see Gunkel, *Genesis*, 193–94; Skinner, *Genesis*, 302–3; von Rad, *Das erste Buch Mose*, 160–61; Rudin-O'Brasky, *The Patriarchs in Hebron and Sodom*, 105, 108; and, most recently, Joyce Louise Rilett Wood, "When Gods Were Men," in *From Babel to Babylon: Essays on Biblical History and Literature in Honour of Brian Peckham* (ed. Joyce Rilett Wood et al.; LHB/OTS 455; New York: T&T Clark, 2006), 285–98. Simpson ("The Book of Genesis," 616) writes: "The hospitality usually … ends in a blessing." This motif is already present in the Ugaritic epic of Aqhat; see Yitzhak Avishur, "The Narrative of Abraham the Host (Genesis 18:1–16a): The Literary Structure and Ugaritic Parallel (CTA 17 [2 Aqht] V: 4–31)," in *Studies in Biblical Narrative: Style, Structure, and the Ancient Near Eastern Literary Background*

exemplary hospitality in this narrative has been pointed out and praised throughout the generations, by traditional Jewish[14] and modern critical[15] commentators alike. Verse 16 constitutes a transitional verse to the second part of the narrative unit, the announcement to Abraham of the impending destruction of Sodom and Abraham's expostulation with God (vv. 17–33).[16] Verse 16aα contains part of the "departure formula" common to the endings of many biblical narratives or of scenes within those narratives:[17]

(Tel Aviv: Archaeological Center Publication, 1999), 57–74; Hebrew orig.: *Beth Mikra* 32 (1987): 166–77; idem, "The Angels' Visit with Abraham and Its Parallels in Ugaritic Literature" [Hebrew], in Weinfeld, *Genesis*, 121–22.

14. See, e.g., b. Shabbat 127a; Lev. Rab., Shemini 11:5 (Mordechai Margalioth, ed., *Leviticus Rabbah* [5 vols. in 2; Jerusalem: Jewish Thelogical Seminary of America, 1993], 2a:224): "When did he approach [God] righteously? When he said 'Do not go on past your servant'" (Gen 18:3); t. Sotah 4 (Moses Samuel Zuckermandel, ed., *Tosefta, Mischna und Boraitha in ihrem Verhältnis zu einander* [2 vols.; Frankfurt am Main: Kauffmann, 1908–1909], 2:298): "'[Abraham] ran three times for the ministering angels,' as it is written: 'When he saw them he ran to them' etc.; 'Abraham hastened to the tent to Sarah'; 'Then Abraham ran to the herd'"; and see Rashi on 18:1–17; Rashbam (R. Shmuel ben Meir) on 18:7–8; Ramban (Nachmanides) on 18:3–7 (Cohen, *Mikra'ot Gedolot*, 1a:160–163; references to Rashbam and Ramban throughout are from this edition); Yehuda Kiel, *Genesis* (3 vols.; Da'at Miqra; Jerusalem: Mossad Harav Kook, 2000), 2:4–10. However, the visit of the angels is not considered one of the "Ten Trials" but a reward for "passing" the sixth test, circumcision, described in the preceding chapter, or a "doctor's visit," to heal him of the operation; see b. B. Metzi'a 86b; Minor Tractates, Kallah Rab. 7:2; Cassuto, *Genesis*, 2:295.

15. Gunkel (*Genesis*, 199), unlike 'Abot de Rabbi Nathan, does consider this narrative a test, because Abraham, not knowing that his guests were divine beings, received them so splendidly. Skinner (*Genesis*, 300) writes: "Hospitality is, so to speak, the logical corollary of passing Abraham's tent." Simpson ("The Book of Genesis," 618) describes "Abraham's prodigal generosity." Sarna (*Genesis*, 129) contends that "Abraham's open-hearted, liberal hospitality towards the total strangers knows no bounds"; and see also Moshe Weinfeld, "Let a Little Water Be Brought," in Weinfeld, *Genesis*, 122; Peleg, "Was Lot a Good Host?"

16. Sarna, *Genesis*, 128.

17. Examples: Gen 22:19; 24:10 (2x); Num 24:25; Judg 19:28; 1 Sam 21:1 (where it indicates that this verse belongs with the preceding chapter). On the departure formula, see, e.g., Isac Leo Seeligmann, "Hebräische Erzählung und die biblische Geschichtsschreibung," *TZ* 18 (1962): 305–25; Shimeon Bar-Efrat, *Narrative Art in the Bible* (trans. Dorothea Shefer-Vanson; JSOTSup 70; Sheffield: Almond Press, 1989), 130–31; Hebrew orig.: *The Art of Narration in the Bible* (2nd ed.; Tel Aviv: Sifriyat Po'alim, 1984), 142–43; Shamai Gelander, "Biblical Narrative," in *Introduction to the Bible* (ed. Zeev Weisman; 6 vols.; Tel-Aviv: Open University, 1988), 4:230–33.

ויקמו משם האנשים— "The men set out from there." Verse 16bβ leads us into the second part of the narrative: וישקפו על פני סדם— "and looked down toward Sodom." The second part of the departure formula does not appear until verse 22a: ויפנו משם האנשים וילכו סדמה— "The two men went on from there to Sodom." The author has thus completely integrated these two parts of the narrative, using a "split departure formula."[18]

Genesis 19 portrays a parallel and very similar[19] hosting of two angels by Lot in Sodom (vv. 1–3) and continues with the deliverance of Lot and his family by the angels (vv. 4–16, 17–22). These verses too are part of a larger narrative unit, which goes on to describe the destruction of Sodom and Gomorrah, Gen 19:23–29, with 19:23 marking the transition between the two parts. Verses 30–38 mark out a separate narrative unit, with a new opening verse and a different topic—the etiological legend of the origins of Moab and Ammon.[20]

---

18. A variant of this "split departure formula" occurs in Judg 19:5–10, in which the Ephraimite sets out three times to return home, but is dissuaded twice by his Bethlehemite father-in-law. Thus, the first part of the formula occurs in vv. 5a and 7a in an abbreviated form: ויקם ללכת "he/the man [the Ephraimite] started to leave." Each time he is persuaded by his father-in-law to tarry another day. On the third day, in v. 9a, the first part of the formula appears again, this time in its full form: ויקם האיש ללכת הוא ופילגשו ונערו, "Then the man, his concubine, and his attendant started to leave," hinting that this time the man will not be persuaded to tarry. Again the father-in-law tries his luck, but the Ephraimite is intent on departing; and so, in 19:10a, the second part of the "split departure formula" appears: ויקם וילך, "He set out...."

19. Some of the similarities—and contrasts—between the two "hospitality" narratives were already noted by the rabbis. See, e.g., Minor Tractates, Kallah Rab. 7:3, which points out that Abraham first offers refreshment, whereas Lot first offers a place to sleep; b. B. Metziʿa 86b–87a discerns that the angels immediately accept Abraham's offer of hospitality, but Lot has to plead with them first; and Gen. Rab. 50:2 (here and throughout, references are to J. Theodor and Chanoch Albeck, eds., *Midrash Bereshit Rabba* [Jerusalem: Wahrmann, 1965], 517), asks why Abraham's visitors are called "men" but Lot's are called "angels."

20. On the ethnological etiological legend see Gunkel, *Genesis*, xxi; on the Moabites and Ammonites specifically, see Eduard Meyer, *Die Israeliten und ihre Nachbarstamme* (Halle an der Saale: Niemeyer, 1906), 311–12.

Weinfeld divides the chapter into two parts, 19:1–29 and 19:30–38; Moshe Weinfeld, "Chapter 18: Introduction," in Weinfeld, *Genesis*, 121. Sarna (*Genesis*, 134) views all three sections as scenes of an integral unit, "for the acts of incest would be unintelligible without the preceding events." This may be so; but the pronounced ethnological etiological nature of 19:30–38 nonetheless sets it apart from the previous sections; and see also Peleg, "Was Lot a Good Host?" 22 n. 1.

Lot's hospitality has been somewhat less favorably received in many traditional Jewish sources[21] and in some modern commentaries;[22] this in line with the inferior position he occupies vis-à-vis Abraham.[23] But on the basis of Gen 18:23, 25, other traditional Jewish sources view Lot as a צדיק "righteous man," a term that lends itself to two very different interpretations: one, that inferred from the biblical text itself, is that Lot was a truly righteous man,[24] but less so than Abraham.[25] Similarly, many modern scholars find nothing wrong with Lot's hospitality.[26]

---

21. A sampling of traditional Jewish commentary: The reason the angels refused Lot's invitation is that he was a "little man" and not a "great man" like Abraham; b. Pesahim 86b, followed by Rashi on Gen 19:2. Tanhuma writes (Vayera 15): "Lot learned [hospitality] from Abraham's deeds" (Salomon Buber, ed., *Midrash Tanhuma haQadum vehaYashan* [Hebrew] [3 vols.; Vilna: Widow Rom & Sons, 1885] 1:93); see also Ramban on 19:3 and Abravanel on 19:1 (R. Isaac Abravanel, *Commentary on the Torah* [Hebrew] [5 vols. in 3; Jerusalem: Sons of Arbil, 1964], 1:248); Sforno on 19:3 (Mordechai Leib Katzenellenbogen, ed., *Torat Hayyim* [Hebrew] [5 vols.; Jerusalem: Mossad Harav Kook, 1986–1993], 1a:223), who interprets משתה as "wine feast," says this fits Lot's character, as we know from his end, while the only time Abraham ever made a wine feast was when his son Isaac was weaned. However, Or haHayyim (R. Hayyim ibn Attar) on 19:3 writes that although Lot made a "feast" (משתה) for the angels, they ate only his unleavened bread, "because Lot didn't observe the Torah like Abraham" (*Miqra'ot Gedolot: The Five Books of the Torah* [5 vols.; New York: Hevrat Tanakh, 1959], 1:225).

22. Speiser (*Genesis*, 139) contrasts Lot's simple, hurried reception with Abraham's hurried one; Weinfeld ("The Figure of Lot," 127) prefers to ignore Lot's hospitality, emphasizing instead his "hapless nature," having been saved twice in this chapter alone by the angels.

23. See, e.g., Minor Tractates, Kallah Rab. 3:1; b. B. Metzi'a 86b–87a; and the sources cited in n. 22 above. Lot was saved only because of Abraham's intercession according to b. Berakhot 54b; Midrash Tanhuma, Vayera 9 (Warsaw: Jasberg, 1875), 26b; R. David Kimhi on Gen 19:16 (Cohen, *Mikra'ot Gedolot*, 1a:175; references to Kimhi throughout are from this edition).

24. Examples: b. Berakhot 54b; b. Yoma 38b; Alfa Beta de-ben Sira, *Tet* (Judah David Eisenstein, ed., *Otzar Midrashim* [Hebrew] [2 vols.; New York: Judah David Eisenstein, 1915], 1:38): "Lot was a completely righteous man"; see also *Zayen* (37) and *Samekh* (41); Ramban on Gen 19:12: "Lot's merits would have saved sons and daughters and sons-in-law, not as Abraham thought."

25. See above n. 23.

26. According to Gunkel (*Genesis*, 207–8), Lot may have thought that the men were poor people of low class but nonetheless urged his hospitality upon the strangers, noting that urging apparently played a great role in ancient hospitality. Simpson ("The Book of Genesis," 627), following RSV on 19:3a, notes that Lot "urged them [the

The second interpretation is that, by comparison with all the other inhabitants of Sodom, Lot was righteous: צדיק בסדום "a righteous man in Sodom," as the modern Hebrew idiom goes.[27] This, of course, is not saying very much. This interpretation can be traced to several factors: (1) when Abraham and Lot decided to part ways, the generous Abraham offered Lot first choice, and Lot chose what appeared to be the more fertile territory;[28] (2) Lot is the eponymous ancestor of Moab and Ammon, two of Israel's unfriendly neighbors during the First Temple period;[29] and (3) a comparison with the description of Noah and its rabbinic interpretation: "Noah was a righteous man in his generations" (Gen 6:9); that is, compared to all the wicked men of his time, Noah was righteous.[30]

The reservations about Lot's hospitality, then, of both ancients and moderns, is fuelled by several factors: his inferior position in comparison with Abraham; his having taken advantage of Abraham when given first choice of land in Gen 13;[31] the choice he actually made—Sodom—even though its inhabitants were evil; and his general haplessness.

One could also point out various apparent deficiencies in Lot's hospitality: whereas Abraham ran from his tent toward the approaching strangers in spite of the heat and bowed himself down (Gen 18:1-2), Lot, in the cooler eventide, merely rose from his seat and bowed down (19:1b); and while Abraham offered his guests a sumptuous meal, putting his whole household to work in the process (18:4-8), Noah merely offered his guests

---

angels] strongly to come to his house" knowing the danger of remaining outside. In a similar vein, von Rad (*Das erste Buch Mose,* 171) writes that only Lot, showing the greatest respect, invited the strangers in, and it was out of apprehension for their safety that he urged them; Rudin-O'Brasky, *The Patriarchs in Hebron and Sodom,* 108, calls Lot "righteous" without any qualification.

27. Some midrashim relate the righteousness of Noah, Lot, and others to the people of their times and places; see Sifre Zuta 27:1 (Hayyim Shaul Horovitz, ed., *Sifre de-ve Rav* [Hebrew] [Jerusalem: Wahrmann, 1966], 316); Midrash Tanhuma-Yelammedenu, Vayera 29:21b (Jacob Mann, ed., *Midrashim from Manuscripts* [Hebrew] [Cincinnati: Hebrew Union College, 1940], 283); *Yalkut Shimoni,* 577. The medieval Jewish commentator R. David Kimhi writes on Gen 19:29: "Even though he was righteous, he wasn't so righteous as to have been saved on his own merits" (Cohen, *Mikra'ot Gedolot,* 1a:179).

28. See above n. 6.
29. See Meyer, *Die Israeliten,* 311-12.
30. B. Sanhedrin 108a; Rashi on Gen 6:9.
31. See above n. 6.

a light snack and a drink (19:3b). Add to this the fact that Abraham's reception of guests is described in seven verses (18:2–8), but Lot's in only three.

One could counter this last assertion with Gunkel's suggested explanations for the brevity of the Lot description: the author, having already given a full description of Abraham's hospitality in Gen 18:1–8, does not wish to tire readers with repetition. Alternatively, writes Gunkel, the narrator may wish to offer further proof of Lot's hospitality in verses 6–8 (in which Lot offers up his daughters to protect his guests).[32]

Taking this one step further, the Lot narrative can be seen as a "mirror narrative"—what Zakovitch calls a "reflection story"—reflecting the Abraham narrative, but contrasting the behavior of the protagonists.[33]

2. Discussion

This essay presents two theses: (1) There is no material difference in the reception of guests by the two protagonists. Lot was as good a host as Abraham and possibly a better one.[34] (2) Genesis 19 does indeed mirror Gen 18, but it is not the behavior of Abraham and Lot that the author wishes to contrast, but that of the angels: in chapter 18, they come to bring good tidings to Abraham; in chapter 19 they come to destroy Sodom.[35]

---

32. Gunkel, *Genesis*, 208.

33. The phenomenon was first noted by Ariella Deem in her comparison of Gen 38 and 2 Sam 11, where she termed it "reverse reflection" ("Cupboard Love: The Story of Amnon and Tamar" [Hebrew], *Hasifrut/Literature* 28 [1979]: 103–4). It was more fully described by Yair Zakovitch, "Reflection Story: Another Dimension for the Valuation of Characters in Biblical Narrative" [Hebrew], *Tarbiz* 54 (1985): 165–76; idem, *Through the Looking Glass: Reflection Stories in the Bible* [Hebrew] (Tel Aviv: HaKibbutz Hameuhad, 1995); see also Jonathan D. Safren, "Balaam and Abraham," *VT* 38 (1988): 105–13.

34. Contra Peleg, "Was Lot a Good Host?" who, on the one hand, admits that Lot was an "exemplary" host (23–24) but then goes on to conclude that Abraham was a better one (45–46). Peleg bases his whole argument on Gen 19:29, which relates that Lot was saved only because of Abraham's intercession, on Lot's being a major character only in this narrative, and on the history of relations between Abraham and Lot. This, it seems to me, is a non sequitur. Conclusions should more correctly be drawn from a comparison of Gen 19:1–29 and Gen 18:1–16, as both belong to the same narrative unit and the one is a reflection of the other.

35. Zakovitch, *Through the Looking Glass*, 82, sees a mirror relationship between Gen 19 and Judg 19 ("The Outrage at Gibeah") but posits no relationship between Gen 19 and 18.

These theses will be demonstrated by comparison of the following parameters: (1) Setting—Place and Time; (2) Greeting; (3) Invitation and Reply; (4) The Repast and Its Preparation; and (5) Aftermath.

2.1. Setting—Place and Time

Abraham (18:1–2a): The LORD appeared to him by the terebinths of Mamre; he was sitting at the entrance of the tent as the day grew hot.

Lot (19:1a): The two angels arrived in Sodom in the evening, as Lot was sitting in the gate of Sodom.

The time of day determines the content of both the invitation and the repast (see below).

Abraham was living in a tent "by the terebinths of Mamre," that is to say, in an open place with unobstructed visibility. He was sitting by his tent in the middle of the day and, looking up, he immediately spotted the three strangers.[36] Lot lived in a city and was sitting "in the gate of Sodom," meaning inside the gate tower or structure. A city gate, "the focal point of all communal activities in an urban center,"[37] was always crowded with passersby, more so in the evening, when throngs of city dwellers were returning from their fields. Canaanite/Israelite city-gate structures[38] often had an L-turn as well, so that potential attackers would not be able to rush straight into the city and, moreover, would have to expose their flanks to any guards in the gate rooms. It would therefore have been difficult to notice approaching strangers, from Lot's vantage point.[39]

---

36. Speiser (*Genesis*, 129) claims that "on a typically hot day ... the landscape turns hazy and one's vision is blurred." This may be true when distance is measured in terms of kilometers, but here the visitors are at the most only a few-score meters distant.

37. Ibid., 138.

38. On Canaanite/Israelite city fortifications, see Ze'ev Herzog, *Das Stadttor in Israel und in den Nachbarländern* (Mainz am Rhein: von Zabern, 1986); Hebrew orig.: "The City Gate in Eretz Israel and the Neighbouring Countries" (Ph.D. diss., Tel-Aviv University, 1986).

39. The midrash, and many traditional commentators in its wake, claim Lot was sitting in the city gate because he had just been appointed judge; see for example: Gen. Rab. 50:3; followed by Rashi on Gen 19:1; Abrabanel and Malbim on Gen 19:1; Keli Yakar (R. Shlomo Ephraim Luntschitz) on 19:9. While sitting there, he was looking for

2.2. Greeting

Abraham (18:2): Looking up, he saw three men standing over against him. As soon as he saw them, he ran from the entrance of the tent to greet them and he bowed to the ground.

Lot (19:1b): When Lot saw them, he rose to greet them and he bowed low with his face to the ground.

The NJPS correctly transmits the intention of the Hebrew וישא עיניו וירא. Abraham had not been looking in the particular direction from which the three "men" had come, but when he did, he saw them. They did not "suddenly" appear out of nowhere;[40] had this been the case, Abraham would have immediately recognized them as divine beings, which he did not.

The Hebrew נצבים עליו in Gen 18:2 is most satisfactorily translated by Fox, "standing over against him."[41] Others translate "standing in front of him,"[42] "standing before him,"[43] "standing beside him" (NJPS), or "standing near him,"[44] but these do not sufficiently capture the flavor of the narrative, as they do not explain why Abraham had to "run" (NJPS) or "rush"[45] from the entrance of his tent to greet the angels. They were standing some distance away, probably by the road, at or near the turn to his tent, and Abraham wanted to intercept them before they passed on, as it did not

---

unsuspecting visitors in order to spirit them away from the evil Sodomites; Gen. Rab. 50:4; Rashi and Ramban on 19:2. Among the moderns, Simpson ("The Book of Genesis," 627) and von Rad (*Das erste Buch Mose,* 171) think that Lot was quite concerned for the safety of the strangers; see above n. 26. But Gunkel (*Genesis,* 207) thinks that Lot was simply resting on a stone bench after his daily exertions, and Westermann (*Genesis,* 2:366–67) claims that the migrant Lot, now a citizen of Sodom, was sitting in the marketplace as befit him in his new status.

40. Contra Gunkel, *Genesis,* 193; von Rad, *Das erste Buch Mose,* 161; and Westermann, *Genesis,* 2:336, who all think that the angels appeared suddenly.

41. Everett Fox, *The Five Books of Moses: Genesis, Exodus, Leviticus, Numbers, Deuteronomy: A New Translation with Introductions, Commentary, and Notes* (New York: Schocken, 1995), 75.

42. RSV; "I נצב," *HALOT* 2:715.

43. Robert Alter, *The Five Books of Moses: A Translation with Commentary* (New York: Norton, 2004), 85.

44. Speiser, *Genesis,* 128.

45. Ibid.

appear to him that they were coming his way. This interpretation is supported by Abraham's words of greeting: "My lords, if it please you, do not go on past your servant."

Abraham "looked up and saw," because he resided in a relatively isolated location and was not expecting strangers. Lot merely "saw." Sitting in the city gate, he was in any case "looking" at all the people entering the city, which is what one would normally do when sitting in the city gate, and especially at this hour.

The difference in vantage point explains why Abraham "rushed" and Lot merely "rose." Abraham, living in open country, could see the strangers while they were still on the road and he ran to intercept them. Lot did not notice them in the throng until they were quite close to him, but as soon he saw them, he rose—there isn't any room to run in a city gate—and bowed down low.

Notice the difference in the language used:

Abraham: וישתחו ארצה —"He bowed to the ground."
Lot: וישתחו אפים ארצה —"He bowed down low with his face to the ground."

Is this merely a stylistic variation?[46] My answer is in the negative, in view of the exchange that follows in each of the two narratives. The narrator purposely intended to indicate that Lot showed greater respect than Abraham toward the strangers.[47] This difference is one of the indications that Lot's hospitality may have been of a higher degree than Abraham's and is indicative of the mirror-relationship between the two narratives.

2.3. Invitation and Reply

Abraham (18:3–5): And he said, "My lords, if it please you, ⁴Let a little water be brought; bathe your feet and recline under the tree. ⁵And let me

---

46. Gunkel (*Genesis*, 207) views the phrase as one of several indications in 19:1b–2a of dependency on 18:2 but sees no other significance in the different wording; Rudin-O'Brasky (*The Patriarchs in Hebron and Sodom*) compares 19:2 in its entirety to Judg 19:20 (104–5) and to parallels from Greek mythology (208–9) but does not attach any significance vis-à-vis Gen 18:5b.

47. Speiser (*Genesis*, 138) finds the difference significant: "This is how courtiers and clients address their superiors in the Amarna Letters."

fetch a morsel of bread that you may refresh yourselves; then go on—seeing that you have come your servant's way." They replied, "Do as you have said."

Lot (19:2–3a): And he said, "Please, my lords, turn aside to your servant's house to spend the night, and bathe your feet; then you may be on your way early." But they said, "No, we will spend the night in the square." But he urged them strongly, so they turned his way and entered his house.

Both Abraham and Lot proffer their hospitality, each with respect to setting and time of day.[48] Both suggest that the guests wash their feet, as in both narratives the angels have come from the dusty way.[49] Abraham offers them a drink of water and a rest under the tree, as it is midday and very hot, and suggests they "refresh" themselves (using the verb סעד)[50] with "a morsel of bread," again because it is midday, and lunchtime.

Lot offers his guests a place to sleep, as it is evening. The sun is setting or has already set, and the Jordan Plain cools down very rapidly, so he does not immediately offer a drink. Moreover, Lot may be concerned for their safety, if their presence should become known to the Sodomites.[51]

Ramban on 19:2[52] interprets the words והשכמתם והלכתם לדרככם to mean that, knowing how evil the men of Sodom were, Lot advised his

---

48. Rashbam on Gen 18:1 understands the difference between the two invitations in precisely this way.

49. See also Gen 24:32; 43:24; Judg 19:21; 2 Sam 11:8.

50. This verb is used when the main object of the feast is food; see Judg 19:5, 8; 1 Kgs 13:6–7; and cf. also Ps 104:15b. It can appear either with or without the direct object לב.

51. Traditional Jewish commentators take special notice of the fact that Lot offers the strangers a place to sleep before anything else, some attributing this to his concern over their welfare; see Minor Tractates, Kallah Rab. 7:4, "If [the Sodomites] had seen them washing ... they would have killed them"; Gen. Rab. 50:4, "Take a circuitous route to me so that you won't be seen coming to me"; and see the authorities mentioned in n. 39 above. Similar opinions have been voiced by some of the modern commentators as well; see Simpson, "The Book of Genesis," 627; Sarna, *Genesis*, 135: "The strangers are urged to get out of town before the people of Sodom become aware of their presence." Peleg ("Was Lot a Good Host?" 23–24), however, does not draw any connection between Lot's urging the angels not to sleep in the street and the dangers that lurk there, but views this as evidence of the narrator's desire "to present Lot as an exemplary host"; and see above n. 26.

52. Followed by Sarna, *Genesis*, 135.

guests to leave very early, but did not take into account the possibility that they would attack the guests as soon as they did. Whether or not this is the literal interpretation of the words, it is certainly suits the context.

The difference in the angels' replies in each case is worthy of note. While Abraham's guests accept his hospitality immediately (18:5b), Lot's guests decline, and it is only after he "urged them strongly" (19:3a) that they accept his invitation and enter his house. This, like the difference in the protagonists' genuflections, is not a chance variation,[53] and results from the difference in the angels' mission: whereas in Gen 18 they had come to bear good tidings to Abraham, now they have come to verify the evil reputation of the Sodomites, and so they have no time for the usual amenities.[54]

The explanation that the refusal is an example of "Oriental politeness"[55] is not acceptable, for a refusal of such a nature would do nothing to advance the plot or understand the motivations of the characters. Moreover, as noted above,[56] Lot, knowing the character of the inhabitants very well, may be concerned for the safety of the strangers.

1.4. The Repast and Its Preparation

Abraham (Gen 18:6–8): Abraham hastened into the tent to Sarah, and said, "Quick, three *seah*s of choice flour! Knead and make cakes!" ⁷Then Abraham ran to the herd, took a calf, tender and choice, and gave it to a

---

53. Gunkel (*Genesis*, 206–7) thinks that the invitation in 19:2a is nothing but a stylistic variant of 18:2, and therefore attaches no particular importance to the angels' refusal in 2b; nor does Rudin-O'Brasky (*The Patriarchs in Hebron and Sodom*, 104–5, 108–9), who limits her discussion of the verse to comparison with Judg 19. On both, see also above n. 49.

The rabbis, however, were mindful of the difference and made various comments on it; see for example Minor Tractates, Derekh Eretz, Pirkei ben Azai 2:2, which interprets the refusal as a ploy to protect Lot's wife and daughters; Gen. Rab. 50:2, "One refuses a little man but not a great one"—a comment made in other midrashic collections as well, and followed by Rashi and Kimhi.

54. Skinner, *Genesis*, 207: "it may contain a hint of the purpose of the visit"; von Rad, *Das erste Buch Mose*, 171: "moreover, they have come—unlike in Hebron—not to visit Lot but for an entirely different purpose" (my trans.); Sarna, *Genesis*, 135: "they must test the inhabitants to learn whether or not their evil reputation is in fact deserved (cf. 18:21)."

55. So Gunkel, *Genesis*, 207–8; followed by Skinner, *Genesis*. Skinner is of two minds here; see previous note.

56. See above nn. 51–52.

servant-boy, who hastened to prepare it. ⁸He took curds and milk and the calf that had been prepared and set these before them; and he waited on them under the tree as they ate.

Lot (Gen 19:3b): He prepared a drinking-feast for them and baked unleavened bread, and they ate.

Three long verses are devoted to Abraham's regalement of his guests but only half a verse to Lot's.⁵⁷ Abraham's menu is the *haute cuisine* of his time,⁵⁸ while Lot serves up only wine and unleavened bread.⁵⁹ Is this consequential?

It is only logical that the time of day and the circumstances determine the type of meal and the extent of the preparations in each narrative,⁶⁰ and therefore there is no intentional difference in these indirect characterizations. Both hosts do their best according to the circumstances, and in both narratives, the host's hospitality goes beyond his original offer.⁶¹

Abraham had originally offered "a little water" and "a morsel of bread," but now he prepares a feast with meat and other delicacies.⁶² The major meal of the day was generally eaten at the end of the day, but guests were a cause for exceptions to the rule⁶³ and since Abraham must prepare the

---

57. Gunkel (*Genesis*, 208) attributes the brevity of the description to its being a rehearsal of 18:1–8. The narrator does not wish to tire his readers with repetitions.

58. Borowski calls it a "special," "complete," or "festive" meal and writes that "it is similar to what is described in the Egyptian story of Sinuhe (ca. twentieth–nineteenth century B.C.E.)"; see Oded Borowski, *Daily Life in Biblical Times* (SBLABS 5; Atlanta: Society of Biblical Literature, 2003), 23, 65.

59. Borowski (ibid., 23) claims that "the same treatment was offered by Abraham's nephew Lot" (referring to his exemplary hospitality), who prepared a "great feast," but if this were so, the narrator would not have written that Lot made a משתה, "drinking feast," and served מצות, "unleavened bread," thus creating a clear distinction between "drinking" and "eating."

60. This was well understood by Kimhi (on Gen 19:3).

61. The Talmud comments: "Such is the way of the righteous; they promise little but perform much" (b. B. Metziʿa 87a). Weinfeld ("Let a Little Water Be Brought," 122) writes that Abraham "didn't want to frighten away his guests, and so he concealed the fuss and bother from them."

62. Meat was not an everyday food but was reserved for special occasions and special guests; on meat dishes, their preparation and consumption, see Borowski, *Daily Life*, 67–68.

63. Joseph invites his brothers to the noontime meal, which includes meat (Gen

meal in haste, he divides the labor between himself and his wife Sarah, he doing the heavier work of slaughtering and preparing the tender, choice calf, with Sarah baking the עגות "cakes"[64] of fine flour. As host, Abraham serves up the food and waits on his guests by himself.

Lot had offered his guests merely a place to sleep, but now he gives them an evening meal, which is normally the cooked meal at the end of the workday.[65] But as the guests were unexpected, the hour is late and Lot wishes to feed his travel-worn (or so he thinks) guests as soon as possible, he bakes unleavened bread all by himself—anyone who has ever seen it done knows that it is a simple process, not taking very long, and not requiring any special assistance. So there is no need for the author to go into details. The time factor is also the reason Lot does not serve up meat, which would have taken some time to prepare.

Instead of meat, and in addition to bread, Lot prepares a משתה "drinking-feast," as one might do for honored guests,[66] or as might take place in the courts of kings.[67] The term משתה is used whenever the consumption of wine or a banquet with wine is intended.[68] The separate mention of bread would thus seem superfluous, because a banquet with wine would presumably include bread, which was a major component of any meal.[69] Note also that the similar description in Judg 19:19 mentions only לחם ויין "bread and wine" and in 19:21 only ויאכלו וישתו "they ate and drank," without using the term משתה. This may be another indication that Lot is giving his guests special treatment, more than customary under such circumstances. The conclusion can then be drawn that the narrator is stressing the special honor Lot bestows upon his guests.[70]

43:16), as does Abraham's meal; see also Judg 19:5–8. On mealtimes, usual and special occasions, see Borowski, *Daily Life,* 74.

64. More properly round, flat loaves of *pita*, "Syrian bread," but not unleavened bread; see "עגה," *HALOT* 2:784. With wife Sarah's assistance, Abraham can offer tastier bread than can Lot.

65. On the evening meal, see Judg 19:19: "bread and wine"; v. 21: "and [they] ate and drank"; and see Borowski, *Daily Life,* 66, 74.

66. See, e.g., Gen 26:30 (Isaac for King Abimelech and his courtiers); 2 Sam 3:20 (David for Abner).

67. See, e.g., 1 Kgs 3:15 (King Solomon for his courtiers); Esth 5:6; 7:2, 7–8 (Queen Esther for King Ahasauerus and his courtier Haman).

68. See "משתה," *HALOT* 2:653.

69. "Bread was a major component of each meal" (Borowski, *Daily Life,* 74).

70. Gen. Rab. 50:4 claims that Lot had learned this from Abraham, by way of

We can see, then, that the type of refreshment offered and the manner of preparing it is dictated by time and circumstances and not by the personalities of the hosts. Both hosts offer the best refreshment possible under the circumstances.

1.5. The Angels' Mission

Abraham (Gen 18:10–16): [10]Then one said, "I will return to you next year, and your wife Sarah shall have a son!" Sarah was listening at the entrance of the tent, which was behind him. [11]Now Abraham and Sarah were old, advanced in years; Sarah had stopped having the periods of women. [12]And Sarah laughed to herself, saying, "Now that I am withered, am I to have enjoyment—with my husband so old?" [13]Then the LORD said to Abraham, "Why did Sarah laugh, saying, 'Shall I in truth bear a child, old as I am?' [14]Is anything too wondrous for the LORD? I will return to you at the time next year, and Sarah shall have a son." [15]Sarah lied, saying, "I did not laugh," for she was frightened. But He replied, "You did laugh." [16]The men set out from there and looked down toward Sodom, Abraham walking with them to see them off.

Lot (Gen 19:4–13): [4]They had not yet lain down, when the townspeople, the men of Sodom, young and old—all the people to the last man—gathered about the house. [5]And they shouted to Lot and said to him, "Where are the men who came to you tonight? Bring them out to us, that we may be intimate with them." [6]So Lot went out to them to the entrance, shut the door behind him, [7]and said, "I beg you, my friends, do not commit such a wrong. [8]Look, I have two daughters who have not known a man. Let me bring them out to you, and you may do to them as you please; but do not do anything to these men, since they have come under the shelter of my roof." [9]But they said, "Stand back! The fellow," they said, "came here as an alien, and already he acts the ruler! Now we will deal worse with you than with them." And they pressed hard against the person of Lot, and moved forward to break the door. [10]But the men stretched out their hands and pulled Lot into the house with them, and shut the door. [11]And the people who were at the entrance of the house, young and old, they struck with

---

belittling Lot's importance, but the word משתה does not appear in Genesis before this verse.

blinding light, so that they were helpless to find the entrance. ¹²Then the men said to Lot, "What else have you here? Sons-in-law, your sons and daughters, or anyone else that you have in the city—bring them out of this place. ¹³For we are about to destroy this place, because the outcry against them before the Lord has become so great that the Lord has sent us to destroy it." ¹⁴So Lot went out and spoke with his sons-in-law, who had married his daughters, and said, "Up, get out of this place, for the Lord is about to destroy the city," But he seemed to his sons-in-law as one who jests.

From here on the two narratives, which have developed up to now in parallel fashion, diverge sharply, and the "mirror-narrative" nature of Gen 19 can be seen more clearly: in each case both the mission and the resulting deportment of the angels are different.

The angels' visit to Abraham continues and ends on a relatively cheerful note. First of all, the heavenly guests bring good news: Sarah is about to conceive and bear a son (v. 10a), a just reward for so good a host, in the manner of the Ugaritic Aqht Epic.[71] It is only during the incident of Sarah's eavesdropping and her "little white lie" (vv. 10b–15) that the true identity of the guests is revealed.[72] Finally, the men rise to set off for Sodom, and Abraham, ever the good host, walks with them to see them off (v. 16), presumably as far as the junction with the road where he had spotted them in the first place—a happy ending as far as Abraham is concerned, but, as we know, it ends only the first part of the "split departure formula." The second part comes after God's revelation to Abraham of his plan to destroy Sodom and Gomorrah (v. 20) and with the final departure of the angels in v. 22a. This first stage of the narrative is immediately followed by Abraham's famous negotiations with the Lord over the fate of the cities (vv. 22b–33), with the final conclusion of the entire unit of the divine visit

---

71. See Avishur's studies, above n. 13.

72. Sarah laughed to herself, thinking the guests would not notice, as in any case she was standing behind them at the entrance to the tent with Abraham facing them; but the angels, being divine, could read her innermost thoughts. The MT reads והוא אחריו, "which [the tent] was behind him [the angel]." The Septuagint and Samaritan Pentateuch read והיא אחריו in 10b, which could be understood as either "she was behind him [the angel]" or "she was behind it [the entrance to the tent]." Either way, Sarah thought she was out of sight and no one could hear her either.

coming only in v. 33, with Yahweh's departure.⁷³ But this need not concern us here.

By contrast, the rest of the angels' visit with Lot (Gen 19:4–16) is dismal. Lot's house is surrounded and attacked by the inhabitants of Sodom (19:4–11). It is in this confrontation with the men of Sodom that Lot proves his mettle. When the Sodomites demand of Lot that he bring out the strangers so that the Sodomites might commit sodomy with them, Lot tries to protect his guests by going outside, shutting the door behind him and reasoning with the assailants. In doing so, he endangers himself. Moreover, to placate the assailants, Lot offers them his two virgin daughters—no small sacrifice at any time but even more so in a patriarchal, tribal society—but to no avail.

Both Lot and his daughters are saved by a literal *deus ex machina*: the two angels pull him back inside, shut the door, and blind the assailants. Only then does Lot become aware of the true nature of his guests. As in the angels' visit to Abraham, they make their divine identity known by performing a deed no human being could possibly do: in the former, by showing they knew Sarah had laughed to herself in silence while not physically visible (18:12–15);⁷⁴ in the latter, by blinding the Sodomites (19:11). This is further evidence of the mirror-nature of the two narratives, more so especially in view of the fact that Sarah is merely rebuked, while the Sodomites are physically incapacitated.

---

73. For a discussion of endings of narrative stages and final conclusions, see Bar-Efrat, *Narrative Art in the Bible*, 130–31 (Heb. 142–43).

74. See above, n. 72. The explanation that it was the announcement of the birth of a child (18:10b) that revealed to Abraham the true identity of his visitors appears to be incorrect. First, similar tidings are also brought by mortals, albeit divinely inspired ones (1 Sam 1:17; 2 Kgs 4:16; Isa 7:14). Second, it is only in v. 13 that the name Yahweh first appears (aside from the introductory v. 1), when the angel asks Abraham why Sarah laughed; so already August Dillmann, *Die Genesis* (5th ed.; KEHAT; Leipzig: Hirzel, 1886), 263. In all the verses in between, whenever one or all of the divine visitors speak, the verb ויאמר/1, "he/they said," appears without any subject. Westermann (*Genesis*, 2:341) claims that there should have been a reaction from Sarah to the angel's rebuke (18:15b) and that the reason that the Tetragrammaton appears in place of איש, "man" is that the messenger represents the one who sends him to deliver the message. This explanation is weak: a narrative can end without an expected reply to a pronouncement, whether the speaker is human, divine, or divinely inspired (see Gen 34:21; 1 Kgs 17:24; 21:29); and the name Yahweh, using Westermann's reasoning, should also have appeared in 18:10.

Then the angels announce that Sodom is about to be destroyed, and only Lot and his family are to be saved (vv. 11–13), a reward for his being the only righteous man in Sodom, and a parallel to Abraham's reward (a son) for his own praiseworthy behavior.

Lot is not taken seriously by his sons-in-law when he urges them to leave the city (19:14). In the end, Lot hesitates—what loving father and grandfather would willingly leave his married daughters and their children to their destruction—and the two angels have to literally drag him and his family outside the city walls (19:15–16).

The verses that have been chosen to end both sections, Gen 18:16 and 19:14, have not been chosen arbitrarily,[75] as in each case they end stages, or acts, in the narratives. In the transitional verse 18:16 (with its completion in 22a), the angels end their visit with Abraham in which they announced the birth of a son and heir, with two heading toward Sodom and one remaining to announce its destruction to Abraham (18:22b).[76]

In 19:13 the angels have likewise ended their visit with Lot, with the announcement of the impending destruction of Sodom. In 19:14 there is a change of venue (as in 18:16, 22a), with Lot leaving his house to make hurried preparations for the flight of his family.

Abraham is not called upon to prove himself in the same way as Lot, so we cannot know what he might have done in Lot's place. However, it is

---

75. Though there has been general agreement about the ending of the "hospitality" and "angels' mission" sections of the Abraham narrative (18:1–8 and 18:9–16) scholars have delineated various borders for the parallel sections in Gen 19. Many hold for 19:1–3 and 19:4–11; see, e.g., Gunkel, *Genesis*, 208; Skinner, *Genesis*, 307; Simpson, "The Book of Genesis," 627; Speiser, *Genesis*, 136–37; Westermann, *Genesis*, 2:362. Sarna (*Genesis*, 134–36) opts for 19:1–5 and 6–11, while von Rad (*Das erste Buch Mose*, 170–71) splits the two sections into three: 19:1–5, 6–8, 9–14.

76. In traditional Jewish sources and commentaries, each angel is sent to perform one mission: the first angel is sent to announce to Abraham the birth of a child, while the other two continue on to Sodom, one to destroy Sodom and the other to save Lot; see, e.g., b. B. Metziʻa 86b; Gen. Rab. 49:32; Ibn Ezra on Gen 18:1 (Cohen, *Mikraʾot Gedolot*, 1a:160); Rashbam on 18:16.

Closest to the traditional Jewish approach is Gunkel (*Genesis*, 199–200), who thinks all three are divine messengers of equal rank. Some critical commentators view one of the angels as either God or an angel of superior rank, and the other two as his attendants; see Dillmann, *Die Genesis*, 261; von Rad, *Das erste Buch Mose*, 199; Speiser, *Genesis*, 138; Sarna, *Genesis*, 129. Westermann (*Genesis*, 2:336, 366) takes no notice of the difference in numbers, preferring instead to stress the narrative function of the angels.

instructive that the narrator has chosen to mention two different details, and not merely one, which point to Lot's readiness to make any effort to protect his guests, who are, after all, strangers: 1) when going out to converse with the Sodomites, he shuts the door behind him (19:6); 2) he is willing to sacrifice his two virgin daughters (19:8). This cannot be by chance.

Moreover, Lot offers up his daughters to the Sodomites not to save himself but his guests. We are afforded with a parallel to Gen 22:1–19, but, as in reflection stories, with contrasts: Abraham is willing to sacrifice his son because of a divine command; Lot offers up his daughters under no divine imperative and with no divine guidance. In addition, then, to the possibility that Gen 19:1–11 is a reflection of 22:1–19, is this not evidence that Lot was a better host than Abraham?

No matter that, in the end, the saver had to be saved—by the angels. Lot's intentions were certainly praiseworthy, and he cannot be blamed for having been one man against many.

3. Conclusions

In conclusion, a reflection- or mirror-structure is displayed in the narratives about the hospitality to strangers displayed by Abraham (Gen 18:1–16) and Lot (Gen 19:1–14). In both stories the angels come to make an important pronouncement: in the former, a happy one; in the latter, a frightening one. In both stories the protagonists display great generosity towards their guests and each is rewarded for his generosity, Abraham with a son and Lot with his life and that of his daughters. In both stories the protagonists exit the scene with the angels. Abraham, of his own volition, accompanies his guests as they leave his home, where he had received them so warmly. Lot's guests drag him out of his home, where he had received them so warmly.

Bibliography

Abravanel, Isaac. *Commentary on the Torah* [Hebrew]. 5 vols. in 3. Jerusalem: Sons of Arbil, 1964.

Alter, Robert. *The Five Books of Moses: A Translation with Commentary*. New York: Norton, 2004.

Avishur, Yitzhak. "The Angels' Visit with Abraham and Its Parallels in Ugaritic Literature" [Hebrew]. Pages 121–22 in *Genesis*. Edited by Moshe Weinfeld. Olam haTanakh; Tel-Aviv: Revivim 1993.

———. "The Narrative of Abraham the Host (Genesis 18:1–16a): The Literary Structure and Ugaritic Parallel (CTA 17 [2 Aqht] V: 4–31)." Pages 57–74 in *Studies in Biblical Narrative: Style, Structure, and the Ancient Near Eastern Literary Background*. Tel Aviv: Archaeological Center Publication, 1999. Originally published in Hebrew in *Beth Mikra* 32 (1987): 166–77.

Bar-Efrat, Shimeon. *Narrative Art in the Bible*. Translated by Dorothea Shefer-Vanson. JSOTSup 70. Sheffield: Almond Press, 1989. Originally published in Hebrew as *The Art of Narration in the Bible*. 2nd ed. Tel Aviv: Sifriyat Po'alim, 1984.

Becker, Hans-Jürgen, ed. *Avot de-Rabbi Natan: Synoptische Edition beider Versionen*. Tübingen: Mohr Siebeck, 2006.

Borowski, Oded. *Daily Life in Biblical Times*. SBLABS 5. Atlanta: Society of Biblical Literature, 2003.

Bowie, Walter Russell. "The Book of Genesis: Exposition." *IB* 1:437–829.

Buber, Salomon, ed. *Midrash Tanhuma haQadum vehaYashan* [Hebrew]. 3 vols. Vilna: Widow Rom & Sons, 1885.

Cassuto, Umberto. *A Commentary on the Book of Genesis: From Noah to Abraham*. Translated by Israel Abrahams. 2 vols. Jerusalem: Magnes, 1964 Originally published in Hebrew as Moshe David Cassuto, *A Commentary on the Book of Genesis: From Noah to Abraham*. 2 vols. Jerusalem: Magnes, 1949.

Cohen, Menahem ed. *Mikra'ot Gedolot haKeter* [Hebrew]. 9 vols. Ramat Gan, Bar-Ilan University, 1992–2007.

Deem, Ariella. "Cupboard Love: The Story of Amnon and Tamar" [Hebrew]. *Hasifrut/Literature* 28 (1979): 100–107.

Dillmann, August. *Die Genesis*. 5th ed. KEHAT. Leipzig: Hirzel, 1886.

Eisenstein, Judah David, ed. *Otzar Midrashim* [Hebrew]. 2 vols. New York: Judah David Eisenstein, 1915.

Fox, Everett. *The Five Books of Moses: Genesis, Exodus, Leviticus, Numbers, Deuteronomy: A New Translation with Introductions, Commentary, and Notes*. New York: Schocken, 1995.

Gelander, Shamai. *Studies in the Book of Genesis* [Hebrew]. 3 vols. Ra'anana: Open University, 2009.

Gunkel, Hermann. *Genesis*. 3rd ed. Göttingen: Vandenhoeck & Ruprecht, 1910. Translated into English by Mark E. Biddle as *Genesis*. Macon, Ga.: Mercer University Press, 1997.

Herzog, Ze'ev. *Das Stadttor in Israel und in den Nachbarländern*. Mainz am Rhein: von Zabern, 1986. Originally published in Hebrew as "The City Gate in Eretz Israel and the Neighbouring Countries." Ph.D. diss., Tel-Aviv University, 1986.

Horovitz, Hayyim Shaul, ed. *Sifre de-ve Rav* [Hebrew]. Jerusalem: Wahrmann, 1966.

Katzenellenbogen, Mordechai Leib, ed. *Torat Hayyim* [Hebrew]. 5 vols. Jerusalem: Mossad Harav Kook, 1986–1993.

Kiel, Yehuda. *Genesis*. 3 vols. Da'at Miqra. Jerusalem: Mossad Harav Kook, 2000.

Levine, Nachman. "Sarah/Sodom: Birth, Destruction, and Synchronic Transaction." *JSOT* 31 (2006): 131–46.

Margalioth, Mordechai, ed. *Leviticus Rabbah*. 5 vols. in 2. Jerusalem: Jewish Thelogical Seminary of America, 1993.

Meyer, Eduard. *Die Israeliten und ihre Nachbarstamme*. Halle an der Saale: Niemeyer, 1906.
Miqra'ot Gedolot: The Five Books of the Torah. 5 vols. New York: Hevrat Tanakh, 1959.
Peleg, Yitzhak (Itzik). "Was Lot a Good Host?" [Hebrew]. *Mo'ed* 18 (2008): 22–41.
Rad, Gerhard von. *Das erste Buch Mose*. 9th ed. ATD 2/4. Göttigen: Vandenhoeck & Ruprecht, 1972.
Rudin-O'Brasky, Talia. *The Patriarchs in Hebron and Sodom (Genesis 18–19)* [Hebrew]. Jerusalem: Hotsa'at Simor, 1982.
Safren, Jonathan D. "Balaam and Abraham." *VT* 38 (1988): 105–13.
Sarna, Nahum M. *Genesis*. JPSTC. Philadelphia: Jewish Publication Society, 1989.
Schechter, Solomon, ed. *Avot de-Rabi Natan*. New York: Bet ha-Midrash le-Rabanim be-Amerikah, 1997.
Seeligmann, Isac Leo. "Hebräische Erzählung und die biblische Geschichtsschreibung." *TZ* 18 (1962): 305–25.
Simpson, Cuthbert A. "The Book of Genesis: Introduction and Exegesis." *IB* 1:437–829.
Skinner, John. *A Critical and Exegetical Commentary on Genesis*. 2nd ed. ICC. Edinburgh: T&T Clark, 1930.
Speiser, Ephraim A. *Genesis*. AB 1. Garden City, N.Y.: Doubleday, 1964.
Theodor, J., and Chanoch Albeck, eds. *Midrash Bereshit Rabba*. Jerusalem: Wahrmann, 1965.
Weinfeld, Moshe. "The Figure of Lot" [Hebrew]. Page 127 in *Genesis*. Edited by Moshe Weinfeld. Olam haTanakh. Tel-Aviv: Revivim 1993.
———. "Let a Little Water Be Brought." Page 122 in *Genesis*. Edited by Moshe Weinfeld. Olam haTanakh. Tel-Aviv: Revivim 1993.
Westermann, Claus. *Genesis*. 3 vols. BK 1. Neukirchen-Vluyn: Neukirchener, 1981.
Wood, Joyce Louise Rilett. "When Gods Were Men." Pages 285–98 in *From Babel to Babylon: Essays on Biblical History and Literature in Honour of Brian Peckham*. Edited by Joyce Rilett Wood et al. LHB/OTS 455. New York: T&T Clark, 2006.
Zakovitch, Yair. "Reflection Story: Another Dimension for the Valuation of Characters in Biblical Narrative" [Hebrew]. *Tarbiz* 54 (1985): 165–76.
———. *Through the Looking Glass: Reflection Stories in the Bible* [Hebrew]. Tel Aviv: HaKibbutz Hameuhad, 1995.
Zuckermandel, Moses Samuel, ed. *Tosefta, Mischna und Boraitha in ihrem Verhältnis zu einander*. 2 vols. Frankfurt am Main: Kauffmann, 1908–1909.

Hospitality and Hostility: Reading Genesis 19 in Light of 2 Samuel 10 (and Vice Versa)

Nathan MacDonald

Genesis 19 and 2 Samuel 10: An Unexplored Parallel

The parallel between Gen 19 and Judg 19 has often been noted by interpreters of both passages. In both texts strangers arriving in a foreign town at dusk are given hospitality by a resident alien. The townsmen threaten to disturb the generous intents of the resident alien by requiring to "know" the strangers. The hapless host offers the females present in the house as an alternative distraction for the townsmen. Ultimately the town and its inhabitants are destroyed. The parallel in Judg 19 when pursued results in a portrayal of the Sodomites in extremely negative terms, which is not inappropriate given the wider context of Gen 18–19. The development of the plot in Judg 19—with its brutal rape of the Levite's concubine and the distribution of her body among the Israelite tribes—places a particular emphasis on sexual violence and this has been important historically for the interpretation of Gen 19.[1]

It is not my intention to argue that we neglect this significant parallel; rather, I would like to make a brief plea for broadening the intertextual

---

1. "Judging by even the most recent commentaries and articles on the narrative (leaving aside the social and cultural representatives thereof), the dominant and indeed still somewhat entrenched paradigm governing its reading remains a (homo)sexual one ... it is possible and even desirable to read the narrative in a manner whereby same-gender sexuality is not the dominant paradigm. ... If one reads the narrative from the perspective of the apparently parallel text in Judges 19, as many do, one will be likely to deal with the data provided by the text in a different manner" (Brian Doyle, "'Knock, Knock, Knockin' on Sodom's Door': The Function of פתח/דלת in Genesis 18–19," *JSOT* 28 [2004]: 433).

conversation partners. Specifically, I want to make the case for the inclusion of 2 Sam 10 in the interpretation of Gen 19. That this might be an interesting innerbiblical parallel has not gone entirely unnoticed, but such observations are rare and are almost always restricted to footnotes or comments made in passing. Fields, for example, notes that the verbal root הפך is used of a city in 2 Sam 10:3. "It may be argued, therefore, that there was an intentional linguistic/narrative connection between the Sodom story and the David/Hanun episode."[2] Unfortunately, he does not pursue this suggestive observation. Similarly, in his discussion of hospitality and hostility Morschauser observes that in 2 Sam 10 David's messengers arrive at the city and are molested by the Ammonites. Morschauser makes no arguments that there are strong intertextual resonances between the passages; rather 2 Sam 10 is one of a number of texts that show there was no tradition in Israel of unqualified hospitality. Foreigners arriving in a town were often treated with suspicion.[3]

Since Gen 19 has received a great deal of interpretative attention, especially in recent years, the case for discovering a significant parallel in 2 Sam 10 needs to be made. The possibility that such a parallel might have been overlooked is at least strengthened by the fact that 2 Sam 10 is judged to be relatively unengaging by most interpreters. In his recent commentary Campbell argues that 2 Sam 10 functions only to set the context for the story of David and Bathsheba.

> The function of this chapter in relation to the narrative that follows needs discussion. What follows in chs. 11–12 is a story about David's behavior with a woman and her husband and its implications for the future of David's family. The story is set within the parameters of a campaign against the Ammonites and a siege of their capital. ... What 2 Sam 10 does is provide a context within which the siege of Rabbah, the chief city of the Ammonites can be understood. Whether a listener or reader

---

2. Weston W. Fields, *Sodom and Gomorrah: History and Motif in Biblical Narrative* (JSOTSup 231; Sheffield: Sheffield Academic Press, 1997), 83 n. 60. Fields's observation occurs in a discussion of Josh 2 as a parallel to Gen 19, where Fields notes that Josh 2 and 2 Sam 10 concern the possible arrival of enemy spies. It is possible, he speculates, that Josh 2 is in an intermediary position between Gen 19 and 2 Sam 10. In my view, there is a stronger intertextual relationship between Gen 19 and 2 Sam 10 than between Gen 19 and Josh 2.

3. Scott Morschauser, "'Hospitality', Hostiles and Hostages: On the Legal Background to Genesis 19.1–9," *JSOT* 27 (2003): 470.

needs this understanding to engage with the story is doubtful. Nevertheless, it is there.[4]

Much of 2 Sam 10 is taken up with reports of battles with the Ammonites and Arameans such that Fokkelmann comments, "Chapter 10 is one of the very few pieces in I/II Sam. which is not absorbing to a high degree, and this applies only after v. 6."[5]

Our particular concern is with the first five verses. In these verses the hostility between David and his Ammonite neighbors is attributed to a diplomatic *faux pas* by the new king of Ammon, Hanun. David sends messengers to offer their condolences to Hanun on the death of his father, and to renew the friendship between Ammon and Israel. Hanun suspects that the overtures of his more powerful neighbor have a different purpose: the spying of the land. The scene is set for hostilities when Hanun humiliates David's messengers who return to Israel in disgrace.

The first link between the two passages as observed by Fields is the use of הפך. The verb is used of the destruction of the cities of Sodom and Gomorrah on a number of occasions: Gen 19:21, 25, 29; Jer 20:16 (כערים); Deut 29:22 (סדם ועמרה אדמה וצבוים); Isa 13:19; Jer 49:18; 50:40 (סדם ועמרה); Amos 4:11; Lam 4:6 (סדם). It is only otherwise used with a city as the object in Jonah 3:4, which is undoubtedly based on the use with Sodom, and here in 2 Sam 10:3 (= 1 Chr 19:3). The meaning of הפך in 2 Sam 10:3 is not without its difficulties. At the beginning of the twentieth century Ehrlich observed that "ולהפכה does not mean 'in order to destroy it', as the expression is usually rendered, for הפך can only have YHWH as the subject in this sense."[6] In addition, the parallel text in 1 Chr 19:3 reorders the wording of 2 Sam 10 so that the relevant actions now read לחקר ולהפך ולרגל. On the conventional translation, this would result in "spying" (רגל) following the overthrow of the city. Ehrlich consequently suggests that הפך must be understood as a synonym of חקר. Ehrlich's suggestion is hardly compelling, especially since it entails proposing an otherwise unattested meaning for הפך. Three observations can be made

---

[4]. Antony F. Campbell, *2 Samuel* (FOTL; Grand Rapids: Eerdmans, 2005), 93.

[5]. J. P. Fokkelmann, *Narrative Art and Poetry in the Books of Samuel: A Full Interpretation Based on Stylistic and Structural Analysis; Vol 1, King David (II Samuel 9–20 and I Kings 1–2)* (Assen: Van Gorcum, 1981), 42.

[6]. Arnold B. Ehrlich, *Randglossen zur hebräischen Bibel* (7 vols.; Hildesheim: Olms, 1968), 3:294.

in response to Ehrlich. First, as we have already seen, הפך is used with the sense "to overthrow, destroy" on the other occasions when a city is the object of the verb. It is gratuitous to suggest the word has another sense. Second, the Chronicler is sometimes given to altering word order (e.g., 2 Chr 23:7; 25:4),[7] and the parallel of 1 Chr 19:3 is complicated by a text-critical problem, for ולהפך is absent from the earliest translations (Greek, Syriac).[8] Third, the cognate מהפכה is used in Isa 1:7 with a human subject: זרים "strangers," though this text is not without problems of its own.[9]

The second link between Gen 19 and 2 Sam 10 is that both stories concern the Ammonites in some way, although the role of Ammon's representative is different in each of the stories. Lot is, of course, the ancestor of both the Ammonites and the Moabites as the concluding story of Gen 19 relates. He offers hospitality to the two strangers and seeks to defend his guests against being interrogated and humiliated by the men of Sodom. In 2 Sam 10, on the other hand, Lot's descendant is inhospitable to David's messengers, taking on the role of the Sodomites.

Third, in both stories foreign messengers, possibly two in both cases,[10] arrive at the city with the inhabitants uncertain about their intentions. The result is confusion and miscommunication, with the hint or reality of sexual shaming and humiliation. In Gen 19 the men of the town surround

---

7. T. Sugimoto, "The Chronicler's Techniques in Quoting Samuel-Kings," *AJBI* 16 (1990): 38.

8. Οὐκ ὅπως ἐξερευνήσωσιν τὴν πόλιν τοῦ κατασκοπῆσαι τὴν γῆν ἤλθον παῖδες αὐτοῦ πρός σέ might well suggest that the Greek translator had the same text as MT but that he recognized ולהפך as difficult and composed a suitable parallel to κατασκοπῆσαι τὴν γῆν.

9. It has often been suggested that זרים be emended to סדם (defended recently by H. G. M. Williamson, *Isaiah 1–5* [ICC; London: T&T Clark, 2006], 50), though some recent commentators have argued against emendation, finding in v. 7 a deliberate wordplay that anticipates the reference to Sodom in v. 9. Thus Watts writes, "Since the line is a deliberate connection between v. 7 with which MT's reading fits and v. 9 where סדם fits, the very tension in the phrase should be seen as intentional and MT's reading sustained" (John D. W. Watts, *Isaiah 1–33* [WBC 24; Waco, Tex.: Word, 1985], 14).

10. From a comprehensive analysis of biblical and ancient Near Eastern evidence, Meier concludes that it was usual for messengers to be sent individually. "There is no justification for the notion that normally two messengers were sent on missions. This might hold true for dangerous missions where one repeatedly does find two messengers in action" (Sam A. Meier, *The Messenger in the Ancient Semitic World* [HSM 45; Atlanta: Scholars Press, 1988], 129). David's messengers in 2 Sam 10 are clearly plural, so it is likely that there were two.

Lot's house and demand that his guests be brought out so that "we may know them" (ונדעה אתם; v. 5). As Pirson and others have argued, there are no decisive indicators that the townsmen are demanding sexual intercourse. Instead, they want to interrogate the men, since they possibly represent a threat to the town just as Joshua's spies were a threat to Jericho.[11] Lot, however, hears what the townsfolk say as an intent to sexually humiliate his guests. He interprets "know" as a demand for sexual intercourse. In exchange he offers his daughters: "Look, I have two daughters that have not known a man [לא־ידעו איש]" (v. 8).[12] If Lot does mishear his neighbors, this would not be surprising since as I have shown this is an important feature of the exchange between Abraham and Yhwh over the fate of Sodom in Gen 18.[13] In 2 Sam 10 David's messengers arrive in order to confirm the existing peaceful relations between Israel and Ammon under the new king. Advised by his princes, the youthful Hanun suspects David has different motives. He communicates his suspicions through the sexual humiliation of David's messengers. "Hanun seized David's servants, shaved off half of their beards, cut their garments in half to the buttocks and expelled them" (2 Sam 10:4). McCarter suggests that "removal of the beard symbolically deprives a man of his masculinity" and the cutting and exposure of the buttocks "suggests symbolic castration."[14] If this is correct, it would form a closer parallel to the symbolic feminization intended through the Sodomites' penetration of Lot's guests.[15]

Fourth, in both cases the messengers come as emissaries from a greater power. The greater power is not necessarily ill-disposed toward

---

11. Ron Pirson, "Does Lot Know about *Yada'*?" (paper delivered at the SBL International Meeting, Edinburgh, 3 July 2006; see pp. 203–13 in this volume); Morschauser, "Hospitality."

12. Pirson (ibid.) is too hesitant at this point: "The sexual connotations of the verb ידע possibly play a role in Gen 19:8, in which Lot presents his own daughters to the crowd, but this is not entirely certain, even though I have included the verse in the list of texts in which the sexual aspect is present."

13. Nathan MacDonald, "Listening to Abraham—Listening to Yhwh: Justice and Mercy in Genesis 18.16–33," *CBQ* 66 (2004): 25–43.

14. P. Kyle McCarter, *II Samuel: A New Translation with Introduction and Commentary* (AB 9; Garden City, N.Y.: Doubleday, 1984), 270. R. P. Gordon, on the other hand, sees the actions as parodies of mourning rituals (*1 and 2 Samuel: A Commentary* [Exeter: Paternoster, 1986], 250).

15. Cf. Tracy M. Lemos, "Shame and Mutilation of Enemies in the Hebrew Bible," *JBL* 125 (2006): 225–41, esp. 232–36.

the recipient, but the humiliation of the messengers, whether attempted or realized, results in the wrath of the greater power and, ultimately, the destruction of the city. In Gen 19 the destruction of the cities of the plain is by no means certain. According to 18:20–21 Yhwh and his messengers have come down in order to ascertain whether the outcry that has come up to heaven is correct. There is much at stake in the conversation between Yhwh and Abraham, as also in the parallel encounter down in Sodom.[16] In 2 Sam 10 Hanun receives men that come bearing David's message of sympathy. Hanun suspects an agonistic motive, though the narrator wishes to emphasize that David's actions are a genuine expression of *hesed*. In both Gen 19 and 2 Sam 10 the abuse of the messengers is a sufficient *casus belli*.

Genesis 19 in Light of 2 Samuel 10

What difference might such a parallel text make for interpreting Gen 19? In the first instance, I think it provides verification for some of the suggestions that have been made about this text by other interpreters in the last ten years. First, within the context of ancient Palestine it is conceivable that the people of Sodom may have had justified fears about strangers arriving late in the day. Their request to know more about the visitors is quite explicable. Second, the question of whether homosexual intercourse is the intent of the men of Sodom is surprisingly difficult to answer. It does not have to be implied in the request "to know the men," but sexual humiliation—including the deprivation of markers of masculinity (whether by shaving beards or anal intercourse)—appears to be a possible action against suspected spies. In the light of 2 Sam 10, Lot's suspicion that this "knowing" may entail the sexual humiliation of his guests is not without some justification. In this case, though, it might be misjudged and appears to be interpreted as an affront by the men of Sodom (19:9). Certainly, the men of Sodom do not perceive the arrival of the two strangers as simply a possible outlet for homosexual desires. Third, and consequently, the writers of Genesis connect the wickedness of the men of Sodom much more to their hostility expressed toward the stranger and their lack of hospitality. Lot and Abraham are the godly paradigm—as already well perceived by the writer to the Hebrews (Heb 13:2); the abuse of Lot's guests is an

---

16. On Gen 18:16–33, see MacDonald, "Listening to Abraham." It is only after the men of Sodom attempt to force their way into Lot's house that the messengers announce the imminent destruction of the city.

extreme expression of the Sodomites' inhospitality, just as was Hanun's conduct toward David's messengers.

Fourth, both stories can be viewed as a reflection on traditions about the lack of hospitality shown by the non-Israelites who live on the other side of the Jordan and around the Dead Sea. Such traditions provide a way of defining Israelite identity as generous and hospitable, while also forming expectations about the Transjordanian "other."[17] These traditions are reflected in a variety of different places in the Old Testament. Thus, at the end of the forty years' sojourn in the wilderness, Israel experiences inhospitality at the hands of her future neighbors, including the descendants of Lot. According to Deut 23:4–5 no Ammonite or Moabite is to be allowed into the assembly of Yhwh even to the tenth generation "because they did not meet you with food and water on your journey out of Egypt." Some of the detailed textual connections, however, suggest that we have more than a common tradition; rather, there is a textual link between Gen 19 and 2 Sam 10.

The book of Genesis offers a prehistory of Israel in which later social, political, and religious realities are reflected, but in ways that are often not straightforward. Genesis 18 and 19 are typical in this respect and the stories about Lot and Abraham are somehow paradigmatic for their descendants. In Gen 18 we are given an account of the overwhelming generosity of Abraham to the three guests that arrive at his tent in the middle of the day. Abraham bows to his guests, offers them water for their feet and has a meal of curds, milk, and meat prepared. Hospitable Abraham will be succeeded by descendants who are to be equally hospitable to the stranger and the poor (cf. Deut 12:18–19; 14:28–29; 16:9–15; 26:1–15). Abraham then intercedes for Sodom. As I have sought to argue elsewhere, this is a dialogue in which Abraham learns the way of Yhwh, a way characterized by mercy. The divine pedagogy proceeds in an unusual manner as Yhwh teaches Abraham his way through a conversation that moves backwards and forwards with Abraham never plumbing the depths of God's generosity.[18] Through this conversation Yhwh instills the values that are to characterize Abraham's descendants (18:17–19).

Abraham's generous hospitality is paralleled in the reception of the angelic visitors in Sodom. This reception includes the aggression of

---

17. See Nathan MacDonald, *Not Bread Alone: The Uses of Food in the Old Testament* (Oxford: Oxford University Press, 2008), 70–99.
18. MacDonald, "Listening to Abraham."

the men of Sodom and the hospitality of Lot. The response of the men of Sodom is clearly meant as a strong contrast to Abraham's generousness. It has already been foreshadowed in the churlishness of the king of Sodom after Abram's defeat of the five kings. While Melchizedek recognizes Abram and brings him bread and wine, the king of Sodom appears surly and Abram has to extract food from him for the nourishment of his companions (Gen 14). The case of Lot is somewhat more ambiguous and scholars have long disagreed about whether Lot's hospitality would have been viewed as commendable or deplorable.[19] Lot also bows down to the strangers and offers them water for their feet, but the meal he offers is only "unleavened bread." It seems to me that it is difficult to pronounce on this issue with confidence, but we should not assume that Lot has transgressed a code of hospitality. What is striking, then, is that in 2 Sam 10 Lot's descendant acts not like his ancestor, but like the Sodomites. Thus, while Abraham is learning mercy for the sake of his descendants, a lesson is being learnt that takes Lot and his descendants in the opposite direction. Lot and his family are learning how to be inhospitable from their neighbors, the people of Sodom.

2 Samuel 10 in Light of Genesis 19

In developing the parallels between 2 Sam 10 and Gen 19 I have highlighted the centrality of hospitality, yet 2 Sam 10 is characterized not by the presence of hospitality but by its absence. Have we flattened the specificities of the text of 2 Sam 10 by bringing it into dialogue with Gen 19? To counter this objection it is important to observe that the dynamics of hospitality, hostility, and misunderstanding are also present in the stories that surround 2 Sam 10. Thus the absence of hospitality in 2 Sam 10 really is an absence, a gaping hole that would have struck the earliest readers. Thus, when we read 2 Sam 10 in the light of Gen 19 we become more attentive to the fact that 2 Sam 10 belongs to a pattern of stories.

The first story of hospitality is found in 2 Sam 9. David seeks out the last survivors from Saul's house to whom he might show חסד. The use of חסד in both 9:1, 3 and 10:2 draws both stories together. The kindness

---

19. See, *inter alia*, Stuart Lasine, "Guest and Host in Judges 19: Lot's Hospitality in an Inverted World," *JSOT* 29 (1984): 37–59; T. D. Alexander, "Lot's Hospitality: A Clue to His Righteousness," *JBL* 104 (1985): 289–91; Victor H. Matthews, "Hospitality and Hostility in Genesis 19 and Judges 19," *BTB* 22 (1992): 3–11.

that David will show is to return to Mephibosheth his grandfather's lands and to give him a place at the king's table. The king's kindness is shown in an act of generous hospitality. The conversations between David and Ziba and then between David and Mephibosheth are no doubt intended to keep the ancient readers and hearers in suspense. Is David genuinely interested in showing חסד to the house of Saul? Will he keep the promise he gave to Jonathan, or will the pressing constraints of *Realpolitik* require that he eliminate the last members of Saul's household? No such tension exists for Mephibosheth, who is not privy to David's oath, and clearly comes to David expecting the worst (vv. 6, 8). Thus, in the first story hostility is expected, but hospitality intended and delivered.

The second story is 2 Sam 10. In this story it is Hanun who is to show hospitality in response to David's generosity. Hanun misunderstands the gesture and interprets it as a hostile act. What was intended as a generous act is transformed into the grounds for hostility.

At first blush the third story in 2 Sam 11, the story of David and Bathsheba, is not obviously about hospitality. David at home in Jerusalem sees the attractive wife of Uriah the Hittite. Taking opportunity of his absence on the battlefield he sleeps with her. When she discovers that she is pregnant, he arranges for Uriah to be killed on the battlefield. There are, however, various indications that this is a story about hospitality, including subtle links to other hospitality stories.

First, when David sees Bathsheba he sends messengers. The sending of messengers provides a parallel to David's sending messengers to Hanun (10:2).[20] Second, David shows hospitality to Uriah, the foreigner, when he returns from battle. On this occasion, however, the elements familiar from Gen 19 and even Judg 19 are in a confused order: the sexual intercourse (between David and Bathsheba) takes place before the hospitality event; David tells Uriah to go home and wash *his own* feet;[21] third, he only

---

20. The expressions in MT 1 Chr 19:2 and 2 Sam 11:4 are identical: וישלח דוד מלאכים. In MT 1 Sam 10:2, on the other hand, the text reads וישלח דוד לנחמו ביד־עבדיו.

21. The "wash your feet" in v. 8 is often understood as either a ritual act at the end of a soldier's vow of sexual abstinence or, more frequently, as a euphemism for sexual relations (Gordon, *1 and 2 Samuel*, 254). Neither of the two references to "washing the feet" that are usually taken as a euphemism (2 Sam 11:8; Song 5:3) are decisive proof that this is the case. While not denying the possibility of a euphemism, it might simply be an expression for making oneself comfortable (Ehrlich, *Randglossen*, 3:296). We

offers food and drink when Uriah fails to go home and sleep with his wife. David's persistence in keeping Uriah in Jerusalem is reminiscent of the story of the Levite and his concubine.[22] As with the other stories in 2 Sam 9–10 David's intent and what is understood by the recipient of his generosity are quite different. David intends for Uriah to sleep with his wife and cover David's tracks. To all other eyes Uriah appears to be delivering a message from the battlefield and receiving the generous hospitality of a grateful liege. In some sense though, his remaining in Jerusalem for a prolonged period makes no sense (vv. 10–12). Third, when Nathan comes to deliver his judgment against David he chooses to use a story of hospitality. Again, David is placed in the role of the generous host. Thus, in the story of David and Bathsheba hospitality is originally intended by David and interpreted as such by the perplexed Uriah, but eventually hospitality turns to hostility.

What we find in 2 Sam 9–11 are three stories about Davidic generosity and hospitality. Second Samuel 9 presents a generous and hospitable David, while 2 Sam 10 has a generous David being met by a hostile Ammonite. In the final story, 2 Sam 11, David appears to be generous and hospitable, but his intent is hostile. I have suggested that in the story of Lot we find the prehistory of his descendants. Hanun's actions are evidence that he has learned from the conduct of Sodom. David, on the other hand, as Abraham's descendant shows his appropriation of the lessons of Gen 18 by acting generously and mercifully to Mephibosheth. But this is not the full story with David. But, how could it be? Hanun is not the only descendent of Lot in the story; David represents the other side of Lot's descendants through his Moabite ancestry. Thus, the stories of 2 Sam 9–11 are a subtle presentation of David's complex heritage: a descendant of Abraham but also the more tarnished line of Lot.

---

should also observe that the phrase is clearly attested a number of times in instances of hospitality (Gen 18:4; 19:2; 24:32; 43:24; Judg 19:21; 1 Sam 25:41).

22. In Judg 19 the Levite stays for three days and seeks to depart on the fourth. He is persuaded to stay another day and does not leave until late on the fifth day. Uriah stays one night, and David promises to keep him another day and send him back after that. It is unclear whether he does or whether David keeps him even longer. The issue turns about how וממחרת (2 Sam 11:12) is to be understood in relation to the surrounding clauses.

Bibliography

Alexander, T. D. "Lot's Hospitality: A Clue to His Righteousness." *JBL* 104 (1985): 289–91.
Campbell, Antony F. *2 Samuel*. FOTL. Grand Rapids: Eerdmans, 2005.
Doyle, Brian. "'Knock, Knock, Knockin' on Sodom's Door': The Function of דלת/ פתח in Genesis 18–19/" *JSOT* 28 (2004): 431–48.
Ehrlich, Arnold B. *Randglossen zur hebräischen Bibel*. 7 vols. Hildesheim: Olms, 1968.
Fields, Weston W. *Sodom and Gomorrah: History and Motif in Biblical Narrative*. JSOTSup 231. Sheffield: Sheffield Academic Press, 1997.
Fokkelmann, J. P. *Narrative Art and Poetry in the Books of Samuel: A Full Interpretation Based on Stylistic and Structural Analysis; Vol 1, King David (II Samuel 9–20 and I Kings 1–2)*. Assen: Van Gorcum, 1981.
Gordon, R. P. *1 and 2 Samuel: A Commentary*. Exeter: Paternoster, 1986.
Lasine, Stuart. "Guest and Host in Judges 19: Lot's Hospitality in an Inverted World." *JSOT* 29 (1984): 37–59.
Lemos, Tracy M. "Shame and Mutilation of Enemies in the Hebrew Bible." *JBL* 125 (2006): 225–41.
MacDonald, Nathan. "Listening to Abraham—Listening to Yhwh: Justice and Mercy in Genesis 18.16–33." *CBQ* 66 (2004): 25–43.
———. *Not Bread Alone: The Uses of Food in the Old Testament*. Oxford: Oxford University Press, 2008.
Matthews, Victor H. "Hospitality and Hostility in Genesis 19 and Judges 19." *BTB* 22 (1992): 3–11.
McCarter, P. Kyle. *II Samuel: A New Translation with Introduction and Commentary*. AB 9. Garden City, N.Y.: Doubleday, 1984.
Meier, Sam A. *The Messenger in the Ancient Semitic World*. HSM 45. Atlanta: Scholars Press, 1988.
Morschauser, Scott. "'Hospitality', Hostiles and Hostages: On the Legal Background to Genesis 19.1–9." *JSOT* 27 (2003): 461–85.
Ron Pirson, "Does Lot Know about *Yada*'?" Paper delivered at the SBL International Meeting, Edinburgh, 3 July 2006.
Sugimoto, T. "The Chronicler's Techniques in Quoting Samuel-Kings." *AJBI* 16 (1990): 30–70.
Watts, John D. W. *Isaiah 1–33*. WBC 24. Waco, Tex.: Word, 1985.
Williamson, H. G. M. *Isaiah 1–5*. ICC. London: T&T Clark, 2006.

Beyond Particularity and Universality: Reflections on Shadal's Commentary to Genesis 18–19

Harlan J. Wechsler

There is no doubt that the particular and the universal are two handles for getting hold of the biblical narrative. Chapters 18 and 19 of Genesis are an apt test case to see these perspectives in action. They may not be exclusive alternatives, however, even when they work together in the same story. Rather, they may merge into a combined phenomenon—a particular mission of the children of Abraham with a universal dimension to it.

I suggest this observation in response to the commentary on these two chapters by a still relatively unknown nineteenth-century Italian Jewish commentator and early master of the craft of the scientific study of Judaism, Rabbi Shmuel David Luzzatto. It is his exposition of Gen 18 and 19 that I would like to share with you.

Shadal

Rabbi Shmuel David Luzzatto is known by the acronym made from the first letters of his three names, Shadal. An Italian rabbi born in Trieste in 1800, he began his studies at the age of five. By eight, he was enamored of the book of Job, inspired by its ideas and its epic poetic style.[1] At nine, he began studying with Mordecai Isaac Cologna whom he later refers to as his principal teacher. Cologna taught him Mishnah, Hebrew grammar, and Bible with the commentaries of Rashi and David Kimhi. At about age

---

1. Morris B. Margolies, *Samuel David Luzzatto: Traditionalist Scholar* (New York: Ktav, 1979), 25.

ten, he began to study Talmud daily under Abraham Eliezer Halevi, chief rabbi of Trieste.

After Napoleon's conquest, when Trieste became part of the new Illyrian republic, the Talmud Torah was reorganized to include German, Italian, French, Latin, mathematics, geography, and history. By 1813, Shadal had become so seriously ill that he had to leave school permanently. From that point on, with the exception of his weekly Talmud study, he was an auto-didact, in both Jewish and secular subjects. Shadal's life was filled with constant trauma, familial, economic, and physical. He suffered the early loss of his mother, of his first wife, and of several children.

The revolution of 1848 brought the economic situation of the Italian Jewish communities into chaos, leading to decreased support for the *Collegio Rabbinico* which was his livelihood, and he was constantly threatened by penury. In 1850 he lost the sight in his left eye. By 1860, he completed the Italian translation of the Pentateuch, Haftarot, and most of the Five Scrolls. His health deteriorated further and as well as suffering from a difficult cough, he eventually approached total blindness. Even so, he devoted himself entirely to the preparation of Yehuda Halevi's Diwan. Shadal died on *Kol Nidre* night, the beginning of the Day of Repentance, September 30, 1865. The compilation of his commentary to the Torah was not published in Padua until 1871. So much for the rewards that accrue to the Lord's toiling servants.

The commentary is a compilation made by Shadal's friends and students. The Italian translation was part of the edition of the Pentateuch with Italian translation of the scriptural text that was published in 1871. It had to wait until 1965 until a separate Hebrew edition made it available to the Hebrew reading public.[2]

Luzzatto's commentary to the Pentateuch is unique in modern commentaries. It is classical and it is modern—classical in that it never ques-

---

2. Samuel David Luzzatto, *Commentary to the Pentateuch* [Hebrew] (Jerusalem: Horev, 1993). For a review of the probable history of the commentary's composition, see Daniel A. Klein's *The Book of Genesis: A Commentary by Shadal* (Northvale, N.J.: Aronson, 1998), xvi–xviii. Shadal's Italian translation of the Pentateuch was published in 1858. The commentary that later accompanied it in 1871 was in Hebrew, resulting in an interesting amalgamation of languages, considering that the text was used in synagogues. The Italian text brought some of the innovative thinking to the unlettered. The Hebrew text was for the learned. And since the Hebrew text was the product of seven more years of his thinking and writing, as well as being the result of his students' selections, it contains conclusions that differ from the Italian.

tions the essential integrity of the text as we have it, though it may quibble with minor details, and that the text is understood primarily from the text itself, and yet modern in that philology is an essential tool and that Shadal will accept or reject scientific hypotheses about why events unfold as they do. As a modern scholar, Shadal also rejects the need to interpret the text only within the confines of rabbinic literature.[3]

But Shadal was not a fundamentalist as we commonly use the term. Scholarship could lead to a deeper understanding of the *peshat*, the straightforward meaning of the text.[4] His commentary to Gen 18 and 19 is a perfect example. As a modern commentator, he takes note of Strabo, Tacitus, and others who comment on the destruction of Sodom.[5] Yet his principal interest is in describing the narrative purpose of the text and the way in which its elements work together to convey theological meanings.[6]

The Test of Hospitality

The unifying theme in Shadal's reading of the two chapters is the notion that both use hospitality as a test to measure certain universal principles central to the divine concern. God appears at the beginning of chapter 18 and by verse 2 we see that there are three men. The relation between God and the men is, of course, one of the intriguing rhetorical devices of the story, not clearly articulated but begging for interpretation. They are, in Shadal's traditional view, angels (מלאכים), divine messengers. But the human form in which they present themselves is, for Shadal, a necessary adjunct of the way in which the test will be carried out. Abraham addresses the leader and sometimes the assembled, immediately offering the strangers a noonday meal—an act of hospitality.

---

3. See Margolies, *Samuel David Luzzatto*, xi–xii.
4. While this is evident from reading the commentary, it is further described by Shadal himself. The Hebrew edition of the commentary is preceded by an introduction which had originally appeared in 1829: "A critical introduction to the text and commentary of the Scripture." This is a partial description of his methodology.
5. As does Nahum M. Sarna, for example, in *Understanding Genesis* (New York: Jewish Theological Seminary of America, 1966), 138.
6. Klein's English translation of Shadal's commentary to Genesis (*The Book of Genesis: A Commentary by Shadal*) opens it up for the English reader. While my translations from the Hebrew are all my own, the English reader can profitably read the commentary through Klein's translation.

Not only does Abraham run to extend favors to his guests—that is obvious—but there are other, less obvious hints about the extent of his hospitality. Shadal points out, for example, that Abraham tells Sarah to take three סאה (שלש סאים) of fine flour—about ninety cups in contemporary baking, a rather large amount. Noting the fact that Ramban finds this perplexing ("We don't know why he made so much bread for three people"), Shadal compares this seemingly superfluous fact to someone bringing many sacrificial offerings. The sheer quantity is an indication of the effort to please. Or, he suggests, perhaps Abraham invited others to the meal to extend yet greater honor to his guests. But since the text does not tell us anything about additional invitees, Shadal finally concludes that the bread was not all for current consumption. It was also food for the road, a useful gift to travelers who were being entertained today but who would also need provisions for tomorrow.

When, in verse 16, the men move on, Abraham walks with them as they depart. To Shadal, Abraham accompanies them דרך כבוד, as a way of showing honor and respect to them. Abraham therefore was not just out for a walk. There was meaning in these actions, for accompanying someone conveys respect.

Concern for the other is also illustrated by what we learn of God's behavior. The Lord says: "Do I hide from Abraham what I am doing?" For Shadal, this verse and the two that follow are not the words of the angel to Abraham but Scripture sharing an aside—what God has said to himself beforehand, a short soliloquy flashback to some divine thinking. But what is the ethical meaning of telling us that God considers sharing his inner life with Abraham? This, too, is a sign of respect and, even more, of affection, דרך חיבה and כבוד, according to Shadal, the way of affection and honor. As Shadal goes on to say: "Like a man who tells his close friend what is in his heart to do, allowing him to express then his own opinion."

Furthermore, the end of the Lord's soliloquy, verse 21—"I will go down to see whether they have acted altogether according to the outcry that has reached me; if not, I will take note"—leads to his conversation with Abraham. That, too, is an indication of honor and respect (and I will return to that because of its *particularistic* significance). It is as if this description reflects modern management techniques, involving subordinates, particularly a respected and favored subordinate, in the decision-making process.

So we now have two important instances of the affection and respect for the other: Abraham's toward the strangers and God's toward Abraham. Yet all of this is really a setup for the crucial test. In a way, of course,

Abraham has been tested and has done well. But this is not the story's purpose. All these lead us to the inquiry that God makes about the behavior of Sodom.

God is going to test the inhabitants of Sodom. Do they respect others? If so, how many of them possess this value: all? none of them? fifty? forty-five? And so forth. But the key point is that the first story is a setup for the second one. Shadal emphasizes that the angels are sent to Sodom to test its inhabitants. If there are righteous among them, they will try to save the guests, or at least they will sit at home and not go out to watch the travesties perpetrated on the visitors.

For Shadal, therefore, hospitality is a *universal* value. That value has been violated by the people of Sodom in the past (or so the word has gotten back to heaven). Hospitality is thus the form of the test. No doubt the value is important but so important is it that the destruction or survival of the city will depend entirely upon it.

Parenthetically I would note that *this* is the traditional rabbinic reading of the sin of Sodom: its inhabitants are misanthropes, unconcerned about other people, persecuting the poor, the wayfarer being a common example of the vulnerable. מעשה סדום, the act of Sodom, or, if you will, "sodomy," is the persecution of the vulnerable. That there may be a sexual dimension to this is yet another indication of lack of respect for fellow human beings.[7]

As Shadal sums up: "It was the way of the world in ancient times to treat guests with honor, and they would provide them with their needs, whereas the people of Sodom were the opposite. ... Not only would they not provide for them but they would abuse them with sodomy."

Sodom Takes the Test

Now of course the people of Sodom fail miserably. Chapter 19 makes this all too obvious. We are tipped off early on through Lot's words. He tells the two

---

7. B. Sanhedrin 109a–b. In the printed edition of Shadal's commentary, this is incorrectly given as b. Sanhedrin 71b. Shadal notes the source in the Bible for this: Ezek 16:49: "Only this was the sin of your sister Sodom: arrogance! She and her daughters had plenty of bread and untroubled tranquility, yet she did not support the poor and the needy." The next verse extends the wrongs to the sexual realm, reflecting the facts of the original story: "In their haughtiness, they committed abomination [תועבה] before me, and so I removed them, as you saw" (Ezek 16:50).

men they should spend the night in his home and then get up early and be on their way. Why send them on so early? Shadal quotes his student Yosef Yareh (as well as giving credit to Abarbanel): They should leave early in the morning before the locals *could gather together to do them harm* (19:1).

Shadal is sensitive to the parallels between chapters 18 and 19, that both Abraham and Lot meet the men visiting at the entry to their respective places, and that both offer food. Yet the reader might assume that Lot's offer is inferior since Lot only offers a משתה, not לחם. Shadal points out that משתה, which literally refers to drink, is apparently a lighter meal, because the major meal was eaten at noontime. In the evening, people would eat a light repast made up principally of wine and that is why it is called a משתה. The key meal of the day, served at noontime, was called לחם.[8] This information should not lead us to think that Lot is less hospitable. They arrived at different times of day and therefore different courtesies were appropriate.

The introduction of the people of Sodom is bad right from the start. For Shadal the repetitive words in verse 4, אנשי העיר and אנשי סדם, are a subtle way of emphasizing their repugnant nature. Look who comes to surround Lot's house in verse 4, the whole people מקצה, which the NJPS translates as "all the people to the last man." For Shadal, קצה emphasizes *from one edge of the city to the other, a huge turnout*. This detail picks up on what Shadal had mentioned before: perhaps somebody would stay home. Somebody, at least, would pass the test. But the point is, already at the beginning of chapter 19, that nobody stays home: not fifty, not forty-five, not even ten—they are all there.

As Shadal comments on verse 5, if one person would gather guests to his home, the entire community would come together, from youths to old people, not so that everyone could abuse them, but to strengthen the abuser by not allowing the people to escape, or to rejoice and have a good time at the suffering and sorrow of the guests. And, he goes on, it is likely that even among themselves the people of the city would treat each other equally outrageously. Therefore guests were sought out as uninitiated playthings. A foreigner would be unaccustomed to these sexual abominations and therefore the locals would be thrilled by these cowering innocents. Knowing this and to appease them, Lot says: "I have two daughters who

---

8. Cf. Gen 37:25: "And they sat down to eat לחם." Joseph's brothers sit down to eat and see a caravan of Ishmaelites passing by. They were eating during the daytime.

have not known a man." Note that there is no mention of the women gathering together. It does not say, for example, from the men to the women, for, Shadal says, "these acts are hateful and repulsive to women, for sodomy lessens the love of males for females and therefore the women would stay at home." The residents of Sodom show their colors. The evidence is in and the punishment forthcoming.

Until here, then, we see the thematic unity of the story, how chapters 18 and 19 serve to make the point of the test so obvious. Abraham succeeds in illustrating an ethical standard—but that is just the beginning. What we learn about Abraham is the background to learning about wrong behavior among his neighbors. The expectation, therefore, is that the ethics are not limited to Abraham. They are *universal*. Likewise, the divine concern is not limited to Abraham. It, too, is *universal* and not only particular.

Lot's Daughters

Universalism is the persistent theme in these chapters, certainly as Shadal understands them. His emphasis is on the universal ethic that is God's concern, a concern that spreads to all people.

Somewhat surprisingly, this is also what Shadal learns from the tale of Lot's daughters. These women escape Sodom with him, leaving behind their husbands who chose to stay in the city and leaving, as it turns out, their mother as a pillar of salt for having tarried and looked behind when the destruction was very much upon them. Lot moves on from Zoar into the mountains. As Shadal understands it, Lot was afraid to stay there since he saw his own dwelling in Zoar as the temporary concession of the angels to his lack of energy. He expected that, in time, the shower of fire and brimstone would make it to that temporary refuge.

As Shadal understands it, the daughters then think about their father's age. Even now we know that he lacks energy. As he gets older, he will certainly lack the strength to wander a great distance to another land and therefore he will not stir sufficiently to take care of marrying them off.

Rashi had understood the phrase in verse 31, "there is not a man on earth to consort with us in the way of all the world," quite literally. Quoting Genesis Rabbah, Rashi says that the daughters assumed the whole world had been destroyed as in the days of the flood.[9] Countering this notion,

---

9. Also E. A. Speiser, *Genesis* (AB 1; Garden City, N.Y.: Doubleday, 1964), 145.

Shadal says that "on earth" does not mean the world but is an expression for "in this area." Though they are living in a cave in the mountains, they are not as alone as it might seem. For, says Shadal, there must have been a nearby settlement which would have been the source of their bread and wine—the wine figuring, of course, so prominently in what lies ahead. For some reason, Lot spurns the fellowship of these neighbors, perhaps realizing that his fraternization with the people of Sodom caused him so much trouble and put him in terrible danger. The locals offer more of the same, he thinks. They are certainly unworthy of his daughters.

The daughters have their own concerns, however. Shadal understands that it was an embarrassment and a source of great suffering for a woman to be childless, as we see with Sarah and Rachel. And beyond that, what will they do when their father dies? As good daughters, they, too, realize that they are in the midst of unsuitable suitors and neighbors, and what will they do should they not have sons to support them?

Thus the ruse of giving their father wine, sleeping with him, and conceiving as a result. Interestingly Shadal does not comment on the reason for getting him drunk. It must have been obvious to Shadal that Lot would not have engaged in these liaisons had he been sober. Which is to say that he knew that incest was wrong, though it does not seem to have troubled his daughters.

The babies are born, and one daughter names her son Moab; the other names her son Ben-Ammi. The text then says: Moab is the father of the Moabites of today, and Ben-Ammi is the father of the Ammonites of today (vv. 37–38). The question is: What does this say about Moab and Ammon?

Shadal takes up this question by mentioning—with no little derision—the understanding of Wilhelm de Wette, the German biblical scholar of the early nineteenth century, who understood this entire story to be manufactured by Israel to express their contempt for the Moabites and the Ammonites.[10]

Such a view is "extremely crazy" (שיגעון גדול), Shadal says. To the contrary, he argues (19:38) that by virtue of this story these nations have

---

10. A view shared later on by Hermann Gunkel, *Genesis* (trans. Mark E. Biddle; Macon, Ga.: Mercer University Press, 1997), 216. To Gunkel, the legend is ethnological in nature; since it became customary to see Moab and Ammon as traditional enemies, "this parentage was assuredly seen as a particular disgrace." This is also James L. Kugel's view: "Modern scholars see this as a nasty swipe at these two nations" (*How to Read the Bible* [New York: Free Press, 2007], 130).

become the relatives of Israel and their brothers and it becomes prohibited for Israel to move against them (להיתגרות). Should Israel have hated them, a stance that would be contrary to the Torah, their origin should never have been from Lot. Rather they would have come from Sodom alone. The tie to Lot, therefore, is crucial and positive.

Note, says Shadal, that the daughters are proud of where their children come from. One is Moab, which Shadal suggests may come from "born from my father's seed." The other is Ben-Ammi, which Shadal sees as stating her pride that her son comes from her people and not from another people. Of course, one wonders: which is her people? Her father's or her mothers? And do not forget, Shadal concludes, that the Torah never condemns the deeds of Lot's daughters, something it surely could have done directly had it wished to. Not only that, we never find that the Moabites and the Ammonites are disparaged and humiliated from Israel's perspective because their mothers were impregnated by their father.

This is the surprise: in a section that we might have understood to focus on a particularistic concern, condemnation of one of Israel's neighbors, Shadal sees the opposite, the forging of brotherhood between Israel and its neighbors. Particularism is transformed into, if not universalism—as in the understanding of the universal obligation of hospitality—at least into brotherhood, another aspect of the universal and the particular. The particular is not by itself nor is it self-centered to the degree that it excludes neighbors. The neighbors rather are brothers—with no derision intended.[11]

Abraham's Special Relation to God

But Shadal has certainly not left out the particularistic side of the story entirely. While he has no comment at all on 19:29, "Thus it was that, when God destroyed the cities of the plain and annihilated the cities where Lot dwelt, God was mindful of Abraham and removed Lot from the midst of the upheaval," he does dwell on the unique relation between Abraham and

---

11. Deut 23:4–5 condemns Moab and Ammon, not allowing the men to marry into Israel. While it might seem therefore that the story of Lot's daughters is a reflection of that condemnation, this is not necessarily the case. Ramban, for example, notes that Israel and these nations had common ancestors and therefore should have been very close with each other. When later Balak, the Moabite king, tries to curse Israel, this is inappropriate behavior for a kinsman. *That*, then, is the reason these nations are condemned: they debase the otherwise close relation they should have had with Israel!

God earlier in the story. I have already mentioned the affection God feels toward Abraham in 18:17: "Do I hide from Abraham what I am doing?" But in my previous mention I stressed the general notion of respect for human beings which is part of the universal message and which is seen so strongly in this special relation.

Genesis 18:18 and 19 stress the unique relation of God with Abraham and his progeny-to-be. "Since Abraham is to become a great and populous nation and all the nations of the earth are to bless themselves by him." That is the reason God wants to take Abraham into his confidence. It goes on: "For I have singled him out, that he may instruct his children and his posterity to keep the way of the Lord by doing what is just and right, in order that the Lord may bring about for Abraham what He has promised him" (18:19). Particularism—here are thy verses.

But according to Shadal, it is not quite that simple. The first verse (18) recalls that God has already decreed great and honorable things for Abraham. As a result, God says that it makes sense for him to treat Abraham with love and respect. According to Shadal, then, this clearly emphasizes the unique particularistic aspect of the story. However, this is shaded slightly differently by his comment on v. 19 that follows.

"The Lord did not choose Abraham for Abraham's sake alone but to be the father of a great nation. Likewise, the choosing of this people is not for *their* sake, but for humankind at large." Not only that, but the verse makes clear, says Shadal, that this particularity or chosenness is not necessary but is contingent on the people's practice of the ways of the Lord. God's condition is their practice of צדקה and משפט, which Shadal defines as follows: צדקה is to do good for others, and משפט is to do no harm to any human being. He quotes Jer 9:22–23: "Let not the wise man glory in his wisdom; Let not the strong man glory in his strength; Let not the rich man glory in his riches. But only in this should one glory: In his earnest devotion to me. For I the Lord act with kindness, משפט, and צדקה in the world."

This is Shadal's point: the children of Abraham are uniquely burdened. Their chosenness is one that has obligations, and the benefits of the unique relationship will come only if they meet the conditions of their obligations to practice goodness toward all others and refrain from harming any human being.

I am not so sure that this is particularity per se. I would rather call it "the mission of the Jews."

Beyond Universality and Particularity

This does not reject the two alternatives of universality and particularity. It brings them together in a way that was poignant for an Italian rabbi living and writing throughout the first two-thirds of the nineteenth century, a period that roughly corresponds to the *Risorgimento*, the process of Italian unification that begins with the end of Napoleonic rule and that continues until the Franco-Prussian War in 1871, a few years after Shadal's death.

It is a period when the status of the Jews in society, their comfort as full participants in the modern state educationally, socially, and politically is a basic part of the consciousness of the community, its leaders and teachers. These issues are precisely the issues that jump off the page so strikingly in Shadal's commentary to Gen 18–19, not because he is necessarily reading into the text the issues that are in the air—though I cannot deny that there may be some truth to that. But reading the Bible, as reading any literature—but especially reading the Bible—is impossible without bringing to that reading the totality of a person's understanding about the meanings of life. Perhaps it was the middle of the nineteenth century that provides the intellectual climate for fostering such insights.

Shadal's approach to the text is always to seek out the *peshat*, the straightforward meaning, which is sometimes not at all simple. His commentary is traditional in that it is thoroughly familiar with the religious and intellectual framework of all other Jewish commentary on the scriptural text, especially that of the midrash, the Talmud, and the medieval commentators. But it has a psychological subtlety and an insight into the parameters of modern Jewish identity that is quite new.

Whether it reflects accurately what the text says I leave to the reader's consideration.

Bibliography

Gunkel, Hermann. *Genesis*. Translated by Mark E. Biddle. Macon, Ga.: Mercer University Press, 1997.

Klein, Daniel A. *The Book of Genesis: A Commentary by Shadal*. Northvale, N.J.: Aronson, 1998.

Kugel, James L. *How to Read the Bible*. New York: Free Press, 2007.

Luzzatto, Samuel David. *Commentary to the Pentateuch* [Hebrew]. Jerusalem: Horev, 1993.

Margolies, Morris B. *Samuel David Luzzatto: Traditionalist Scholar*. New York: Ktav, 1979.

Sarna, Nahum M. *Understanding Genesis*. New York: Jewish Theological Seminary of America, 1966.
Speiser, E. A. *Genesis*. AB 1. Garden City, N.Y.: Doubleday, 1964.

Does Lot Know about Yada‘?*

Ron Pirson

It is striking that in a short space of time in the early twenty-first century, several articles were published on Gen 18–19, three in the *Journal for the Study of the Old Testament* and one in the *Catholic Biblical Quarterly*.[1] As if that were not enough, 2004 saw the publication of the volume *Sodom's Sin: Genesis 18–19 and Its Interpretations*, edited by Ed Noort and Eibert Tigchelaar.[2]

Since Gen 18–19 is without doubt an interesting text, these different publications are most rewarding to read. Nonetheless, enough problems and issues remain for others to shed their light on this most intriguing narrative. For reasons of space, I shall limit myself here to the episode in which Lot receives his nocturnal visitors (19:4–11). In particular, I wish to deal with the issue of what the "men of Sodom ... from the youngest to the oldest (אנשי סדם ... מנער ועד־זקן)" desire from or with Lot's two guests. Or perhaps: what they definitely do not desire.

In his article "The Sin of Sodom," Brian Doyle provides a short overview of the three accusations, the three types of "sin," with which the history of interpretation has charged the men of Sodom.[3] The first accusa-

---

* Translated from the Dutch by Pierre Van Hecke.

1. Scott Morschauser, "'Hospitality', Hostiles and Hostages: On the Legal Background to Genesis 19.1–9," *JSOT* 27 (2003): 461–85; Brian Doyle, "'Knock, Knock, Knockin' on Sodom's Door': The Function of פתח/דלת in Genesis 18-19," *JSOT* 28 (2004): 431–48; Thomas M. Bolin, "The Role of Exchange in Ancient Mediterranean Religion and Its Implications for Reading Genesis 18-19," *JSOT* 29 (2004): 37–56; Nathan MacDonald, "Listening to Abraham—Listening to Yhwh: Divine Justice and Mercy in Genesis 18,16-33," *CBQ* 66 (2004): 25–43.

2. Ed Noort and Eibert Tigchelaar, eds., *Sodom's Sin: Genesis 18-19 and Its Interpretations* (TBN 7; Leiden: Brill, 2004).

3. Brian Doyle, "The Sin of Sodom: *yada‘, yada‘, yada‘*? A Reading of the Mamre-

tion is that they wanted to engage in a sexual encounter with Lot's guests. The second sin proposed in the secondary literature is that they wanted to violate Lot's hospitality towards his guests. The third, and most recent, charge brought against the men of Sodom is that of "shaming": they wish to shame the guests, whether sexually or otherwise.

In this paper I shall deal with the verb ידע in Gen 19, especially with reference to verse 5. Most modern translations leave little to the imagination in rendering the expression ונדעה אתם. The JPS translation reads: "Bring them out to us, so that we may be intimate with them," while the Revised English Bible translates: "so that we may have intercourse with them," and the Good News Bible explains: "the men wanted to have sex with them." The NRSV is remarkably sober and renders more literally "so that we may know them," a translation also found in the older translations such as ASV and KJV.

According to the *Theological Lexicon of the Old Testament*, the verb ידע has the connotation of "sexual intercourse: man with woman..., woman with man..., and homosexual intercourse."[4] Genesis 19:5 and 8 are included among the seventeen cases in which such a meaning would apply.

In his commentary, Hamilton points to the position defended by some scholars, namely, that the verb ידע does not have a sexual connotation in Gen 19:5 but goes more in the direction of "getting to know someone." Hamilton could not disagree more; he regards this interpretation as "wild and fanciful." From what Lot says about his daughters in verse 8, Hamilton concludes, it is crystal clear what the meaning of ידע is: "the issue is intercourse and not friendship."[5]

Sodom Narrative in Genesis 18-19," *Theology and Sexuality* 9 (1998): 84-85.

4. Luise Schottroff, "ידע," *TLOT* 2:515; cf. G. Johannes Botterweck, "ידע," *TDOT* 5:464, even though he does not list more than 16 cases—Gen 24:16 is lacking. See also *HAL* 2:374; *NIDOTTE* 2:411; and *DCH* 4:100.

5. Victor P. Hamilton, *The Book of Genesis: Chapters 18–50* (Grand Rapids: Eerdmans, 1995), 34. Robert I. Letellier also understands ידע in Gen 19:5 as "knowing sexually" (*Day in Mamre, Night in Sodom: Abraham and Lot in Genesis 18 and 19* [Leiden: Kok, 1995], 146-47). Loader even speaks of a "homosexual *mob rape*" (J. A. Loader, *A Tale of Two Cities: Sodom and Gomorrah in the Old Testament, Early Jewish and Early Christian Traditions* [Kampen: Kok, 1990], 37). Compare also R. Christopher Heard, *Dynamics of Diselection: Ambiguity in Genesis 12–36 and Ethnic Boundaries in Post-Exilic Judah* (SemeiaSt 39; Atlanta: Society of Biblical Literature, 2001), 47-61, esp.

In one of the articles I listed above, Scott Morschauser makes an interesting proposal, by sketching the juridical background of Gen 19:1–9 in the context of the ancient Near East. Morschauser starts from the assumption, suggested by the account in Gen 14, that Sodom is a city in wartime. At the outset of the story in chapter 19, Lot stands in the city gates, as one who mounts the guard: he has to make sure that no spy or saboteur enters the city. Consequently, he takes the visitors to his home without informing his fellow citizens. For that reason, the men of Sodom want to grill the visitors and ascertain the purpose of their visit—hence the use of the verb ידע. Lot refuses them permission to interrogate, but, rather, proposes to give his daughters as a kind of pledge. Although I consider Morschauser's hypothesis interesting, I am not fully convinced. Nonetheless, I am persuaded by Morschauser's position that ידע should not be understood in a sexual way.[6] Brian Doyle, on the other hand, defends the latter interpretation, rejected by Hamilton as "wild and fanciful." Doyle considers it possible and even desirable not to read the text in the light of the sexual connotation of the verb ידע.[7]

I would like to take the issue one step further by maintaining that it is actually impossible to read the text in this sense, at least so far as 19:5 is concerned. Or let me put it somewhat more cautiously: I believe the arguments in favor of a sexual interpretation lose out to the arguments against.

Analysis of ידע

In order to support my claims, I shall investigate more closely the instances of the verb ידע which the dictionaries and theological lexica (*TLOT*, *TDOT*, *NIDOTTE*) consider to have a sexual connotation. As mentioned above, seventeen such cases have been discerned, all of them in the *qal*

52–55; Weston W. Fields, *Sodom and Gomorrah: History and Motif in Biblical Narrative* (JSOTSup 231; Sheffield: Sheffield Academic Press, 1997), 122–23.

6. In 1992 Matthews suggested that Lot is guilty by showing hospitality to guests while being a nonindigenous inhabitant of the city (Victor H. Matthews, "Hospitality and Hostility in Genesis 19 and Judges 19," *BTB* 22 [1992]: 4: "Lot has no right to offer these strangers hospitality.... he cannot represent the city in this matter").

7. Doyle, "Knock, Knock, Knockin' on Sodom's Door," 433. In his commentary, Henk Jagersma dissociates himself from the sexual meaning: "Here, however, the verb indicates that the inhabitants of Sodom want to know what kind of people Lot has taken into his home" (*Genesis 1:1–25:11* [Verklaring van de Hebreeuwse Bijbel; Nijkerk: Callenbach, 1995], 217, my trans.).

formation. Needless to say, investigating the over eight hundred cases of ידע in the *qal* would greatly exceed the scope of the present paper.[8]

In my semantic analysis, I shall take a closer look at a number of formal aspects with regard to the verb ידע: (1) What is the verb's subject? (2) What is the verb's object? (3) Does the verb govern a preposition, and if so, which one? (4) Is the clause including the verb part of a narrative or of a discursive text?

Let me briefly explain the different issues. As far as the first two are concerned, it is clear that the use of a particular subject and object affect a verb's interpretation. For example, in Gen 23:20 it is clear that the verb קום with שדה as its subject cannot have its usual meaning of "to rise." These aspects therefore need little explanation. The same is true for the third issue: it needs little or no comment that the use of a preposition deeply affects the meaning of the verb: "to run into" is something altogether different than "to run over" or "to run out."

In my opinion, however, it is likewise important to make a distinction with regard to the textual context in which the clause, and the verb, occurs, that is, the distinction between a narrative and a discursive context. As we will see, the discursive context is of utmost importance for a correct understanding of a concept. The story's characters need not agree with the narrator's text, nor vice versa. The narrator may use a word in a particular way, while the character may understand it in a different way. (In the New Testament, this phenomenon is very well-known in the so-called "Johannine misunderstandings," where the narrator and the character Jesus understand some terms in one way, while the other interlocutors in the story understand the same terms in a different way altogether.)

Besides those more general aspects of subject, object and text type, the immediate context of a word or clause constituent also plays an important role. As we will see, it is often the context that determines whether or not ידע has sexual connotations.

---

8. The dictionaries (*TLOT*, *TDOT*, *DCH*, and *NIDOTTE*) all agree that ידע *qal* occurs 822 times in the Hebrew Bible.

	Subject / Object	Narrator's text (N) / Direct speech (D)	prep. / nota acc.	context
Gen 4:1	S: man / Adam O: Eve, his wife	N	את	הרה ילד
Gen 4:17	S: Cain O: his wife	N	את	הרה ילד
Gen 4:25	S: man / Adam O: his wife	N	את	בן ילד
Gen 19:5	S: we O: them (the men)	D	את	—
Gen 19:8	S: they (daughters) O: a man	D	—	איש
Gen 24:16	S: a man O: her (Rebecca)	N	—	איש בתולה
Gen 38:26	S: Judah O: her (Tamar)	N	—	הרה ילד
Num 31:17	S: woman O: man (איש, זכר)	D	—	זכר שכב
Num 31:18	S: women O: [man] (זכר, etc.)	D	—	זכר שכב
Num 31:35	S: women O: [man] (זכר, etc.)	N	—	זכר שכב
Judg 11:39	S: Jephthah's daughter O: man	N	—	איש בתולה

Judg 19:22	S: we O: him	D	—	—
Judg 19:25	S: the men O: her (concubine)	N	את	ענה בתולה
Judg 21:11	S: every woman O: [man]	D	—	זכר שכב
Judg 21:12	S: virgin O: man	N	—	זכר שכב איש בתולה
1 Sam 1:19	S: Elkana O: Hannah	N	את	הרה ילד בן
1 Kgs 1:4	S: David O: her (Abishag)	N	—	שכב בתולה

In the table above, all the instances of the verb ידע with alleged sexual connotations are listed, with mention of the subject and object, of the text type in which the verb occurs, and of the preposition, if any, governed by the verb. In the far right column, the lexemes from the immediate context are listed that guide the interpretation of the verb ידע, namely, verbs as הרה, ילד, and שכב and nouns as זכר and בתולה. My analysis yields the following results:

(1) Eleven instances occur in narrator's text, six in character's text.[9]

(2) Seven times the subject is feminine, ten times it is masculine, with the following distribution: in the narrator's text eight instances have a masculine subject and a feminine object, while in three cases the subject is feminine and the object is masculine. In the character's texts, three

---

9. Jan Fokkelman proposes the inclusion of Gen 38:26 as a whole in Judah's direct speech ("Genesis 37 and 38 at the Interface of Structural Analysis and Hermeneutics," in *Literary Structure and Rhetorical Strategies in the Hebrew Bible* [ed. L. J. de Regt et al.; Assen: Van Gorcum; Winona Lake, Ind.: Eisenbrauns, 1996], 152–87, esp. 173). If one adopts this proposal, the proportion of narrator's texts versus character texts becomes ten to seven.

instances have a masculine subject and a feminine object, and two cases have a feminine subject and a masculine object.

(3) Only in one case is the object plural, namely, Gen 19:5.

(4) There are six texts in which the subject is plural, namely, Gen 19:5, 8; Num 31:18, 35; Judg 19:22, 25.

(5) There are six texts in which ידע is followed by the *nota accusativi*—five cases in narrator's text, and one in character's text. There are no cases in which ידע governs a prepositional object.

(6) In four texts, the object takes the form of a pronominal suffix. Three cases are found in narrator's text and one in character's text: Gen 24:16; 38:26; Judg 19:22; 1 Kgs 1:4.

(7) The negated construction לא ידע occurs seven times; five times with a feminine subject (Gen 19:8; Num 31:18, 35; Judg 11:39; 21:12), twice with a masculine subject (Gen 24:16; 1 Kgs 1:4). Perhaps Gen 38:26 should also be included in the latter category.

(8) There are two more texts besides with a feminine subject who did know a man (Num 31:17; Judg 21:11)—expressed by means of the participle.

(9) In all texts but two (Gen 19:5; Judg 19:22) the verb ידע is clustered with words related to procreation or lying together with, such as ילד, הרה, and שכב.

Interpretation of Genesis 19?

(1) There are fifteen cases in which the sexual aspect of ידע is certainly predominant: Gen 4:1; 17:25; 19:8; 24:16; 38:26; Num 31:17, 18, 35; Judg 11:39; 19:25; 21:11, 12; 1 Sam 1:19; 1 Kgs 1:4.

All these cases have a number of common characteristics that justify grouping them together. In the context of each one, procreation and sexuality play an explicit role. This can be seen clearly in texts in which a man "knows" a woman, after which she becomes pregnant and gives birth to a child (four cases). In Gen 38:26, the larger context, namely, the preceding story of Judah and Tamar's sleeping together and of her becoming pregnant, makes it very clear that "he did not know her again" has sexual meaning. The sexual aspect is self-evident too when it is said that a woman has not "known" a man (or, on the contrary, has known a man), or that a man does not "know" a woman (see points 7 and 8 of the preceding paragraph: nine cases in total). It is beyond doubt that sexual contact, or rather sexual abuse, is intended in Judg 19:25. In total, fifteen cases of the verb ידע have a sexual connotation.

(2) Two texts do not share the characteristics mentioned in the previous section, namely, Gen 19:5 and Judg 19:22. In Gen 19:5 (just as in Judg 19:22, which should be the subject of a different study) the verb ידע cannot be interpreted as "knowing in the biblical sense," in other words with a sexual connotation. Neither the context, nor the way in which the verb is used, supports this interpretation. No one would think of reading the verb in a sexual way in Gen 18:19, for example: when it is written that Yhwh knew Abraham, no one would conceive of anything sexual there.[10] In my opinion, the men of Sodom are not interested in having sex with Lot's guests. They want to get to know them. I am not sure whether the reason for this is the one Morschauser proposes in his article, but whatever the reason might be, the men of Sodom do not have sexual motives.

I am, of course, fully aware of the fact that the narrator himself characterizes the men of Sodom very negatively, which does not seem to support their innocence. See, for example, Gen 13:13: "The inhabitants of Sodom were very wicked sinners against the Lord" and 18:20: "The Lord said: 'The outrage of Sodom and Gomorrah is so great, and their sin is so grave.'"[11] One could also argue that indeed the Sodomites' reaction to Lot's words proves them to be wicked. But would not the inhabitants of Sodom be angry with Lot? First, Lot blames them for having evil plans (v. 6), even before knowing what they really want. Second, he shamelessly addresses them as his "brothers" (v. 6), while they themselves rightly[12] consider him a foreigner or גר (v. 9).[13] Furthermore, he bluntly accuses them of wanting to go to bed with his visitors (v. 8); people have been killed for lesser things. When the Sodomites say in v. 9 that "we will deal worse with you than with them," they therefore mean: "we will deal worse with you than you thought we would deal with your guests."

(3) The sexual connotations of the verb ידע possibly play a role in Gen 19:8, in which Lot presents his own daughters to the crowd, but this is not entirely certain, even though I have included the verse in the list of texts in which the sexual aspect is present.[14] But if Lot indeed understood the Sod-

---

10. This form, *qatal* plus suffixed object, is the same as in Gen 24:16 and 1 Kgs 1:4 (in both cases preceded by לא).

11. See also outside of Gen: Jer 23:14; Ezek 16:46–50; Jude 7.

12. See Gen 13.

13. Compare with Abraham's courteous words to the Hittites in Gen 24.

14. lxx translates ידע in v. 5 as συγγινομαι and as γινωσκω in v. 8 (see also Doyle, "The Sin of Sodom," 92). Targum Neofiti and Targum Pseudo-Jonathan translate the

omites' use of the verb ידע as "having intercourse with," this could reveal more about Lot than about his fellow citizens. Here the difference in types of discourse proves to play a central role. Genesis 19:8 is character's text; as I have mentioned above, in that type of discourse, the meaning that one character ascribes to a word does not necessarily coincide with what a different interlocutor understands by that same word.

That Lot would misinterpret his fellow citizens fits perfectly with the way in which Lot is portrayed in Gen 19. He is not exactly one of the brightest. If the men of Sodom really were looking for sex—with Lot's male guests—what use would his daughters be to them?[15] Moreover, Lot presents them as "two daughters who have not known a man," that is to say, as two virgins. Even apart from the question whether it is sexually interesting to sleep with a virgin, the argument of virginity is only valid for one or two men in the city; for all the others they would not be virgins any longer anyway.

That Lot is not one of the brightest also becomes apparent somewhat later in the text. His visitors urge him to evacuate his family from the city since they have come to destroy it.[16] So Lot goes to his sons-in-law and tells them to flee since the Lord will destroy the city. The narrator then reports: "But they did not take him seriously" (REB) or, translated differently, "But he seemed to his sons-in-laws as one who jests" (JPS). How could it not be so? Obviously, his sons-in-laws have heard Lot's proposal, since "all the inhabitants of the city" were present at his house. How could they take seriously someone who has just proposed that their future wives may be used sexually by the whole city?

---

verse differently. The former reads ונחכם ("that we may know them": "a verb which very seldom conveys the sexual connotation of Hebrew ידע" [Florentino García Martínez, "Sodom and Gomorrah in the Targumim," in Noort and Tigchelaar, *Sodom's Sin*, 90]), while Targum Pseudo-Jonathan renders ונשמש ("so that we have sexual relations with them").

15. In my opinion, it is a weak bid to consider Lot's proposal as irony: in that way, all troubling passages can be termed irony. Moreover, Lot has not shown to be particularly good at irony anywhere else in the story.

16. By the way, Lot does not seem convinced of the need to leave: in the morning he is still at home (see 19:15–16).

Conclusions

(1) The verb ידע in Gen 19:5 has *no* sexual meaning, nor has it the meaning of nonphysical "humiliation" or "shaming."

(2) Probably there are more texts in which ידע occurs and in which the criteria mentioned above play a role. Those texts have hitherto been left out of consideration when dealing with the sexual connotation of the verb. Further research could demonstrate that in some instances a sexual aspect is present that had not been recognized earlier, or that in other texts dealing with sexuality in which the verb ידע occurs, the verb should be understood as "knowing" in the biblical sense.

(3) In the light of the preceding, a translation as in the Revised English Bible "that we may have intercourse with them" cannot be maintained. Translations like this one deprive the reader of the Hebrew text's ambiguous character, and opt for the least likely interpretation, that is, the sexual one.

Bibliography

Bolin, Thomas M. "The Role of Exchange in Ancient Mediterranean Religion and Its Implications for Reading Genesis 18-19." *JSOT* 29 (2004): 37–56.

Doyle, Brian. "'Knock, Knock, Knockin' on Sodom's Door': The Function of דלת/פתח in Genesis 18-19." *JSOT* 28 (2004): 431–48.

———. "The Sin of Sodom: *yada', yada', yada'*? A Reading of the Mamre-Sodom Narrative in Genesis 18-19." *Theology and Sexuality* 9 (1998): 84–100.

Fields, Weston W. *Sodom and Gomorrah: History and Motif in Biblical Narrative.* JSOTSup 231. Sheffield: Sheffield Academic Press, 1997.

Fokkelman, Jan. "Genesis 37 and 38 at the Interface of Structural Analysis and Hermeneutics." Pages 152–87 in *Literary Structure and Rhetorical Strategies in the Hebrew Bible*. Edited by L. J. de Regt et al. Assen: Van Gorcum; Winona Lake, Ind.: Eisenbrauns, 1996.

García Martínez, Florentino. "Sodom and Gomorrah in the Targumim." Pages 83–96 in *Sodom's Sin: Genesis 18-19 and Its Interpretations*. Edited by Ed Noort and Eibert Tigchelaar. TBN 7. Leiden: Brill, 2004.

Hamilton, Victor P. *The Book of Genesis: Chapters 18–50*. Grand Rapids: Eerdmans, 1995.

Heard, R. Christopher. *Dynamics of Diselection: Ambiguity in Genesis 12–36 and Ethnic Boundaries in Post-Exilic Judah*. SemeiaSt 39. Atlanta: Society of Biblical Literature, 2001.

Jagersma, Henk. *Genesis 1:1–25:11*. Verklaring van de Hebreeuwse Bijbel. Nijkerk: Callenbach, 1995.

Letellier, Robert I. *Day in Mamre, Night in Sodom: Abraham and Lot in Genesis 18 and 19.* Leiden: Kok, 1995.
Loader, J. A. *A Tale of Two Cities: Sodom and Gomorrah in the Old Testament, Early Jewish and Early Christian Traditions.* Kampen: Kok, 1990.
MacDonald, Nathan. "Listening to Abraham—Listening to Yhwh: Divine Justice and Mercy in Genesis 18,16-33." *CBQ* 66 (2004): 25–43.
Matthews, Victor H. "Hospitality and Hostility in Genesis 19 and Judges 19." *BTB* 22 (1992): 3–11.
Morschauser, Scott. "'Hospitality', Hostiles and Hostages: On the Legal Background to Genesis 19.1–9." *JSOT* 27 (2003): 461–85.
Noort, Ed, and Eibert Tigchelaar, eds. *Sodom's Sin: Genesis 18-19 and Its Interpretations.* TBN 7. Leiden: Brill, 2004.

CONTRIBUTORS

Calum Carmichael is a professor of comparative literature and adjunct professor of law at Cornell University. Fellowships received include the Guggenheim and the Nation Endowment for the Humanities. He is the author of eleven books that focus primarily on biblical law and is the editor of Studies in Comparative Legal History (University of California, Berkeley), a six-volume series devoted to the work of David Daube, and has edited five volumes on different aspects of law and literature. His latest book, *The Book of Numbers as a Critique of Genesis 25–50*, is forthcoming with Yale University Press.

Diana Lipton read English at Oxford University and earned her Ph.D. in biblical studies at Cambridge University. Formerly a Fellow of Newnham College, Cambridge, and a Reader in Hebrew Bible and Jewish Studies at King's College London, she is now a visting lecturer at Tel Aviv University. Her publications include *Revisions of the Night: Politics and Promises in the Patriarchal Dreams of Genesis* (Sheffield Academic Press, 1999) and *Longing for Egypt and Other Unexpected Biblical Tales* (Sheffield Phoenix Press, 2008).

William John Lyons received his B.A., M.A. and Ph.D. from the University of Sheffield and is now Senior Lecturer in Biblical Interpretation in the Department of Theology and Religious Studies at the University of Bristol. His publications include *Canon and Praxis: The Canonical Approach and the Sodom Narrative* (Sheffield Academic Press, 2002) and, as co-editor, *New Directions in Qumran Studies* (Continuum, 2005) and *The Way the World Ends? The Apocalypse of John in Ideology and Culture* (Sheffield Phoenix Press, 2009).

Nathan MacDonald studied theology at the Universities of Cambridge and Durham. He is Reader in Old Testament at the University of St.

Andrews and Leader of the Sofja-Kovalevskaja Research Team at the Georg-August-Universität Göttingen. His publications include *Deuteronomy and the Meaning of "Monotheism"* (Mohr Siebeck, 2003), *Not Bread Alone* (Oxford University Press, 2008) and *What Did the Ancient Israelites Eat?* (Eerdmans, 2008).

Amira Meir earned her Ph.D. in Medieval Jewish Commentary of the Pentateuchal Poetry at McGill University. She was the head of Biblical Studies in Beit Berl College in Israel and has lectured at the Hebrew Union College in Jerusalem and New York, University College London, and the Gregorian University, Rome. Her publications deal primarily with biblical commentary.

Yitzhak (Itzik) Peleg is the Head of Biblical Studies in Beit Berl College, a member of Kibbutz Ein Hashofet, and editor of *MOED: Annual for Jewish Studies*. His publications include, among others, "Going Up and Going Down: A Key to Interpreting Jacob's Dream," *ZAW* 116 (2004): 1–11; "'Yet Forty Days, and Nineveh Shall Be Overthrown' (Jonah 3:4) Two Readings of the Book of Jonah," in *God's Word for Our World* (London: T&T Clark, 2004), 262–74; and "The Peace Vision of the End of Days in Isaiah (2:2–5) and the Peace Vision in Micah" (4:1–5)" [Hebrew], *Shnaton: An Annual for Biblical and Ancient Near Eastern Studies* 22 (2010): 27–50.

T. A. Perry has taught the Hebrew Bible, Sephardic studies, and comparative literature at Ben Gurion University and the University of Connecticut. He has published dozens of articles and eleven books, including *Dialogues with Kohelet, Wisdom Literature and the Structure of Proverbs, The Honeymoon Is Over: Jonah's Arguments with God*, and *God's Twilight Zone: Wisdom in the Hebrew Bible*. His forthcoming books are *Joyous Vanity: Kohelet's Guide to Living Well* and *Dream-Kisses: Spiritual Eroticism and the Biblical Tradition*. He is Acting Chair of the Program in Christian and Jewish Learning at Boston College.

Ron Pirson was a University Lecturer in Old Testament Exegesis at the Faculty of Theology and Religious Studies at the University of Tilburg, Netherlands. After a degree in Theology and a doctorate on the Joseph cycle in Genesis 37–50, he began his career in Tilburg, where he was responsible for teaching the Old Testament. He was a much-loved teacher who also contributed regularly to international congresses and was editor of *Schrift*, an academic journal of biblical studies aimed at serious nonspecialists.

Jonathan D. Safren is Senior Lecturer (emeritus) in Hebrew Bible at Beit Berl College, Israel. He earned his Ph.D. in Hebrew and Cognate Studies at Hebrew Union College in 1979 and has published in Assyriology and Hebrew Bible

Meg Warner completed graduate studies in law at the Universities of Bristol and Western Australia and undertook doctoral work in biblical studies at the Melbourne College of Divinity. She was the inaugural recipient of the Morna Sturrock Doctoral Fellowship at Trinity College Theological School in Melbourne, where she was later appointed Lecturer in Biblical Studies, teaching Hebrew Bible in the United Faculty of Theology.

Harlan J. Wechsler taught Jewish philosophy and the history of Jewish ethics at The Jewish Theological Seminary of America for over thirty years. He is rabbi of Congregation Or Zarua in New York City and is engaged in research on the theology of commentaries to the Bible.

Ellen van Wolde read Theology and Biblical Studies at Nijmegen and Rome and Semiotics in Bologna. She earned her Ph.D. (cum laude) in Biblical Studies at Nijmegen. She was for sixteen years a Professor of Exegesis Old Testament and Hebrew at Tilburg University and has been Professor Exegesis Old Testament and Source Texts of Judaism at the Radboud University in Nijmegen since 2009. Her publications include *A Semiotic Analysis of Genesis 2–3* (1989), *Words Become Worlds* (1994), *Stories of the Beginning* (1996), *Job 28: Cognition in Context* (2003), and *Reframing Biblical Studies: When Language and Text Meet Culture, Cognition, and Contexts* (2009).

Index of Ancient Sources

Hebrew Bible/Old Testament

Genesis
1	7
1–11	7
1:22	51
3:5	132 n. 8
3:22	132 n. 8
4–11	9
4:1	132 n. 8, 207, 209
4:9	121
4:10	76, 82 n. 8
4:17	132 n. 9, 207
4:25	132 n. 9, 207
6:2	114 n. 5
6:9	135 n. 17, 163, 163 n. 30
7	121 n. 19
8:1	141 n. 33
9:1	51
9:8–17	124
9:22–25	105
11:27	148
11:27–30	7
11:28	148
11:31	149, 152, 152 n. 64, 153
12	11
12–19	16–17
12–25	94
12–26	26
12–50	x
12:1	8, 35
12:1–3	6, 18, 26
12:1–4	149
12:1–10	94 n. 43
12:3	9
12:5	149, 149 n. 55, 153
12:7	6, 8, 18
12:10–13	8 n. 21
12:10–20	11, 109 n. 8, 149
12:11–14:24	94 n. 44
12:20	150 n. 58
13	12, 94, 163, 210 n. 12
13:1	150, 150 n. 58
13:2	150
13:5	150, 150 n. 59
13:6	150
13:7	150
13:8	151
13:8–9	8, 150
13:10	8, 158
13:10–13	28
13:11	114 n. 5
13:12	8
13:12–13	95
13:13	8, 210
13:18–19	140 n. 31
14	8 n. 21, 92, 96, 117 n. 10, 186, 205
14:1–16	8
14:11–12	95
14:12–16	151
14:13–24	95
14:19	95
14:21	95
14:22	95
15–17	94 n. 43
15–18	31 n. 14
15:2	7 n. 21, 8, 8 n. 21
15:18	8
16	x
16:1–4	8 n. 21

Genesis (cont.)

17	119, 121, 141 n. 33
17:2–14	9
17:7	66, 66 n. 47
17:15–21	9
17:16	121 n. 20
17:18	8 n. 21
17:23–27	115 n. 6
17:25	209
18	9–11, 27 n. 3, 27–28 n. 5, 28–29, 31 n. 14, 33–34, 36 n. 20, 38, 45, 54, 84, 91 n. 37, 101, 104–5, 107–8, 110, 116–17, 117 n. 10, 118, 120 n. 19, 122, 124, 130, 130 n. 3, 140, 142–44, 154, 159, 164, 164 n. 35, 169, 183, 185, 188, 191, 193, 196–97
18–19	ix, xi, xiv, 3, 6 n. 14, 14, 18, 21, 29 n. 10, 30–35, 40–41, 43, 47, 51, 54, 71, 88–89, 91–92, 94, 94 n. 44, 96, 99, 113, 123–24, 129 n. 1, 132 n. 10, 140 n. 32, 143, 148 n. 50, 159, 159 nn. 10–11, 179, 201, 203
18–20	26, 28–29, 39, 91
18:1	9, 35, 105, 120 n. 19, 144, 168, 174 n. 74, 175 n. 76
18:1–2	4, 163, 165
18:1–6	159 n. 11
18:1–8	159, 164, 170 n. 57, 175 n. 75
18:1–16	41, 147, 159 n. 11, 164 n. 34, 176
18:1–17	160 n. 14
18:2	35, 144, 166, 167 n. 46, 169 n. 53, 193
18:2–8	39, 164
18:3	9, 152, 160 n. 14
18:3–4	144
18:3–5	167
18:3–7	160 n. 14
18:3–8	135 n. 18
18:4	144–45, 188 n. 21
18:4–8	163
18:5	167 n. 46, 169
18:5–8	145
18:6	35
18:6–8	146, 164, 169
18:7–8	160 n. 14
18:9	35, 121, 145
18:9–14	135 n. 18
18:9–15	159
18:9–16	175 n. 75
18:10	9, 35, 173, 173 n. 72, 174 n. 74
18:10–13	139 n. 30
18:10–15	173
18:10–16	172
18:12	119, 122
18:12–15	105, 174
18:13	120 n. 19, 121, 174 n. 74
18:14	9
18:15	119, 119 n. 15, 121 n. 20, 174 n. 74
18:16	54, 120 n. 19, 140 nn. 31–32, 144, 160–61, 173, 175, 175 n. 76, 194
18:16–33	184 n. 16
18:17	54, 120 n. 19, 200
18:17–18	54
18:17–19	9, 18, 54, 185
18:17–21	9
18:17–33	140 n. 31, 160
18:17–19:38	159 n. 11
18:18	35, 63, 200
18:19	10, 36, 39, 53–57, 67, 89, 113–14, 114 n. 5, 115 n. 6, 116, 118, 122–25, 200, 210
18:20	30, 73, 83, 116, 120 n. 19, 173, 210
18:20–21	54, 71, 83, 89, 184
18:21	30, 71, 83, 89, 90 n. 36, 116, 194
18:22	30, 35, 89, 120 n. 19, 140 n. 32, 144, 161, 173, 175
18:22–32	11
18:22–33	116, 173
18:23	30, 89, 116, 142, 142 n. 38, 162
18:24	30, 84 n. 16, 101, 119, 122, 142 n. 38
18:24–32	8 n. 21
18:25	10, 30, 35, 89, 89 n. 35, 90, 94–95, 99, 102, 117, 124, 162
18:26	30, 35, 120 n. 19

INDEX OF ANCIENT SOURCES

18:26–29 90
18:27 39
18:28 30, 142 n. 38
18:31 142 n. 38
18:32 37, 102, 142 n. 38
18:32–33 40
18:33 120 n. 19, 174
19 7, 10, 27 n. 3, 27–28 n. 5, 29, 31, 34, 89 n. 35, 91 n. 37, 92, 94, 96, 101–2, 104–5, 107–8, 110, 116–17, 117 n. 10, 118, 122, 124, 130 nn. 3–4, 136, 136 n. 22, 144, 147 nn. 47–48, 151–54, 164 n. 35, 173, 179–80, 180 n. 2, 182, 184–87, 191, 193, 195–97, 204–5, 211
19:1 30, 129 n. 1, 131, 137, 139–40, 143–44, 151, 161, 162 n. 21, 163–65, 165 n. 39, 166, 196
19:1–2 167 n. 46
19:1–3 135 n. 18, 161, 175 n. 75
19:1–5 130, 175 n. 75
19:1–9 205
19:1–10 139
19:1–11 139, 176
19:1–14 176
19:1–26 140 n. 31
19:1–29 129, 129 n. 1, 161 n. 20, 164 n. 34
19:2 10, 131, 144–45, 162 n. 21, 166 n. 39, 167 n. 46, 168, 169 n. 53, 188 n. 21
19:2–3 168
19:3 10, 131, 134, 137, 144, 147 n. 47, 162 n. 21, 162–63 n. 24, 164, 169–70, 170 n. 60
19:4 93, 104, 131, 138, 145, 196
19:4–5 10
19:4–11 39, 134, 146 n. 45, 174, 175 n. 75, 203
19:4–13 172–73
19:4–16 161, 174
19:5 71, 91–92, 132, 132 n. 9, 133, 136–37, 145, 183, 196, 204, 204 n. 5, 205, 207, 209–10, 210 n. 14, 212
19:5–9 134, 134 n. 16
19:6 91, 137, 176, 210
19:6–8 175 n. 75
19:6–11 175 n. 75
19:7 90, 134
19:8 10–11, 37, 90, 94, 132 n. 9, 133, 138, 176, 183, 183 n. 12, 204, 207, 209–10, 210 n. 14, 211
19:9 39, 91–92, 96, 117, 117 n. 10, 134, 165 n. 39, 184, 210
19:9–14 175 n. 75
19:10 117, 137, 158
19:10–22 135
19:11 92, 174
19:11–13 10, 175
19:11–22 139
19:12 30, 32, 90, 162 n. 24
19:12–25 135 n. 18
19:13 32, 71–73, 83, 89, 89 n. 35, 135–36, 139, 139 n. 30, 142 n. 38, 175
19:14 30, 32, 94, 104 n. 5, 142 n. 38, 175
19:15 30, 90, 142 n. 38, 154
19:15–16 158, 175, 211 n. 16
19:16 10, 130 n. 5, 135, 142 n. 39, 162 n. 23
19:17 90, 138, 142 n. 38
19:17–22 161
19:18 10
19:18–23 10
19:19 30, 138
19:20 30
19:21 46, 171, 181
19:22 30, 33, 90
19:23 32, 90, 139, 161
19:23–29 161
19:24 139, 139 n. 30, 151 n. 61
19:25 181
19:26 10, 32, 104
19:27 140 nn. 31–32
19:27–28 140, 140 n. 31
19:29 11, 13, 32, 35, 118 n. 12, 130 n. 5, 140, 140 n. 32, 141, 141 n. 33, 142, 142 n. 37, 143, 147, 151–52, 154, 158, 163 n. 27, 164 n. 34, 181, 199

Genesis (cont.)

19:30	10, 129 n. 1, 143 n. 40
19:30–38	11, 35, 105, 142 n. 39, 161, 161 n. 20
19:31	38, 104 n. 5, 133, 197
19:32	38, 103
19:36–38	105
19:37–38	198
19:38	198
20	27 n. 3, 28, 33, 36, 41, 108
20–25	94 n. 43
20:1–18	11
20:4	28, 35–36
20:6	109
20:7	35
20:9	90 n. 36
20:10	90 n. 36
20:12	37
20:17	36
21	x, 36, 109
21:1	120
22	110, 119, 121, 121 n. 19
22:1–19	176
22:7–9	120 n. 17
22:9	121
22:10	121
22:12	121
22:13	121
22:15–18	113, 125 n. 26
22:19	160 n. 17
23:20	206
24	210 n. 13
24:10	160 n. 17
24:16	132 n. 9, 146 n. 44, 204 n. 4, 207, 209, 210 n. 10
24:32	168 n. 49, 188 n. 21
25:22	54
26–32	x
26:3–5	113, 125 n. 26
26:5	121
26:30	171 n. 66
27:34	73, 75 n. 3, 76, 82 n. 8
29:13	146 n. 44
30:1–24	108
30:14–16	108
33:4	146 n. 44
34	106
34:21	174 n. 74
35:9–12	106
37:25	196 n. 8
38	164 n. 33
38:26	132 n. 9, 207, 208 n. 9, 209
39:17	133
41:55	76
43:16	170–71 n. 63
43:24	168 n. 49, 188 n. 21
44:18	89 n. 34
49	106
49:5–7	106

Exodus

1:7	51
2:23	76
3:7	73, 75 n. 5
3:9	73
5:8	77
5:15	77
8:8	77, 82 n. 8
11:6	73, 75 n. 6
12:30	73, 75 n. 6
12:49	124
14:10	77
14:15	77
15:25	77, 82 n. 8
17:4	77, 82 n. 8
22:21–22	75 n. 5
22:22	73, 77
22:26	77
23:12	65, 65 n. 45
24:14	89 n. 34
32–33	34
32:9–14	17
32:10	17
32:11	34
32:12	34
32:13	34
32:14	18
32:27	34
32:32	35
33:12	61, 61 n. 32, 114 n. 5

INDEX OF ANCIENT SOURCES

33:13	67, 67 n. 48	31:35	207, 209
33:17	58, 58 n. 23, 114 n. 5		
		Deuteronomy	
Leviticus		1–34	106
2:13	122 n. 22	1:17	89 n. 35
5:20–26	119–20, 120 n. 19	2:9	13
5:21	119	2:19	13
5:22	119	4:6	101
5:25	121	4:8	101
5:26	121	6:1–2	115 n. 6
7:1–6	121	6:1–3	115 n. 6
7:2	121	6:2	115 n. 6
7:5	121	6:20–25	115 n. 6
17–26	38	8:16	55
18:2–4	106	12:18–19	185
18:7	105, 110	14:28–29	185
18:9	37	16:9–15	185
18:18	108	17:8	89 n. 35
18:18–21	101, 110	17:9	89 n. 35, 90
18:19	107–8	17:11	89 n. 35
18:20	108	17:16	109 n. 8
18:21	110	17:17	109 n. 8
24:22	124	22:24	77, 82 n. 8
26	125 n. 26	22:27	77, 82 n. 8
26:40–45	125 n. 26	23:2	106
26:44–45	123 n. 23	23:2–6	101, 105, 110
		23:3–6	106–7
Numbers		23:4	33, 36
5:5–8	120 n. 19	23:4–5	38, 185, 199
9:14	124	23:7	40–41
11:2	77	25:1	89 n. 34
12:13	77, 82 n. 8	25:17–19	39, 107
14:11–12	17	26:1–15	185
14:13–17	18	26:7	77
14:19	34	28	106, 125 n. 26
15:29	28 n. 7	29:22	46, 181
17:11	135	32:8–9	96–97, 99
18:19	122 n. 22	33:8–11	106
18:35	132 n. 9	33:21	115 n. 6
20:16	77	34:10	114 n. 5
22:4	107		
22:6	107	Joshua	
24:25	160 n. 17	2	130, 135–36, 180 n. 2
31:17	132 n. 9, 207, 209	2:1	136–37, 137 n. 24
31:18	207, 209	2:2	136–37, 137 n. 24

Joshua (cont.)

2:3	137, 137 n. 24
2:4	137 n. 24
2:4–5	137
2:5	137
2:7	137
2:8	138
2:12	138–39
2:16	138
5:13	133
6	136 n. 22
6:17	136, 136 n. 22, 138
6:22–23	136, 136 n. 22
6:25	136, 136 n. 22
24:7	77

Judges

3:9	77
3:15	77
4:3	77
6:6	77
6:7	77
10:10	78
10:12	78
10:14	78
11:39	132 n. 9, 207, 209
12:2	78, 82 n. 8
19	129 n. 2, 143 n. 39, 164 n. 35, 169 n. 53, 179, 179 n. 1, 187, 188 n. 22
19:2	132 n. 10
19:5	161 n. 18, 168 n. 50
19:5–10	161 n. 18
19:7	161 n. 18
19:8	168 n. 50
19:9	161 n. 18
19:10	161 n. 18
19:19	171 n. 65
19:20	167 n. 46
19:21	168 n. 49, 171 n. 65, 188 n. 21
19:22	132 n. 9, 208–10
19:25	132 n. 9, 208–9
19:28	160 n. 17
21:11	208–9
21:11–12	132 n. 9
21:12	208–9

1 Samuel

1:17	174 n. 74
1:19	132 n. 9, 208–9
3	45 n. 3
4:12	78
4:13	82 n. 8
4:14	73, 75 n. 5
5:10	78
7:8	78, 82 n. 8
7:9	78
8:18	78
9:16	73, 75 n. 5
10:17	82 n. 8
11:4	108 n. 7
11:5	108 n. 7
12:8	78
12:10	78
14:38	89 n. 34
15:11	78
21:1	160 n. 17
25:41	188 n. 21
28:12	78

2 Samuel

3:20	171 n. 66
7:20	114 n. 5
8:2	13
9	186, 188
9–10	188
9–11	188
9:1	186
9:3	186
9:6	187
9:8	187
10	179–80, 180 n. 2, 181–82, 182 n. 10, 183–88
10:2	186–87, 187 n. 20
10:3	180–81
10:4	183
10:6	181
11	164 n. 33, 187–88
11–12	180
11:4	187 n. 20
11:8	168 n. 49, 187 n. 21
11:10–12	188

INDEX OF ANCIENT SOURCES

11:12	188 n. 22	15:5	74, 75 n. 5, 79
12:14	34	15:8	74, 75 n. 6
13:19	78	19:20	79
13:27	134 n. 16	26:17	79
15:6	89 n. 35	30:19	79
19:5	78	33:7	79
19:29	78	41:1	89 n. 34
22:27	103	42:2	79
		46:7	79
1 Kings		52:1–2	157 n. 1
1:4	132 n. 9, 208–9, 210 n. 10	57:13	79
3:15	171 n. 67	63:7–10	135 n. 19
3:28	90	65:14	79
13:6–7	168 n. 50	65:19	74, 76 n. 7
17:9–10	43		
17:24	174 n. 74	Jeremiah	
20:30	82 n. 8	1:5	114 n. 5
20:39	78	4:5–9	39
21:29	174 n. 74	9:22–23	200
22:19	97	11:11	79
22:32	78	11:12	79
		18:22	74, 76 n. 7
2 Kings		20:8	79, 82 n. 8, 88 n. 29
2:12	82 n. 8	20:16	74, 76 n. 7, 181
3:24	13	22:20	80
4:1	79	23:14	210 n. 11
4:14	82 n. 8	23:18	64 n. 42
4:16	174 n. 74	25:34	80
4:40	79	25:36	74, 75 n. 4
6:5	79	30:15	80
6:26	79	32:19	60
8:3	79, 82 n. 8	47:2	80
8:5	79, 82 n. 8	48	13
18:1	47 n. 7	48:3	74, 75 n. 6
		48:4	74, 75 n. 4
Isaiah		48:5	74
1:7	182, 182 n. 9	48:20	80
1:9	182 n. 9	48:31	80, 82 n. 8
5:7	73, 76 n. 7	48:34	74
6:8–10	39	49:3	80
6:13	37	49:18	181
7:14	174 n. 74	49:21	75 n. 6
13:19	181	50:27	59 n. 27
14:31	79	50:40	181
15:4	79	50:46	74, 76 n. 6

Jeremiah (cont.)
51:54 — 74, 76 n. 6

Ezekiel
3:6–21 — 39
3:20 — 40
9:8 — 80
11:13 — 80
14 — 27–29, 28 n. 5, 29 n. 10, 30, 32–34, 36 n. 21, 39–40
14:12–23 — 29
14:13 — 30
14:14 — 30, 32
14:15 — 30
14:16 — 30, 32–33
14:18 — 30, 32–33
14:19 — 32
14:20 — 30, 32–33
14:21 — 30, 32
14:22 — 30, 33
16:46–50 — 210 n. 11
16:49 — 195 n. 7
16:50 — 195 n. 7
18 — 29, 31
18:21 — 31
21:15 — 55
21:17 — 80
27:28 — 74, 75 n. 4
27:30 — 80
33 — 38–39
33:2 — 38
33:7 — 38
33:10 — 38
33:11 — 38
33:12 — 38
33:12–13 — 38
33:14–15 — 38
33:15 — 38
33:23 — 29
33:25 — 38

Hosea
7:14 — 80
8:2 — 80
11:9 — 34

Joel
1:14 — 80

Amos
2:1–3 — 13
3:2 — 114–15 n. 5
4:11 — 181

Jonah
1–2 — 48
1:1 — 47 n. 7
1:2 — 45 n. 2, 46
1:2–3 — 43
1:5 — 80
2 — 47
3 — 44–45, 47 n. 9
3:2–3 — 46
3:4 — 46, 181
3:10 — 45
3:10–4:3 — 44
4 — 44–45
4:1 — 45 n. 2
4:1–3 — 45
4:2 — 44
4:3 — 47
4:4 — 48
4:5 — 44, 49 n. 13
4:8 — 47
4:10 — 50
4:11 — 50

Micah
3:4 — 80

Habbakuk
1:2–4 — 88 n. 29
2:11 — 80

Zephaniah
1:10 — 74, 76 n. 6

Psalms
9:13 — 74, 75 n. 4
18:26 — 103
22:6 — 80

INDEX OF ANCIENT SOURCES

23	ix, xi	Ruth	
33:5	64 n. 41	2:1	58, 58 nn. 21 and 26
33:15	60	3:2	58, 58 n. 22
33:18	59	4:17–22	13
34:18	80		
77:2	81, 82 n. 8	Song of Songs	
78:38	34	5:3	187 n. 21
82	96–99		
82:1	98	Qoheleth	
82:1–5	98	9:17	74, 75 n. 4
82:6	98		
82:7	98	Lamentations	
82:8	98	2:18	81
88:2	81	3:8	81, 82 n. 8
101:6–7	63	4:6	181
104:15	168 n. 50		
107:6	81	Esther	
107:13	81	4:1	75, 75 n. 3, 81, 82 n. 8
107:19	81	5:6	171 n. 67
107:28	81	7:2	171 n. 67
142:2	81, 82 n. 8	7:7–8	171 n. 67
142:6	81, 82 n. 8	9:31	75, 75 n. 5
144:3	61, 61 n. 33		
		Ezra	
Job		3:4	89 n. 35
16:18	74, 75 n. 3, 75 n. 5	9:2	124
19:7	81, 82 n. 8, 88 n. 29	9:4	124
22:7	107	10:6	124
22:8	107		
27:9	74, 75 nn. 3 and 5	Nehemiah	
31:16	107	5:1	75, 75 n. 4
31:17	107	5:6	75 n. 5
31:31	107	9:4	81
31:38	81	9:7–8	53
34:28	74, 75 n. 4	9:9	75, 75 n. 5, 76 n. 6
35:12	81	9:27	81
36:7	59, 60 n. 29	9:28	81
38–41	104		
		1 Chronicles	
Proverbs		5:20	81
14:34	39 n. 26	19:2	187 n. 20
21:13	74, 75 n. 4	19:3	181–82
25:21	107		
29:12	63	2 Chronicles	
		8:14	89 n. 35

2 Chronicles (cont.)
13:14	81
18:31	81
19:6	89 n. 35
23:7	182
25:4	182
32:20	81

New Testament

Matthew
1:5	13

Romans
3	31 n. 14
4	31, 31 n. 14
11	20, 31 n. 14

Hebrews
13:2	184

Jude
7	210 n. 11

Deuterocanonical Books

2 Esdras
3:13	157 n. 1
4:2	104
7:36	157 n. 1

Judith
8:26	157 n. 1

1 Maccabees
2:52	157 n. 1

2 Maccabees
1:2	157 n. 1

Prayer of Manasseh
1:7	157 n. 1

Sirach
44:19–20	157 n. 1

Old Testament Pseudepigrapha

Jubilees
12:12–15	148–49 n. 54

Dead Sea Scrolls

4QDeut^q
32:8–9	97

4QDeut^j
32:8–9	97

Targumim

Targum Onkelos
Gen 18:19	56

Targum Neofiti
Gen 19:8	210–11 n. 14

Targum Pseudo-Jonathan
Gen 19:8	210–11 n. 14

Greco-Roman Literature

Aeschylus, *Suppliant Maidens*
403	103

Ovid, *Metamorphoses*
8.611–724	131 n. 6

Rabbinic Works

m. 'Abot
5:3	157 n. 2

t. Sotah
4	160 n. 14

b. Avodah Zarah
4a, b	31

b. Baba Batra
10b	39 n. 26

INDEX OF ANCIENT SOURCES

b. Baba Metzi'a
- 86b — 160 n. 14, 175 n. 76
- 86b–87a — 161 n. 19, 162 n. 23
- 87a — 170 n. 61

b. Berakhot
- 54b — 162 nn. 23–24

b. Pesahim
- 86b — 162 n. 21

b. Sanhedrin
- 71b — 195 n. 7
- 108a — 163 n. 30
- 109a–b — 195 n. 7

b. Shabbat
- 127a — 160 n. 14

b. Yoma
- 38b — 162 n. 24

Midrash and Related Literature

'Abot de Rabbi Nathan
- A 33 — 157 n. 2
- B 36 — 157 n. 2

Alfa Beta de-Ben Sira
- Tet — 162 n. 24

Derekh Eretz, Pirkei ben Azai
- 2:2 — 169 n. 53

Exodus Rabbah
- 2:6 — 67 n. 52

Genesis Rabbah
- 39:13 — 148 n. 50
- 49:4 — 62 n. 36
- 49:32 — 175 n. 76
- 50:2 — 161 n. 19, 169 n. 53
- 50:3 — 165 n. 39
- 50:4 — 145–46, 165 n. 39, 168 n. 51, 171–72 n. 70

Kallah Rabbati
- 3:1 — 162 n. 23
- 7:2 — 160 n. 14
- 7:3 — 161 n. 19
- 7:4 — 168 n. 51

Leviticus Rabbah
- 11:5 — 160 n. 14

Midrash Tanhuma, Vayera
- 9 — 162 n. 23
- 29:21b — 163 n. 27

Sifre Zuta
- 27:1 — 163 n. 27

Early Christian Writings

Augustine of Hippo, *City of God*
- 18.46 — 20 n. 53

John Chrysostom — 20 n. 53

Ambrose of Milan — 20 n. 53

Jewish Interpreters

Abrabanel, Isaac ben Judah 56, 56 n. 18, 162 n. 21, 165 n. 39
Bahya ben Asher 55, 55 n. 10, 59–61, 60 n. 30, 61 nn. 31 and 34, 65
Behor Shor 55, 55 n. 9, 65–67
Hizkiya bar Manoach (Hazkuni) 55, 55 n. 11, 58, 65–67
ibn Attar, Hayyim 162 n. 21
Ibn Ezra, Abraham (Raba) 55–56, 56 n. 13, 175 n. 76
Kimhi, David (Radak) 55, 55 n. 12, 57, 62, 65–67, 132 n. 10, 135 n. 20, 162 n. 23, 163 n. 27, 169 n. 53, 170 n. 60, 191
Leibush, Meir (Malbim) 165 n. 39
Luntschitz, Shlomo Ephraim 165 n. 39
Moses ben Maimon (Rambam) 63, 63 nn. 37–38, 67 n. 52, 160 n. 14

Moshe ben Nahman (Ramban)   56,
  56 n. 14, 59, 61, 61 nn. 31 and 33,
  63–67, 135, 135 n. 20, 141 n. 35, 162
  nn. 21 and 24, 165 n. 39, 168
Rashi (Shelomo Izhaki)   55, 55 n. 7,
  57–58, 62, 64–67, 133, 133 n. 11, 141
  n. 35, 146 n. 43, 158 n. 6, 160 n. 14,
  163 n. 30, 165–66 n. 39, 169 n. 53, 191,
  197
Sa'adia Ga'on (Rasag)   55–56, 55 n. 6
Sforno, Ovadia   56, 56 n. 15, 62, 62 n.
  35, 65–66, 66 n. 47, 67, 162 n. 21
Shmuel ben Meir (Rashbam)   55, 55 n.
  8, 57, 160 n. 14, 168 n. 48, 175 n. 76

Index of Modern Authors

Albeck, Chanoch   62 n. 36, 68, 161 n. 19, 178
Albertz, Rainer   114 n. 3, 125
Alexander, T. D.   186 n. 19, 189
Alter, Robert   54, 54 n. 1, 56, 56 n. 17, 68, 166 n. 43, 176
Amit, Yairah   129–30 n. 2, 143, 143 n. 41
Ansbacher, B. Mordechai   17 nn. 42 and 45, 22
Avishur, Yitzhak   159–60 n. 13, 173 n. 71, 177
Bar-Efrat, Shimeon   141 n. 34, 146 n. 46, 155, 160 n. 17, 174 n. 73, 177
Barth, Karl   3 n. 2, 6
Bartor, Assnat   109 n. 8, 111
Bechtel, Lyn   92, 92 n. 39, 93, 93 n. 40, 94, 94 nn. 41–42, 99, 115 n. 5, 117 n. 10, 125
Becker, Hans-Jürgen   157 n. 2, 177
Ben Zvi, Ehud   44, 44 n. 1, 52
Ben-Sasson, Haim Hillel   16 n. 30, 17 n. 45, 22
Berenbaum, Michael   17 nn. 33–34, 23
Blenkinsopp, Joseph   27–28 n. 5, 41
Bolin, Thomas M.   38 n. 24, 39 n. 25, 41, 118, 118 n. 13, 125, 203 n. 1, 212
Borowski, Oded   170 nn. 58–59, 170–71 nn. 62–63, 171 nn. 65 and 69, 177
Bovati, Pietro   84–88, 84 nn. 14–15, 85–88 nn. 17–28, 88 nn. 30–32, 90, 91, 91 n. 37, 92, 99, 116, 116 n. 7, 125
Bowie, Walter Russell   158 n. 6, 177
Boyce, Richard N.   84, 84 nn. 11–13, 90–91, 99
Brenner, Rachel Feldhay   6 n. 13, 22
Brett, Mark G.   7 n. 21, 8 nn. 23 and 25, 11, 11 n. 29, 13 n. 32, 22, 29 n. 9, 40, 40 n. 28, 41, 114 n. 3, 124 n. 25, 125
Browning, Christopher R.   15 nn. 34–36, 16 n. 40, 17 n. 41, 22
Bruckner, James K.   83, 83 n. 10, 88–89, 89 nn. 33 and 35–36, 90–91, 91 nn. 37–38, 99
Buber, Martin   58 n. 25, 68
Buber, Salomon   162 n. 21, 177
Campbell, Antony F.   180, 181 n. 4, 189
Carmichael, Calum   106 n. 6, 110 n. 10, 111
Carpenter, J. Estlin   54 n. 2, 68
Carr, David M.   113, 113 nn. 1–2, 114 n. 4, 115 n. 6, 123, 125, 125 n. 27
Carroll, James   20 n. 53, 22
Cassuto, Umberto   157 n. 2, 158 nn. 5 and 7–8, 160 n. 14, 177
Chavel, Charles B.   59 n. 28, 61 n. 33, 64 n. 42, 65 n. 46, 68
Childs, Brevard S.   3, 3–4 n. 2, 4, 4 n. 3, 5, 5–6 n. 10, 6, 6 n. 12, 14, 22
Clines, David J. A.   6, 6–7 n. 15, 7, 7 nn. 17–18, 22
Cohen, Menachem   132 n. 10, 133 n. 11, 135 n. 20, 141 n. 35, 146 n. 43, 155, 158 n. 6, 160 n. 14, 162 n. 23, 163 n. 27, 175 n. 76, 177
Cotter, David W.   7 n. 21, 11 n. 29, 22
Daube, David   102, 102 n. 1, 110 n. 9, 111
Davies, Philip R.   8 n. 22, 22
Davis, Avrohom   58 n. 24, 62 n. 36, 64 n. 43, 68

Deem, Ariella 164 n. 33 177
Dillmann, August 174 n. 74, 175 n. 76, 177
Dolinko, David 103 n. 2, 111
Doyle, Brian 35–36 n. 20, 41, 179 n. 1, 189, 203, 203 n. 1, 203–4 n. 3, 205, 205 n. 7, 210–11 n. 14, 212
Ehrlich, Arnold B. 181–82, 181 n. 6, 187 n. 21, 189
Eisenstein, Judah David 162 n. 24, 177
Even-Shoshan, Abraham 57, 57 n. 19, 68
Fackenheim, Emil L. 5, 5–6 n. 10, 6, 6 n. 11, 18, 18 n. 47, 19, 19 nn. 49–51, 21, 23
Fassberg, Steven 55, 55 n. 5, 68
Fields, Weston W. 118, 118 n. 11, 125, 180, 180 n. 2, 189, 205 n. 5, 212
Fokkelmann, J. P. 181, 181 n. 5, 189, 208 n. 9, 212
Fox, Everett 166, 166 n. 41, 177
Fretheim, Terence E. 7–8 n. 21, 23
Garber, Zev 6 n. 13, 23
García Martínez, Florentino 211 n. 14, 212
Garner, Brian 103 n. 4, 111
Garsiel, Moshe 130 n. 3, 144 n. 42, 155
Gelander, Shamai 158 n. 6, 160 n. 17, 177
Gordon, R. P. 183 n. 14, 187 n. 21, 189
Greenberg, Moshe 28 n. 6, 29 n. 10, 31, 31 n. 15, 36 n. 21, 41
Gunkel, Hermann 54 n. 3, 68, 118, 118 n. 11, 126, 158 n. 6, 159 nn. 11 and 13, 160 n. 15, 161 n. 20, 162 n. 26, 164, 164 n. 32, 166 nn. 39–40, 167 n. 46, 169 n. 53, 169 nn. 55 and 57, 175 nn. 75–76, 177, 198 n. 10, 201
Hamilton, Victor P. 104 n. 5, 111, 204, 204 n. 5, 205, 212
Heard, R. Christopher 124 n. 24, 126, 204 n. 5, 212
Hecke, Pierre van ix, xi
Helyer, Larry R. 8, 8 n. 24, 11–12 n. 30, 23

Hepner, Gershon W. 37 n. 22, 41, 114 n. 4, 120–21, 126
Herzog, Ze'ev 165 n. 38, 177
Hoffman, Schlomo 16 n. 38, 23
Holladay, William L. 67, 67 n. 51, 68
Horovitz, Hayyim Shaul 163 n. 27, 177
Horowitz, Elliott S. 19 n. 52, 23
Jagersma, Henk 205 n. 7, 212
Joyce, Paul M. 27 n. 4, 29 n. 10, 31 nn. 11 and 13, 41
Kaminsky, Joel S. 114 n. 5, 124 n. 24, 125 n. 26, 126
Katz, Steven T. 18, 18 n. 48, 19 n. 51, 23
Katzenellenbogen, Mordechai Leib 162 n. 21, 177
Kiel, Yehudah 160 n. 14, 177
Klein, Daniel A. 192 n. 2, 193 n. 6, 201
Knohl, Israel 120 n. 19, 126
Kochan, Lionel 17 nn. 33–34, 23
Kogut, Simcha 65, 65 n. 44, 68
Kugel, James L. 198 n. 10, 201
Lasine, Stuart 186 n. 19, 189
Leibowitz, Nehama 58, 58 n. 25, 67, 67 n. 49, 68, 150 n. 59, 155
Lemos, Tracy M. 183 n. 15, 189
Letellier, Robert I. 204 n. 5, 213
Levinas, Emmanuel 48, 48, n. 11, 52
Levine, Nachman 7 n. 21, 23, 159 n. 10, 177
Lipton, Diana ix, xi, 17 n. 3, 41
Loader, J. A. 204 n. 5, 213
Luzzatto, Samuel David (Shadal) 191–92, 192 n. 2, 193–201
Lyons, William John 4, 4 n. 5, 7 nn. 15–16 and 19–20, 9 n. 27, 10 n. 28, 11 n. 30, 12 n. 31, 13 n. 32
MacDonald, Nathan 31 n. 12, 35 n. 19, 41, 183 n. 13, 184 n. 16, 185 nn. 17–18, 189, 203, 213
Malul, Meir 132 n. 9, 155
Margalioth, Mordechai 160 n. 14, 177
Margolies, Morris B. 191 n. 1, 193 n. 3, 201
Matthews, Victor H. 186 n. 19, 189, 205 n. 6, 213

INDEX OF MODERN AUTHORS

McCarter, P. Kyle 183, 183 n. 14, 189
Mecklenburg, Jacob Tzevi 67 n. 48, 68
Meier, Sam A. 182 n. 10, 189
Meir, Amira ix, xi
Meyer, Eduard 161 n. 20, 163 n. 29, 178
Milgrom, Jacob 28 n. 7, 41, 120 n. 19, 126
Moore, James F. 6 n. 13, 23
Morschauser, Scott 180, 180 n. 3, 183 n. 11, 189, 203 n. 1, 205, 210, 213
Muffs, Yochanan 34, 34 n. 16, 41
Noort, Ed 203, 203 n. 2, 213
Peleg, Yitzhak (Itzik) ix, xi, 132 n. 8, 138 n. 25, 159 n. 10, 160 n. 15, 161 n. 20, 164 n. 34, 168 n. 51, 178
Perry, T. A. 43 n. *, 45 n. 2, 46 nn. 4 and 6, 47 nn. 8–9, 48 nn. 10 and 12, 49 n. 13, 50 n. 14, 52, 52 n. 17
Pirson, Ron ix–x, xi–xiv, xv–xvi, vxii–xviii, 3, 3 n. 1, 71, 132 n. 10, 183, 183 nn. 11–12, 189
Pocock, J. G. A. 109 n. 8, 111
Polak, Frank 135 n. 18, 155
Rad, Gerhard von 140 n. 32, 141–42, 142 n. 37, 155, 158, 158 n. 9, 159 nn. 11 and 13, 163 n. 26, 166 nn. 39–40, 169 n. 54, 175 n. 75, 178
Römer, Thomas 114 n. 3, 126
Roth, John K. 19 n. 51, 23
Rubenstein, Richard 19 n. 51, 23
Rudin-O'Brasky, Talia 130–31 n. 6, 134 n. 15, 139 nn. 29–30, 146 n. 45, 147 n. 47, 148 nn. 50 and 53, 149 n. 56, 150 n. 58, 151 n. 62, 155, 159 n. 10, 163 n. 26, 167 n. 46, 169 n. 53, 178
Safren, Jonathan D. 164 n. 33, 178
Sarna, Nahum 134 n. 14, 141, 141 n. 36, 142–43 n. 39, 155, 159 n. 11, 160 nn. 15–16, 161 n. 20, 168 nn. 51–52, 169 n. 54, 175 nn. 75–76, 178, 193 n. 5, 202
Sasson, Jack M. 47, 47 n. 9, 52
Schechter, Solomon 157 n. 2, 178
Scheffler, Wolfgang 16 n. 39, 23
Seeligmann, Isac Leo 160 n. 17, 178

Shakespeare, William 25
Shinan, Avigdor 151 n. 61, 156
Simon, Uriel 50 nn. 15–16, 52, 147 n. 48, 148, 148 n. 51, 149 n. 57, 152, 152 n. 63, 155
Simpson, Cuthbert A. 159 n. 11, 160 n. 15, 162–63 n. 26, 166 n. 39, 168 n. 51, 175 n. 75, 178
Skinner, John 54, 54 n. 3, 56, 56 n. 17, 68, 140 n. 32, 150 n. 58, 155, 159 nn. 11 and 13, 160 n. 15, 169 nn. 54–55, 175 n. 75, 178
Smith, Mark S. 97, 97 n. 46, 98 n. 47, 99, 99 n. 48
Smith, Richard G. 115 n. 6, 126
Smith-Christopher, Daniel L. 27 n. 2, 41
Speiser, Ephraim A. 56, 56 n. 17, 68, 140 n. 32, 155, 158 n. 6, 162 n. 22, 165 nn. 36–37, 166 nn. 44–45, 167 n. 47, 175 nn. 75–76, 178, 197 n. 9, 202
Steinberg, Naomi 7, 7 n. 21, 23
Sternberg, Meir 46, 46 n. 5, 52
Sugimoto, T. 182 n. 7, 189
Theodor, J. 62 n. 36, 68, 161 n. 19, 178
Tigchelaar, Eibert 203, 203 n. 2, 213
Toensing, Holly J. 9 n. 26, 23
Tolkien, J. R. R. xii–xiv, xvii n. 1
Tov, Emmanuel 97, 97 n. 45, 99
Turner, Laurence A. 8, 8 n. 22, 23
Vogels, Walter 11–12 n. 30, 23
Walzer, Michael 40, 40 n. 27, 41
Warner, Megan 114 n. 4, 126
Watts, John D. W. 182 n. 9, 189
Weinfeld, Moshe 63, 63 n. 40, 67, 67 n. 50, 68, 148, 148 n. 52, 155, 157, 157 n. 3, 158 n. 4, 160 nn. 13 and 15, 161 n. 20, 162 n. 22, 170 n. 61, 178
Wenham, Gordon 54, 54 n. 4, 68
Westermann, Claus 114 n. 5, 126, 129 n. 2, 134 n. 15, 140 n. 31, 141 n. 33, 155, 159 n. 11, 166 nn. 39–40, 174 n. 74, 175 nn. 75–76, 178
Wette, Wilhelm de 198
Weyrauch, Walter 103 n. 3, 111
Williamson, H. G. M. 182 n. 9, 189

Wolde, Ellen van   ix, 72 n. 1, 100, 115 n. 5, 116 n. 7
Wood, Joyce Louise Rilett 159 n. 13, 178
Yarchin, William   4 n. 3, 23
Yri, Kjell Magne   85 n. 19, 100
Zakovitch, Yair   130 n. 4, 136, 136 nn. 21–22, 139 nn. 26–28, 147 n. 49, 148 n. 54, 149 n. 55, 151 n. 61, 155–156, 164, 164 nn. 33 and 35, 178
Zimmerer, Jürgen   15 n. 37, 23
Zimmerli, Walther   31 n. 13, 35 n. 17, 41
Zuckermandel, Moses Samuel   160 n. 14, 178

www.ingramcontent.com/pod-product-compliance
Lightning Source LLC
Chambersburg PA
CBHW021756230426
43669CB00006B/93